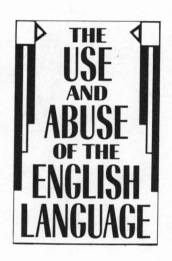

THE USE AND ABUSE OF THE ENGLISH LANGUAGE

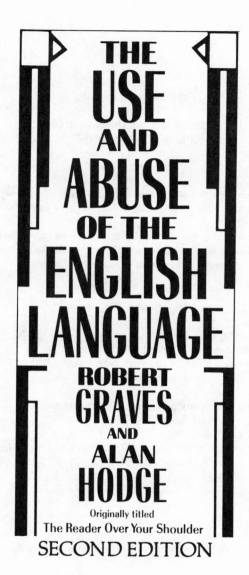

THE USE AND ABUSE OF THE ENGLISH LANGUAGE

ROBERT GRAVES
AND
ALAN HODGE

Originally titled
The Reader Over Your Shoulder

SECOND EDITION

PARAGON HOUSE
NEW YORK

First Paragon Edition, 1990

Published in the United States by
Paragon House Publishers
90 Fifth Avenue
New York, NY 10011

Library of Congress Cataloging-in-Publication Data

Graves, Robert, 1895-
    [Reader over your shoulder]
    The use and abuse of the English language / Robert Graves and
Alan Hodge. — 1st Paragon ed.
        p.   cm.
    Reprint. Originally published: The reader over your shoulder.
2nd ed. London : J. Cape, 1947.
    ISBN 1-55778-317-9
    1. English language—Style.   2. English prose literature—History
and criticism.   I. Hodge, Alan, 1915-   II. Title.
PE1421.G74   1990
808'.042—dc20   89-38022
                                                                  CIP

Manufactured in the United States of America

CONTENTS

Part I
The Reader Over Your Shoulder

Part II
Examinations and Fair Copies

Acknowledgements

We thank all those writers who have allowed us to make critical use of the passages from their books which we quote in Part II, p. 175; we have asked (and been granted) permission wherever the material used seemed to exceed in length or importance the critic's legitimate allowance. The following publishers have asked us to make formal acknowledgements to them: Messrs. Ernest Benn on behalf of Sir Leonard Woolley, Cambridge University Press on behalf of Sir James Jeans, Professors Bertrand Russell and A. N. Whitehead, The National Council for Civil Liberties on behalf of Sir Norman Angell, Messrs. John Murray on behalf of Sir Cyril Norwood, Messrs. George Routledge on behalf of Professor I. A. Richards.

Finally we thank our friends Norman Cameron, Patricia Carey, Clifford Dalton, John Dennis, Margaret Frame, John Graves, Francis Hemming, Basil Liddell Hart, Colin McFadyean, Thomas Matthews, James Reeves, Darcy Sullivan, Virginia Wimperis and Gilbert Yates for various assistance in preparing this book.

To
Jenny Nicholson

Part I

THE
READER
OVER YOUR
SHOULDER

1

The Peculiar Qualities
of English

The most ancient European languages—those that have longest avoided infiltration by other languages—are the most complicated in their grammer and syntax. The age of a language can be roughly guessed by a count of its declensions, conjugations, moods, tenses, voices, cases, genders and numbers. Latin is clearly less ancient than Greek, since it has no 'middle voice', no 'dual number' and no 'optative mood'[1]—thus in Latin at least seven words are needed to express the sentence 'If only you two thieves had drowned yourselves', but in Greek only four. French is clearly less ancient than Latin, since it has no separate neuter gender and does not decline its nouns; also, its conjugations are far simpler. English is clearly less ancient than French: except for its pronouns, it is free of gender differentiation.

Grammatical simplicity is the mark of a vernacular. The word 'vernacular', formed from the Roman historian Varro's phrase *vernacula verba*, 'unliterary expressions used by slaves or serfs', has often since been used loosely to mean 'the native language of a peasantry'; but few of Varro's slaves can have been native Italians—they may have been Greeks, Bithynians, Africans or Germans—and the language they spoke among themselves was a mixed lingo, sometimes called 'camp Latin', which later developed in Italy into modern Italian, in Spain into Spanish, in France into French. Properly speaking, then, a vernacular is a lingo, or language of domestic convenience, compounded of the languages spoken by master and alien

---

[1] These denote respectively: action done for oneself (between the active and passive *voices*); reference to two people (between the singular and plural *numbers*); expression of a wish (supplementing the indicative and subjunctive *moods*).

slave. It has a less complicated grammar and syntax than the languages from which it springs, but rapidly accumulates words as the slaves become freedmen, and their children are born as freemen, and finally their great-grandchildren, marrying into their masters' families, are accepted as cultured people with full rights as citizens. The historical origins of German, which is not very primitive in structure, are obscure; modern German, however, is not a vernacular in Varro's sense, but a late artificial compound of several kindred dialects, with a far smaller vocabulary of early borrowings from the Latin and Greek than the other languages of Western Europe.

English is a vernacular of vernaculars. It began in the eleventh century as the lingo used between the Norman-French conquerors and their Anglo-Saxon serfs, and though it became a literary language in the fourteenth century has never crystallized in the way that Italian, French and Spanish have done. A proof of this is that no writer of English would be credited with a perfect literary style merely because he had exactly modelled himself on some native paragon—say, Addison in England, or Emerson in the United States—as Italians, Spaniards and Frenchmen might be after modelling themselves, respectively, on Boccaccio, Cervantes and Bossuet. To write English well, it is generally agreed, is not to imitate, but to evolve a style peculiarly suited to one's own temperament, environment and purposes. English has never been jealously watched over by a learned Academy, as French has been since the seventeenth century; nor protected against innovations either by literary professionalism, as with Italian, or, as with Spanish, by the natural decorum of the greater part of those who use it. It is, indeed, an immense, formless aggregate not merely of foreign assimilations and local dialects but of occupational and household dialects and personal eccentricities.

The general European view is that English is an illogical, chaotic language, unsuited for clear thinking; and it is easy to understand this view, for no other European language admits of such shoddy treatment. Yet, on the other hand, none other admits of such poetic exquisiteness, and often the apparent chaos is only the untidiness of a workshop in which a great deal of repair and other work is in progress: the benches are crowded, the corners piled with lumber, but the old workman can lay his hand on whatever spare parts or accessories he needs or at least on the right tools and materials for improvising them. French is a language of fixed models: it has none of this workshop untidiness and few facilities for improvisation. In French, one chooses the finished phrase nearest to one's purpose and, if there is nothing that can be 'made to do', a long time is spent getting the Works—the Academy—to supply or approve a new model. Each method has its own advantages. The English method tends to ambiguity and obscurity of expression in any but the most careful writing; the French to limitation of thought. The late Sir Henry Head was once preparing an address on neurology for a learned society in Paris. He wrote it in what he hoped was French, but took the precaution of asking a French professor to see that it was correctly phrased. The manuscript was returned marked: *'pas français', 'pas français', 'pas français'*, with suggested alterations; but almost every *'pas français'* could be matched with a *'pas vrai'*, because the amendments in *français* impaired the force of the argument.

As for the view that English is illogical: it certainly differs greatly in character from French, Italian, Spanish and German, which are claimed to be logical languages. These are all able codifications of as much racial experience as can be translated into speech: theoretically, each separate object, process or quality is given a registered label and ever afterwards recognized by label rather than by individual quality. Logical languages are therefore also rhetorical languages, rhetoric being the emotionally persuasive use of labels, with little concern for the things to which they are tied. English has always tended to be a language of 'conceits': that is, except for the purely syntactical parts of speech, which are in general colourless, the vocabulary is not fully dissociated from the imagery out of which it has developed—words are pictures rather than hieroglyphs.

Matthew Arnold, who as a critic did insufficient justice to the peculiar genius of the English language, suggested in his essay on the 'Influence of Literary Academies' (1875) that:

'The power of French Literature is in its prose-writers, the power of English Literature in its poets. While the fame of many poets of France depends on the qualities of intelligence they exhibit, qualities which are the distincitive support of prose, many of the prose-writers . . . depend wholly for their fame on the imaginative qualities they exhibit, which are the distinctive support of poetry.'

The truth is, that the French are not plagued by their metaphors tending to get out of hand and hamper the argument; whereas English writers of prose or poetry find that, so soon as a gust of natural feeling snatches away the merely verbal disguise in which their phrases are dressed, the pictorial images stand out sharply and either enliven and enforce the argument or desert it and go on a digressive ramble. English writers seldom have any feeling for purity of literary form in the Classical sense: it is both their strength and their weakness that imaginative exuberance breaks down literary restraint.

'Fixed' English, which may be dated from Dr. Johnson's *Dictionary*, completed in 1755, fulfils the need of a safer, less ambitious language arranged on the same system and dedicated to the same uses as French—a language of agreed preconceptions. 'Fixed' English makes possible a French-English, English-French, or a German-English, English-German dictionary. Each foreign label has its English counterpart: 'Glory' is matched (not very satisfactorily) with *'la gloire'* and *'der Ruhm';* *'le matelot'* and *'der Matrose'* with 'sailor'. 'Fixed' English compares well enough with other languages, but is often more mechanically, and therefore more correctly, employed by foreigners than by those whose mother-tongue it is and who are always inclined to slip back into free English. 'Fixed' English is an easy language to learn, like colloquial Arabic; but of free English, as of scholarly Arabic, no wise person will ever claim final mastery—there is no discovered end to either language. 'Fixed' English is never more than momentarily fixed. The conventional, hotel-manager English that foreigners learn is always a little stilted and a little out of date by the time that the book from which they learn it is published; and twenty years later the book will read very quaintly.

English, whether 'fixed' or 'free', has certain unusual advantages in structure. In the first place, it is almost uninflected and has no genders. The Romance and Germanic languages, not having had occasion to simplify themselves to the same degree, still retain their genders and inflections. There is no logical justification for genders. They are a decorative survival from a primitive time when the supposed sex of all concepts—trees, diseases, cooking implements—had to be considered for the sake of religious convention or taboo. Yet even new scientific words have to decide, so soon as coined, on their hypothetical sex. Writers of the Romance and Germanic languages have an aesthetic objection to a genderless language. But when a language is used for international exchange of ideas the practical disadvantages of gender are generally admitted to outweigh its decorative qualities. Gender is illogical, in being used partly to express actual sex, e.g. *le garçon, la femme,* and partly to dress words up, e.g. *la masculinité, le féminisme; le festin, la fête.* If one does wish to give sex-characteristics to concrete objects or abstractions (as, for example, masculinity to 'sword' and 'pen' and femininity to 'Parliament'), the existing gender is an actual hindrance to any such renewal of mythology. An inflected tense has a certain beauty from which writers in these languages refuse to be parted; but, for merely practical uses, an inflected tense such as *je serai, tu seras, il sera, nous serons, vous serez, ils seront* seems unnecessary to Britons and Americans, particularly since the French have dropped noun and adjective inflections almost as completely as they have.

The eventual disappearance of Norman-French from England after the Conquest was never in doubt once Anglo-Saxon had been simplified to meet the needs of the French-speaking invaders. Anglo-Saxon was deficient in words to fit the new methods of trade and government, and these had to be borrowed from French, which had a closer connexion with Rome, the source of all contemporary civilization. Passing the stage of Broken Saxon, the new vernacular developed an easy grammar and syntax, a modification of Anglo-Saxon, but with French turns wherever a legal or literary subtlety was needed. The vocabulary, though enormously enriched with Norman-French and Latin words of advanced culture, remained Anglo-Saxon in foundation: English words of Anglo-Saxon origin, though not half so numerous as Romance words, are used about five times as often. One feature of the happy-go-lucky development of English was that adjectives were made to do service for nouns, nouns for verbs, and so on; until by Elizabethan times it could be said that all parts of speech in English were interchangeable.

This interchangeability is a great help to accurate expression; for example, where an adjective formed in the usual way from a noun has wandered slightly from its original sense. If one wishes to discuss the inflections of a verb and does not wish to write 'verbal inflections', because 'verbal' means 'of a word' rather than 'of a verb', one is free to write 'verb inflections', using a noun for an adjective.

Further gains to English in this early period were: the wide choice of prefixes and suffixes which the pooling of the wealth of both languages gave, the use of auxiliary words to help out the verb tenses, and the new freedom won by prepositions. There is a greater richness of prepositions in English than in any other language of Western Europe: for instance, the French *de* has to bear the whole burden of the English prepositions 'of', 'from', 'out', and *à* of 'at', 'to', 'till', while German has no separation between 'of' and 'from'; 'into' and 'out of' are double prepositions with no equivalent in either French or German.

The British have long been conscious of the extreme subtlety of their language. James Clarence Mangan, in his humorous essay *My Bugle and How I Blow It*, published in the early 1830's, wrote about one use of the preposition 'in':

'I am the Man in the Cloak. In other words, I am by no manner of means the Man *of* the Cloak or the Man *under* the Cloak. The Germans call me *"Der Mensch mit dem Mantel"*, the Man with the Cloak. This is a deplorable error in the nomenclature of that otherwise intelligent people: because my cloak is not part and parcel of myself. The cloak is outside and the man is inside, but each is a distinct entity. I admit you may say, "The Man with the Greasy Countenance", thus also Slawken-Bergius (*vide* "Tristram Shandy") calls his hero "The Stranger with the Nose", for, however long, the nose was an integral part of the individual. With me the case is a horse of a different colour. I do not put my cloak on and off, I grant, but I can do so when I please: and therefore it is obvious to the meanest capacity that I am the Man *in* the Cloak and no mistake.'

Mangan's objection to the German idiom could have been strengthened by an opposite objection to the French *'l'homme à la redingote'*, where greater emphasis is laid on the cloak than on the man. Mangan, as he says, is not 'the Man *of* the Cloak'; yet, *'l'homme dans la redingote'* is no more French than *'Der Mensch in dem Mantel'* is German. And nearly three centuries before Mangan Sir Philip Sidney had written in his *Apology for Poetry:*

> 'English giveth us great occasion to the right use of matter and manner, being indeed capable of any excellent exercising of it. I know some will say that it is a mingled language. And why not so much the better, taking the best of both the other? Another will say it wanteth Grammar. Nay, truly it hath that praise, that it wanteth not Grammar, for Grammar it might have, but it needs not; being so easy of itself and so void of those cumbersome differences of Cases, Genders, Moods, and Teneses, which I think was a piece of the Tower of Babylon's curse, that a man should be put to school to learn his mother tongue. But for the uttering sweetly and properly the conceits of the mind, which is the end of speech, that it hath equally with any other tongue in the world: and is particularly happy in compositions of two or three words together, near the Greek, far beyond the Latin: which is one of the greatest beauties can be in a language.'

The growth of English as a common language of conqueror and conquered had one great disadvantage: the slowness with which it arrived at a common convention for the pronunciation and spelling of words. Neither the French nor the Anglo-Saxons could form their mouths properly for the management of the others' language, particularly of the vowels; yet the French scribes had to write Saxon words in their legal records, and the Saxon scribes in submitting accounts in writing had to adopt a convention of spelling which their masters would understand. Each district, too, had its different dialect. East Midland finally became the dominant one, but words were brought into it from other dialects with different spelling conventions; when at last a general convention was agreed upon, it was (and remains) a tissue of inconsistencies—the most serious handicap to English as a language for international use.

The termination *-ough*, for instance, occurs in words as differently sounded as 'rough', 'bough', 'cough', 'thorough', 'though', 'through', and 'hiccough': the *gh* represents what was once an Anglo-Saxon guttural corresponding with the Greek letter *chi*. This guttural the Norman-French could not, or would not, pronounce: either they made an *f* sound of it or they sounded the vowel and left out the consonant altogether. It is probable that this habit became fashionable among people of Saxon blood who wished to pass as members of the ruling caste, and except in the North, where it lasted much later and still survives in many dialect words, the *gh* passed out of the spoken language and, in the written, remains merely as an historic relic. To the different pronunciation of vowels in different parts of the country, these -ough words are sufficient witnesses; as in the *ch* in 'Church', 'Christian', 'chivalry' and 'pibroch' to the inconsistency of the spelling convention. The trouble was that the scribes had only twenty-six letters (of which x, k, and q were redundant) to express forty-three common sounds. They tried various methods, such as doubling a consonant to show that the vowel which came before was short, e.g. 'batter', and putting a final 'e' after a consonant to show that the vowel was long, e.g. 'bone'. None of these methods could be used consistently while the pronunciation was still so various; and the scribes did all that could be expected of them, short of inventing a new alphabet.

Spelling conventions have changed continually ever since and are not yet stabilized. The word 'mutton', before its spelling was thus fixed early in the reign of James I, had been spelt: 'moltoun', 'motoun', 'motone', 'motene', 'motonne', 'motton', 'mouton', 'muton', 'muttoun', 'mutown' and 'mutten'. 'Button', stabilized at about the same time, had had a still greater range of spelling variations including 'botheum' and 'buttowne'. Yet even after this newly borrowed Romance words in '*-on*' were not similarly Englished as '-on': *balon, marron, musqueton, salon,* were spelt 'balloon', 'marroon', 'musketoon', 'saloon'. This 'oo', which also represented the narrow vowel in the word 'good', was then confused with the broader 'oo' sound as in 'food' and 'moon'. In more recent times the English have either spelt and pronounced the newly borrowed words in *-on* in the French way, if they are words of limited use, such as *soupçon* and *raison d'être*; or, if they are words capable of popular use, they have Englished them much as they did the words first borrowed. So *bâton*, as in 'conductor's baton', is made to rhyme with *fatten*; and on the barrack-square *échelon* has come to rhyme with 'stretch along'. However, on the whole the English-speaking peoples have become more willing to pronounce and spell foreign words as they are spelt and pronounced in their countries of origin. Broadcasting assists this tendency: for example, 'garridge' for 'garage' would have become general in Britain but for the French pronunciation insisted on by the B.B.C. This new respect for accuracy of pronunciation has made things rather worse than before. For instance, the Irish word 'lough', not long borrowed, has added one more pitfall to the pronunciation of words in '-ough'. Conscientious English travellers to Ireland try to manage the sound, but the dictionaries compromise by directing that it shall be prounouced 'lok'—'k' is at any rate a guttural and nearer to the original sound than 'f'.

Certain advantages have been derived even from these confusions. Where there has been more than one pronunciation of a word, it has very often been split into two words, each devoted to a different sense and usually spelt differently. 'Through' and 'thorough' provide an instance of differentiation both of spelling and pronunciation; 'flower' 'flour' 'gest' and 'jest' of differentiation in spelling only. It sometimes happens that the same word is borrowed more than once from the same language, the first borrowing having already changed in sense. Thus the second borrowing becomes a new English word and, the spelling convention having meanwhile also changed, is easily distinguished from the early borrowing. The word 'saloon' was the eighteenth-century English equivalent of the French *salon*, meaning a reception-room in a palace or great house. In early Victorian times it began to be vulgarized, and now has come to mean merely a large room in a commercial establishment. *Salon*, borrowed again, means the reception-room of a

lady of fashion, where wits and notabilities assemble for mutual
entertainment. Similarly, 'antick', with its more modern forms
'antic' and 'antique', present very different views of things anti-
quated.

In accepting English, one must accept the inconsistent spelling cheerfully, not only for the practical service it has given in
the differentiation of meaning, but on its own account, as one
learns to accept and even love the irregularities of a friend's
face. There is to the English eye something distasteful in phonetic spelling. Attempts to force it upon the language, though
supported by all the logic in the world, are unavailing—'because of the ugly look the words have—too much "k" and "z"
and "ay".' One would have less objection to phonetic or 'simplified' spelling if it could be introduced retrospectively in one's
grandfather's days; but nobody likes to make such sacrifices for
the sake of his grandchildren.

As the regularizing of spelling and pronunciation on a ra-
tional basis has never succeeded, so the permanent limiting of
particular words to particular senses, the fixing of English, has
never come to much. There have been professorial panjan-
drums who have undertaken the reformation of the language as
their life's task; there have even been short periods, usually
after a time of national disturbance, when the governing classes
have had fits of tidiness and thought about putting the dictionary into better order. But English has always resisted attempts
to cramp its growth. Alexander Gil (Headmaster of St. Paul's
School when Milton was a pupil) wrote in 1619 in his *Logonomia
Anglica* to complain of the 'new mange in speaking and writing',
for which he held Chaucer originally responsible.

'O harsh lips! I now hear all around me such words as
common, vices, envy, malice; even *virtue, study, justice, pity, mercy,
compassion, profit, commodity, colour, grace, favour, acceptance.* But
whither, I pray in all the world, have you banished those
words which our forefathers used for these new-fangled ones?
Are our words to be exiled like our citizens? Is the new bar-
baric invasion to extirpate the English tongue? O ye Englishmen, on you, I say, I call in whose veins that blood flows,
retain, retain what yet remains of our native speech, and

whatever vestiges of our forefathers are yet to be seen, on these plant your footsteps.'

He was not heeded, nor were the literary oligarchs of the early and middle eighteenth century who tried to impose 'decorum' permanently on English. We find Jonathan Swift vainly protesting in his *Bickerstaff Papers* (1723) against: the 'abundance of polysyllables introduced by the late war, *speculations, operations, preliminaries, ambassadors, communication, circumvallation, battalions*'; and at the same time against such slang as *'banter, uppish, bamboozle, kidney, mob, sham, bully, shuffling* and *palming'*—just as in October 1941 a Mr. Faning wrote to the *Daily Telegraph:*

'Sir—I view with concern the increasing introduction of German words into our language—such words as "blitz", "panzer", "luftwaffe" and others.

Surely it is sad to reflect on the ease with which Germany can invade our language, if not our shores!

If no check is put upon this practice these horrible words will become incorporated into our English vocabulary. German is uncouth and hardly fit for a civilized nation.'

Nobody will ever succeed in annulling the natural right, which every English-speaking person can claim, of borrowing words from foreign languages, coining words, making new distinctions in sense between alternative forms of the same word, resurrecting ancient words, or using whatever grammatical oddities he may please—provided he can satisfy his neighbours, colleagues, or readers, that the coining, the distinction, the borrowing, the resurrection, or the grammatical oddity is necessary. The proof of necessity will be that they adopt the form themselves.

The practice of making new words by declaration is of long standing. For example, the word 'mumpsimus', meaning 'an erroneous doctrinal view obstinately adhered to', was first put into currency by Henry VIII, in a speech from the throne in 1545. He remarked, 'Some be too stiff in their old mumpsimus, others be too busy and curious in their sumpsimus.' He was referring to the familiar story of a priest who, on being reproved for reading in the Mass *'quod in ore mumpsimus'* instead of *quod in ore sumpsimus'* ('which we have taken in our mouths'), his Missal being miscopied, replied that he had read it with an *m* for forty years, 'and I will not change my old mumpsimus for your new sumpsimus.' The word has held its own since, though the doctrinal sense has lost its importance compared with the scholastic sense: it now means 'an established manuscript-reading which, though obviously incorrect, is retained blindly by old-fashioned scholars'.

In several countries the declaration of an individual is not enough to settle a word, even though this is built up regularly from native material or correctly formed from Latin or Greek. The declaration has to be endorsed by the Ministry of Fine Arts or the recommendation of a university committee or learned society. The English word 'defeatism' is formed from the French word *défaitisme* current in 1915, which is not officially French: that is to say, in the early Twenties Marshal Foch, as a member of the *Académie Française*, vetoed its adoption into the Dictionary, on the ground that it was an un-French concept and intolerable. It appears apologetically, however, in A. Dauzat's *Dictionnaire Etymologique*, 1938, as: '1904, appliqué aux Russes; vulgarisé 1915.'

A passage from Lewis Carroll's *Alice Through the Looking-Glass*.

'Humpty-Dumpty said: "There's glory for you." "I don't know what you mean by 'glory,'" Alice said. Humpty-Dumpty smiled contemptuously. "Of course you don't till I tell you. I meant, 'There's a nice knock-down argument for you!'" "But 'glory' doesn't mean 'a nice knock-down argument',," Alice objected. "When *I* use a word," Humpty-Dumpty said in rather a scornful tone, "it means just what I choose it to mean, neither more nor less." "The question is," said Alice, "whether you *can* make words mean so many different things." "The question is," said Humpty Dumpty, "which is to be Master—that's all." Alice was too much puzzled to say anything, so after a minute Humpty-Dumpty began again. "They've a temper, some of them—particularly verbs, they're the proudest—adjectives you can do anything with, but not verbs—however, *I* can manage the whole lot of them! IMPENETRABILITY! That's what I say!"

"Would you tell me, please," said Alice, "what that means?" "Now you talk like a reasonable child," said Humpty-Dumpty, looking very much pleased. "I meant by 'impenetrability' that we've had enough of that subject, and it would be just as well if you'd mention what you mean to do next, as I don't suppose you mean to stop here the rest of your life." "That's a great deal to make one word mean," Alice said in a thoughtful tone. "When I make a word do a lot of work like that," said Humpty-Dumpty, "I always pay it extra." "Oh!" said Alice. She was too much puzzled to make any other remark. "Ah, you should see 'em come round me of a Saturday night," Humpty-Dumpty went on, wagging his head gravely from side to side, "for to get their wages, you know." '

Lewis Carroll himself added several words to the language; and not only in the United States, where novelty of expression is widely exploited as a proof of national vigour, but in Great Britain too, enterprising people are constantly doing the same. The greater part of their inventions has only a local and temporary currency; but a residue satisfies a national demand and sticks in the general vocabulary. Wars, politics and the popularization of scientific inventions are the chief causes of new words gaining wide currency; often these are forgotten again within the year. (One cannot yet tell whether the word 'quisling' will outlast the Nazi technique of preparing for the invasion of a country by political infiltration.) English dictionaries are collections of precedents, rather than official code-books of meaning.

In the United States, intelligent writers sometimes use a far less rigidly grammatical prose than British-born writers would dare. This is from an article (1941) by Otis Ferguson, about 'The Spirits of Rhythm', a negro orchestra:

'[First it was] . . . Douglas Daniels and Leo Watson, who sang, played and messed around with their feet down any cab rank in St. Louis, to coax pennies ringing on to the sidewalk. . . .

They started with ukeleles, because at the time of "Yes, We Have No Bananas" every kid going to school had about a dollar's worth of ukelele under his arm, whack it every chance he got. They started innocent of music as any kind of exercise and even to-day, as Doug says, there isn't a one of them could read a note as big as that table. But they have an active book of arrangements that can keep them going all night; and while it's all in their heads and something they have got up through playing together, you couldn't start out old and get a book like that for less than a thousand dollars.

Their act is what the record labels call vocal with inst. accomp., the inst. at present being a guitar, two tipples (a small-size guitar, using only the first four strings) and a double-bass. But that gives you no idea. The truth is, with just the four of them playing along they have more balance, depth and lift than any of the bands they are supposed to "relieve" on the stand. . . .

Twenty desks of violins in your local grade-school symphony may make more noise than the four instruments of the Budapest Quartet without getting the power in music, and a half-acre of Goldman Band can take Nola at around 380 to the minute without getting the sense of motion of one good two-finger piano player doing Lazy. . . .

They picked up Teddy Bunn in Washington. Teddy Bunn is the present guitar player. He is a perfectly terrible man, but has the mostest fun, and seems to be resigned to music, though there was a time when somehow or other he got hold of an electric guitar and he was playing electric all over the place, and those were not happy days. He is one of the most brilliant men in the business, and keep your pockets sewed up.'

This is good English in its unconventional way. Mr. Ferguson is taking the same liberties with prose as 'The Spirits' took with music, just to make his write-up fit the subject—there are negroish conversational inflexions throughout; for example, the abrupt 'whack it every chance he got', the emphatic 'there isn't a one of them', and the swift change of tone in 'and keep your pockets sewed up.' He admires 'The Spirits' as showing musical genius and 'plays along' with them without finding their racy speech any more comical than their music. Some of these inflexions may one day become incorporated in the main vocabulary of English.

2

The Present Confusion
of English Prose

There is not, and cannot be, any permanent model of literary English; but there are everywhere obvious differences between written and spoken English. A speaker reinforces his meaning with gestures and vocal inflexions, and if the people he addresses still do not understand they can ask for further explanation; whereas a writer, not enjoying either of these advantages, must formulate and observe certain literary principles if he wishes to be completely understood. Granted, he may not always wish to be so understood: a good deal of play is made in English with deliberate looseness of phrase.[1] But the only relevant standard by which to judge any straightforward piece of prose is the ease with which it conveys its full intended sense to the readers to whom it is addressed, rather than its correctness by the laws of formal English grammar. A disadvantage of English grammar, as taught in schools until recently,[2] is that it is not originally English, nor even Latin. It is Alexandrian-Greek grammar modified to serve a language of altogether different habits; and it is often inadequate to its task—just as formal English prosody (designed on the Greek model) is inadequate to serve English poetry. The vernacular freedom of English allows many meanings, complex and simple, to be struck from the interplay of words, which in Greek or Latin or even French would be ruled out by the formal relationships insisted on by grammatic logic. How could one adequately translate into any

[1] The Balfour declaration, for example, which promised the Jews a 'National Home in Palestine' may well have been disingenuous rather than merely careless: while not alarming our Arab allies it allowed ardent Zionists to understand the word 'in' as meaning 'consisting of' rather than 'situated within the borders of'.

[2] In modern schools the 'grammar of function' is now taught.

of these languages the passage by Otis Ferguson quoted at the
end of Chapter One, or the following from E. E. Cummings's
carefully written Introduction to his *Collected Poems* (1938)?

'The poems to come are for you and for me and are not for
mostpeople
—it's no use trying to pretend that mostpeople and ourselves are alike. Mostpeople have less in common with ourselves than the squarerootofminusone. You and I are human
beings; mostpeople are snobs. . . .
You and I wear the dangerous looseness of doom and find
it becoming Life, for eternal us, is now; and now is much too
busy being a little more than everything to seem anything,
catastrophic included.
Life, for mostpeople, simply isn't. Take the socalled standard of living. What do mostpeople mean by "living"? They
don't mean living. They mean the latest and closest plural
approximation to singular prenatal passivity which science,
in its finite but unbounded wisdom, has succeeded in selling
their wives. If science could fail, a mountain's a mammal.
Mostpeople's wives can spot a genuine delusion of embryonic
omnipotence immediately and will accept no substitutes
—luckily for us, a mountain is a mammal. The plusormi-
nus movie to end moving, the strictly scientific parlour-game
of real unreality, the tyranny conceived in misconception
and dedicated to the proposition that every man is a woman
and any woman a king, hasn't a wheel to stand on. What
their most synthetic not to mention transparent majesty,
mrsandmr collective foetus, would improbably call a ghost is
walking. He isn't an undream of anaesthetized impersons, or
a cosmic comfortstation, or a transcendentally sterilized look-
iesoundiefeelietastiesmellie. He is a little more than everything, he is democracy; he is alive: he is ourselves.'

Cummings, it will be noted, has his own typographical conventions and metaphysical vocabulary and, being a true poet, a
broad enough mind to reconcile eternal and diurnal terms. But
he and Otis Ferguson were alike writing, in the passages
quoted, not for 'mostpeople' but for a small special public: each
knew the conventional rules of English prose but had something

particular to say that he believed could not be said except by breaking them. It is seldom that the passionate necessity arises for writing so peculiarly and, when it does, only a small special public can be expected to understand. Our book concerns English as it should be written for the large general public always, and for a small special public on any but the most unusual occasions.

There is an instinctive mistrust of grammarians in Britain ad the United States, and a pride in following one's natural course in writing. Deliberate obscurity is rare. We suggest that whenever anyone sits down to write he should imagine a crowd of his prospective readers (rather than a grammarian in cap and gown) looking over his shoulder. They will be asking such questions as: 'What does this sentence mean?' 'Why do you trouble to tell me that again?' 'Why have you chosen such a ridiculous metaphor?' 'Must I really read this long, limping sentence?' 'Haven't you got your ideas muddled here?' By anticipating and listing as many questions of this sort as possible, the writer will discover certain tests of intelligibility to which he may regularly submit his work before he sends it off to the printer.

No writer should fail to reckon with modern reading habits. As each year until the fall of France more and more reading matter was obtruded on people's notice, they had to protect themselves in some way from having their whole leisure time engrossed by it. How much of the averagely interesting book is actually read nowadays by the averagely interested person? It can only be a small part, and of that small part a good deal is lost because, though the eye goes through the motions of reading, the mind does not necessarily register the sense. Even when a book is being read with the most literal attention—a fair example is proof-reading by the author, his friends and members of the publishing firm and printing house—scores of errors pass by undetected.[1]

[1] Why so many well-educated people spell badly is because they were quick-brained as children and learned to take in two or three words at a time, before going to school and learning exceptions to the ordinary spelling rules. Thus they may never, since nursery days, have *read* a word which they habitually mis-spell (though they may come across it twenty times a week); but see it as they think it should be. We have found 'Aircraftman' spelt correctly only once in American journals against the scores of times we have seen it spelt 'Aircraftsman'.

It is not that modern people are less intelligent than their grandparents: only that, being busier, they are less careful. They must learn to take short cuts, skimming through the columns of a newspaper, flicking over the pages of a book or magazine, deciding at each new paragraph or page whether to read it either attentively or cursorily, or whether to let it go unread. There is a running commentary in the mind. For example, in reading a *Life of Napoleon*: 'page 9 . . . yes, he is still talking about Napoleon's childhood and the romantic scenery of Corsica . . . something about James Boswell and Corsican independence . . . tradition of banditry . . . now back to the family origins again . . . wait a minute . . . no . . . his mother . . . more about her . . . yes . . . French Revolution . . . page 24, more about the French Revolution . . . still more . . . page 31, not interested . . . ah . . . Chapter 2, now he's at the military school. . . . I can begin here . . . but oughtn't to waste time over this early part . . . in the artillery, was he? . . . but when do we get to the the Italian campaign?' And even when the reader does get to the Italian compaign and settles down comfortably to the story, he seldom reads a sentence through, word by word. Usually, he takes it in either with a single comprehensive glance as he would a stream or a field of cows that he was passing in the train, or with a series of glances, four or five words to a glance. And unless he has some special reason for studying the narrative closely, or is in an unusually industrious mood, he will not trouble about any tactical and geographical niceties of the campaign that are not presented with lively emphasis and perfect clarity. And, more serious still from the author's point of view, he will not stop when the eye is checked by some obscurity or fancifulness of language, but will leave the point unresolved and pass on. If there are many such obstructions he will skim over them until his eye alights on a clear passage again.

Imaginative readers rewrite books to suit their own taste, omitting and mentally altering as they read. And most readers automatically correct obvious errors in sense as well as misprints. Such a slip as 'Cain's murder by Abel did not go unavenged' would almost certainly pass unnoticed by every reader who was familiar from childhood with the Bible story:

he would read it as 'Cain's murder of Abel' or 'Abel's murder by Cain'. And if some Hebrew scholar perhaps wished to report an alternative legend in which it was Cain, not Abel, who was murdered, this point would have to be underscored emphatically before educated people could be expected to read the story correctly. Writers who use such unfamiliar words as 'aerobat', 'comport', 'dietic', 'sublimination' find them so often altered by typists and printers into 'acrobat', 'comfort', 'dietetic' and 'sublimation' that most readers may be presumed to do the same in their minds. The old catch of asking someone to repeat the verse:

> Tobacco, Tobacco, Tobacco!
> When you're sick it makes you well,
> And it makes you well when you're sick,
> Tobacco, Tobacco, Tobacco!

is the point here. Nine intelligent people out of ten will reverse the order of the words in the third line, to change the repetition into an antithesis:

> And when you're well it makes you sick.

We do not suggest that writers should indulge busy readers by writing down to them—given them nothing but short messages simply phrased; but only that sentences and paragraphs should follow one another so easily and inevitably, and with such economy of phrase, that a reader will have no encouragement to skip.

There is a hasty way of writing which is a counterpart to the hasty way of reading. It is becoming more common every year and raising less and less protest. A speech, or an article, has to be written by a certain day; there are the usual interruptions and distractions. The writer is hurried but confident, with a fairly clear notion of what he wants to say. He dashes down or dictates a first draft, reads it through quickly, or has it read back to him, makes a few verbal alterations, calls it done and immediately turns to some other business. The greater the haste in which the draft is written, the closer will it come to ordinary conversational style; and will therefore have a certain intimate charm of expression, unless of course he has trained himself to think wholly in clichés. But it is likely to contain repetitions, contradictions, muddled sequences of ideas, dropped threads, hastily chosen phrases, irrelevancies, queer variations of tense and case—especially when he is writing on a topic new to him and not merely repeating his own or someone else's remembered phrases. And phrases that seemed good enough to him in his haste—useful stand-ins for the star phrases he could not quite command—will often not only fail to convey a particular meaning to the reader but will make a blank of the whole passage.

It is not only single words and phrases that are used as stand-ins. Someone is asked, perhaps, for a article on the Rebuilding of London, or on God and the War, or on the German National Character. He has probably two or three quite good points to make but feels that an article of this sort needs a general philosophical or historical setting. He is himself neither a philosopher nor a historian and has therefore to vamp out a rhetorical introduction and conclusion. The busy eye, reading such an article, understandingly discounts the stand-in paragraphs and goes straight for the points, which in the popular press are often considerately printed in heavy type; but, in doing so, is liable to miss whatever of importance may be embedded in the rhetoric.

In spoken English haste has been the chief cause of the increasing confusion. People in important positions use a ragged conversational style that in the leisured Eighties would have been attributed to drink, mental decay or vicious upbringing. The rank and file have followed suit. The tempo of life in the United States of America is faster than in Britain and conversational looseness in Congress has been carried further than in the Houses of Parliament. The haywire innovations[1] of conversational English—not merely the slang vocabulary but the logical confusion—have worked their way into literary prose, chiefly

[1] To appreciate the force of 'haywire' one must have seen the confusion caused in an American hayfield when the wire cable, intended to secure a huge stack against tornadoes, has slipped and tangled itself in coils among the fallen hay and the haymakers.

because the growing prejudice against academic writing as pompous and sterile of ideas tempts writers to disguise their commonplaces.

Probably the habit of dictation to a typist has been responsible for a good deal of the confusion. Business and official letters and reports were once drafted by the person responsible and then, after careful emendation, given to a junior clerk for copying. They are now dictated to a shorthand typist (whose chief recommendation is usually her speed) and very often are not even read back before they are typed. Few people are capable of composing a difficult report or letter so that all the sentences of a paragraph are neatly related, unless they write it our for themselves and are able constantly to glance up and down the page, altering and erasing. Sometimes the typist is not only part of the office-equipment but an audience: the employer will wish to give an impression of fluency and infallibility rather than fumble and fuss over words. Though nine letters out of ten write themselves, their subjects being so familiar and their phrasing so formalized, the tenth, which deals with an unusual case, will present a literary problem from which there is no escape even with the business-man's lifebelt 'Comma, on the basis of which' and his breeches-buoy 'Paragraph, under the circumstances, therefore'. The employer blusters through somehow; the efficient typist quickly reduced the muddle to a clear page of typescript; and it then acquires so authoritative a look that it is usually signed and sent off without emendation.

Reluctance to disturb the orderliness of a typewritten or manuscript page is often responsible for clumsy composition. The writer has an after-thought, and instead of recasting his sentence to include it, tags it on at the end. For example:

'*The pupils at Smith Town Engineering College were negroes* [here he remembers that most of them were too light-coloured to be called negroes] *or rather mulattoes* [but here he remembers two or three of inky blackness] *for the most part;* [here he remembers the staff] *as were also the majority of the teachers, except for a Chinese demonstrator in physics* [here he does not want to suggest that any white men taught] *and some negroes.*'

A neater form of the sentence is:

'Most of the pupils, and also of the teachers, at Smith
Town Engineering College were mulattoes; the remainder,
except for a Chinese demonstrator in physics, were negroes.'

The difference between conversational and written English
can be seen from the following statement attributed to Dr.
Hugh Dalton, M.P., then Minister of Economic Warfare, at a
Press Conference in 1940:

'I have here as an emblem of the success of the blockade a
portion of a cable which once belonged to a German plane.
Normally this would be made of rubber containing a copper wire. Shortage of rubber is evident from the fact that
within a very thin coating of rubber the wire is held within a
glass contraption. Glass beads enclose the copper wire.'

No doubt Dr. Dalton made himself clear by passing the piece of
cable round for inspection. But a talk, when printed, cannot
take the place of descriptive writing. It was legitimate for Dr.
Dalton to refer offhandedly to a 'glass contraption', and then,
when interest was aroused, to concentrate attention on the glass
beads and raise his voice in emphasis; by so doing he avoided
the apparent contrast between 'contraption' and 'beads'. But
whoever in his Ministry prepared the official 'hand-out' forgot
that newspaper readers would not be able to examine the 'emblem'; and that these conversational remarks would therefore
not describe it adequately and would fail as propaganda. Newspaper readers would naturally raise the following points:

*Within a very thin coating of rubber the wire is held within a glass
contraption.* Where is the coating of rubber? Between the wire
and the glass contraption? Or outside the glass contraption?
  *Shortage of rubber is evident from the fact that within a very thin
coating of rubber the wire is held within a glass contraption.* How is it
evident? Might not glass be better than rubber for the purpose? To make this quite clear, the purpose of the coating
should have been stated.

An emblem of the success of the blockade. The swastika is an emblem. So are: a broken obelisk, a lily, a broad arrow, an olive branch. This piece of cable has no such hieroglyphic character. It is either 'evidence' of the success of the blocade, or a 'token' of it.

Within a very thin coating of rubber the wire is held within a glass contraption. Glass beads enclose the copper wire. If the glass contraption consists of beads, the word is surely not 'coating', because this would mean that each bead was coated, but 'enclose'? Also the reintroduction of the word 'copper' makes an unintentional contrast between the two 'wires'. They are really the same thing.

The wire is held within a glass contraption . . . Glass beads enclose the copper wire. The second statement seems to be an amplification of the first.

Normally this would be made of rubber containing a copper wire. This is like saying that a pond consists of duck-weed and mud with water in the middle. The wire is the cable; the rubber is merely the insulation.

A cable which once belonged to a German plane. 'Once' seems long ago for so immediate a conclusion as Dr. Dalton was drawing. Did the inflexions of his voice convey a further message? The severity of German losses in aircraft?

If Dr. Dalton's Publicity Officer had been doing his work properly this is what the public would have read in the newspapers:

'This piece of cable, taken from a wrecked German plane, is evidence of the success of our blockade. Hitherto the Germans have made their cables of copper wire thickly sheathed with rubber. Now, as you see, they pack the wire in glass beads, held together by a very thin rubber envelope. Only a severe rubber shortage can have reduced them to this insecure insulating device.'

In the Commons debate immediately following the announcement that Great Britain was at war with Germany, Mr. Gallagher, the Communist member, spoke under emotional stress. This is a verbatim report from *Hansard:*

'I tried to impress on the House at the time of Munich, and now that disaster is threatening to come on the whole of Europe I want to ask, whether it is possible to get this House, representing as it does the people of the country, seriously to discuss a complete change of Government, in order to get a Government that will seek to save the young manhood of this country, and bring the war to a speedy end, instead of concerning itself with spreading the war.'

People speak like this in moments of passion, and contrive somehow to make themselves understood. Perfection of phrasing is not necessary in public speaking: indeed, Charles James Fox, who was an authority on Parliamentary rhetoric, said that a speech which read well was 'a damned bad one' when spoken. This is how Mr. Gallagher might have amended his speech for *Hansard* before the Library copies were printed:

'I asked the House an important question during the crisis which was resolved by the Munich Conference. Now that disaster once more threatens all Europe, I shall repeat it: Can we not, as representatives of the British people, seriously discuss a change of Government? Can we not appoint a Government which will try to preserve the lives of our young manhood, and concern itself rather with smothering war than with spreading war further?'

To haste as a cause of confusion must be added distraction. Normally, except for those who work in the early hours of the morning, or who live up a long country lane, it is almost impossible to avoid being disturbed by incidental noises of traffic, industry, schools, and the wireless, or by the telephone, or by callers. Few people can immediately switch their minds from one complicated subject to another, and presently switch back again, without losing something in the process. Most business men and journalists claim that they are accustomed to noise and can 'work through anything'. But this does not mean that they are not affected by noise: part of the brain must be employed in sorting out the noises and discounting them. The intense concentration achieved when one writes in complete silence, security and leisure, with the mental senses cognizant of every possible aspect of the theme as it develops—this was always rare and is now rarer than ever. Modern conditions of living encourage habitual distraction and, though there are still opportunities for comparative quiet, most people feel that they are not really alive unless they are in close touch with their fellow men—and close touch involves constant disturbance. Hart Crane, a leading American poet of the Nineteen-Twenties, decided that he could not write his best except with a radio or victrola playing jazz at him and street-noises coming up through the open window. He considered that distraction was the chief principle of modern living; he cultivated it, distractedly, and committed suicide in his early thirties.

A third general cause of confusion has been timidity. A fear of feeling definitely committed to any statement that might cause trouble or inconvenience seems to haunt almost everyone in Britain who holds a public position, however unimportant.

A fourth cause of confusion has been dividedness of mind. When people have to write from a point of view which is not really their own, they are apt to betray this by hedging, blustering, an uneasy choice of words, a syntactical looseness. We mean, for example, Cabinet Ministers expressing the view of a Cabinet from which they have often considered resigning; priests, assailed by honest doubt, who must continue to enunciate church dogma; Communists uneasily following the party-line; officials relaying to the public some order from headquarters of which they disapprove; critics borrowing aesthetic standards not properly understood.

British writers excel in straightforward narrative, once they have finished their introductory generalizations and got into their narrative stride. But they tend to be embarrassed by any autobiographical element. What was a rhetorical device in the Classical schools of oratory—*meiosis* or under-emphasis—and came into facetious use in Victorian times (e.g. 'Pedestrianism in November is a matter of not a little unpleasantness'), is now second nature to most Englishmen, and has lost its original ironic purpose. It now means modesty: 'At four thousand I ran into a spot of bother—a couple of Ju.88s who dived at me from a cloud and one of them didn't do my port engine any too

much good, but I managed to put paid to him—the crew baled
out—and then I watched the other go down in bits and
pieces—not a pretty sight—well, I met a passing Messerschmitt
on the way home. . . .' Conversationally this style can be
charming, but in prose it makes for irrelevancy, material omission, faulty connexion, logical weakness and, eventually, boredom.

There is no natural safeguard in the English language
against the faults of haste, distraction, timidity, dividedness of
mind, modesty. English does not run on its own rails, as French
does, with a simply managed mechanism of knobs and levers, so
that any army officer or provincial mayor can always, at a
minute's notice, glide into a graceful speech in celebration of
any local or national event, however unexpected. The fact is,
that English has altogether too many resources for the ordinary
person, and nobody holds it against him if he speaks or writes
badly. The only English dictionary with any pretension to completeness as a collection of literary precedents, the *Oxford English
Dictionary*, is of the size and price of an encyclopedia; and
pocket-dictionaries do not distinguish sufficiently between
shades of meaning in closely associated words: for example,
between the adjectives 'silvery', 'silvern', 'silver', 'silvered', 'ar-
gent', 'argentine', 'argentic', 'argentous'. Just as all practising
lawyers have ready access to a complete legal library, so all
professional writers (and every other writer who can afford it)
should possess or have ready access to the big *Oxford English
Dictionary*. But how many trouble about the real meanings of
words? Most of them are content to rub along with a Thesaurus—which lumps words together in groups of so-called synonyms, without definitions—and an octavo dictionary. One
would not expect a barrister to prepare a complicated insurance or testamentary case with only *Everyman's Handy Guide to the
Law* to help him; and there are very few books which one can
write decently without consulting at every few pages a dictionary of at least two quarto volumes—*Webster's*, or the shorter
Oxford English Dictionary—to make sure of a word's antecedents
and meaning.

To write English perfectly is impossible in practice: occasional ambiguities or slight improprieties of phrase are discover-

able in every book—there has never been a writer who did not have some blind spot in his reading eye. Even to write it well is difficult. The alternative chosen by those who cannot carry on their daily business without constantly writing reports, demands and orders is a dialect of limited vocabulary with no pretence to the literary graces, designed as a vehicle of restricted meaning. 'Officialese', 'legal English' and 'business English' merge into one another as the general service dialect of impersonality, for use in every case where people are not private individuals but merely (according to the context) the public, the electorate, the parties concerned, age groups, man power, personnel, consumers. We discuss this dialect at length in Chapter Four.

Some of the chief contentions in this chapter are borne out by Mr. H. G. Andrews, poet and English teacher in a West Country school, who writes:

'The presence of the wireless set in eight million English homes makes the job of teaching much harder in these days, especially where the Government system allots only one teacher to forty or fifty children. The child is so used to a background of noise, mainly vocal, that he has acquired the habit of ignoring its import. . . .

'It is difficult to get boys to grasp the bare essentials of the language, let alone think logically. The standard of good English in these uncertain, disorderly days is imposed by the few on the very many, and the few grow daily more slack and slipshod in their maintenance of the standard. Writers in the Select Press and for the B.B.C. come sprawling arsy versy over the most obvious trip-wires. The increasingly confused state of educated prose has been a chief symptom of the sickness of our wrong-headed civilization during the last twenty years. . . . It is dispiriting to teach the elements of English composition to boys most of whom will not set pen to paper more than a dozen times a year, after they leave school, and then only to sign their names on an indicated dotted line. It would be stupid to teach my boys the analytical syntax that bought a blight on my own boyhood: I teach them such functional grammar as will help them to compose a straightforward, sensible narrative paragraph with the commas and stops in the right places. I do not bother them with any considerations of euphony—as Lewis Carroll's Duchess said to Alice: "Take care of the sense and the sounds will take care of themselves!" '

3

Where is Good English to Be Found?

Experts in every scientific or learned subject communicate with one another in a distinct technical dialect; and when, now and then, one of them is asked for a popular lecture of book on his own subject, it is seldom that he is able to translate his ideas into an English immediately intelligible to his readers. Usually he has only a meagre general vocabulary. The language which, say, a theologian, an electrical engineer and a morbid-psychologist would use amongst themselves if they were thrown into contact would probably be a loose, schoolboy slang—their common dialect before they began to specialize. Three hundred years ago a correspondingly diverse goup of experts, whenever they had difficulty in making themselves understood to one another in English, could fall back on Latin. The reason for stabilizing all learned terms in Latin, helped out with a little Greek, was to avoid the looseness of vernacular expression: each plant, planet or physical phenomenon was fixed in the corpus of knowledge by being given a unique and inalienable name. Botanists, with great advantage to themselves, have kept faithfully to a single Latin register of terms; other scientists, including zoologists, have not done so, nor have philosophers, and their subjects are consequently full of overlapping, ambiguous and contradictory terms. A conscientious scientist, historian or philosopher, wishing to master every aspect of his subject, must now learn not merely one language, Latin, but three or four— French, German, Italian, perhaps Russian—often more. Even so, he cannot always be sure that the meaning of a certain word in a foreign language is exactly equivalent to its counterpart in his own. There is no international lexicon of scientific and learned terms, and the international Scientific Congress of 1922 failed to agree even to a proposal for limiting to nine the languages in which scientific works might be written in order to qualify for international recognition.

The recent substitution in most British schools of French and English for Latin has had on the whole a vicious effect on English prose. The pupil in the old-fashioned grammar-school was faced with the problem of finding English equivalents to Latin phrases and so became aware of the peculiar properties of English. The teaching of French does not have the same illuminating effect, either because it is closer in structure and spirit to English than Latin is or because it has been taught without the tradition of scholarly discipline that clings to a long-studied dead language. The clue to the appropriate use of a great many English words is to be found in their Latin originals, which occur in French only in degenerate forms: especially important is a knowledge of the effect of Latin prepositions on the verbs to which they are prefixed. Moreover, Latin, though surpassed by English in richness of vocabulary and flexibility of grammar, did for centuries put a useful check on any literary bad manners in which writers of English might feel inclined to indulge. A useful test of the logic of metaphorical English prose is to translate it into Latin.

The following editorial comment from a leading London weekly (1941) is typical of what will not pass the test:

> 'The next few weeks may decide whether the Easter egg which Matsuoka and Molotoff laid in the Kremlin last Sunday is just a shell, or full of dynamite. Although fresh from the nest, it already emits several displeasing odours.'

The Latin point of view would be that a man cannot lay an egg, still less can two men; that Easter eggs are either real eggs, in which case they contain a yolk and a white, or artificial eggs, in which case they are not 'laid'; that if the egg were just a shell it would not smell, nor would it if it were filled with dynamite; that one egg can only emit one odour, not several. The passage is therefore untranslatable. The Romans, though they had a broad sense of stage humour and enjoyed absurd jokes at the baths and at banquets, kept their prose free from extravagance.

It is unfortunate that English, which has for some time been the most widely used language in the world—the chief language of trade, and the national or administrative language of six hundred million people—should be so difficult a one—and that there should be no short cuts to learning it.[1] There are, however, compensations for this difficulty. Frenchmen who make errors in English are not obliged to feel the same embarrassment as Englishmen who, speaking French, mistake the gender of some simple household utensil: for, however strange their accent, they are unlikely to use English more clumsily than a great many people whose mother-tongue it is.

Situations arise in English unparalleled in more rigidly grammatical languages. If an intelligent foreigner were asked to translate into English a simple Latin sentence *'Mala fortuna semper obruet talem qualis ego'*, he would probably write: 'Misfortune will always overwhelm such as I', and justify it grammatically by pointing out that 'such' was accusative, the object of the word 'overwhelm', and was followed by an independent clause 'as I', with the word 'am' understood. He would be right; and only wrong if he decided that 'such as me' was ungrammatical—on the ground that in no sane language can nominative and accusative be used alternatively in the same phrase, and that in all Romance and Germanic languages the nominative would be used. However, 'such as me', treated as a declinable compound pronoun, has been used in English since at least 1412, when Hoccleve wrote:

> Earthern vessel, to such a man as me.
> Full fitting is. . . .

---

[1]One well-advertised expedient is 'Basic English' ('British American Scientific International Commercial'), a self-denying restriction of language to a vocabulary of 850 words—carefully selected as serving all international needs and designed to have technical vocabularies built on to it, like shelves of a sectional bookcase. This has its advantages as a simply-learned, artificial language for foreigners to use to foreigners, but it does not help English-speaking people to speak or write English better. They find it extremely difficult to confine themselves to such a meagre ration of words, especially of verbs: to remember that they must say not 'I wrote a letter' but 'I put a letter down on paper'; and not 'I read a letter' but 'I went through a letter'. If there is any virtue in a dialect that dispenses with a number of common words, 'Basic' is outdone by the picturesque trade-English used in West Africa. The Nigerian official who wishes to announce a total eclipse of the sun to his black subordinates says: 'Him kerosene b'long Jesus Christ by'm-by all done, b——r up, finish.'

It may be assumed that, though grammatically there are two alternatives, 'such as I' and 'such as me', one of them will be more suitable than the other to the context. In no book of usages will the foreigner find any ruling upon this. However, a writer sensitive to the emotional logic of English would probably write 'Misfortune will always overwhelm such as me', but (if the sense had to be reversed) 'Misfortune will never overwhelm such as I'. His feeling would be that the phrase 'such as me' bows passively before misfortune, whereas 'such as I' resists it actively and uprightly.

Or, what is the plural of 'formula'? The dictionary allows a choice of either 'formulae' or 'formulas', but suggests no rule for deciding when to use which. Probably most sensitive people would write: 'Professor Brown advised his pupils to memorize a number of thermodynamic formulae,' but 'The Foreign Minister, before signing the pact, was offered a choice of three formulas.' The Latin plural tends to be used in scientific contexts, the English plural in non-scientific ones. Prose-writers, however, meet this sort of problem less frequently than poets, nor are they obliged so often to transcend conventional usage or to coin new words.

One of the differences in English between prose and poetry is that, while the prose writer must nowadays assume his reader to be a busy person whose eye sweeps along the page at a fairly steady rate, seldom pausing long even at key passages, the poet, unless he is a suicidal Hart Crane, still assumes his reader to have perfect leisure and patience for dwelling on each word in a poem and appreciating its relation with every other. Prose, in fact, is expected to reveal its full content at first reading: poetry only at third or fourth. The first glance at a poem takes in its prose sense as a base on which to build up the poetic sense. For example, the following stanza from Keats's *La Belle Dame Sans Merci* presents a simple story situation:

> I saw pale kings and princes too,
>> Pale warriors, death pale were they all—
> They cried 'La Belle Dame Sans Merci
>> Thee hath in thrall.'

Having grasped so much, one considers the lines in poetic terms. 'What literary context do these pale kings, princes and warriors recall? What force has the repetition of the word "pale"? And who or what is *La Belle Dame Sans Merci*? Why has she a mediaeval French name?' One is free to interpret her fatal person according to personal experience. To Keats, she seems to have been a mixture of Fanny Brawne, with whom he was hopelessly in love, Consumption, which had carried off his brother Tom and was to kill him too, and the intractable Spirit of Poetry. One notes how the conventional phrase 'She has enthralled you', by being resolved into its original elements, recovers its metaphorical force of 'has you in slavery'; and how the subsidiary rhyme of *merci* with *thee* echoes in the mind and gives 'thee' the force of 'thee too'; and how the variation of vowel-sounds gives iridescence to the lines; and how well-suited to the sense the alliteration is; and what a shiver comes with the word 'warriors'.

Poetic meaning, then, is contained in the complicated correspondence between the words used, regarded both as sense and as sound, and in latent meanings of the words evoked by the rhythmic spell. The unusual juxtaposition of two words may carry a weight of meaning over which a thoughtful reader will spend as much time as over a page or more of prose argument. In ordinary prose one does not look for correspondences of this sort, or for latent meanings. Reading as prose the sentence 'La Belle Dame Sans Merci hath thee in thrall' one would miss the rhyme of *merci* and 'thee' and, mentally accentuating the first syllable of *merci*, would give no greater stress to 'thee' than to 'hath'.

If, therefore, a prose writer has some thought to express that has occurred to him with poetic knottiness, he must either prepare the reader for this knot by unmistakable warnings, and help him slowly to disentangle it by subsequent comment; or he must withhold the knot and provide a prose equivalent instead. It would, for example, be unwise to write in prose: 'Reprisals in war are a mad and vicious spiral', and expect the reader to take this odd metaphor in his stride. Either he would automatically read it as 'a vicious circle'; or his reaction would be 'Why not "vicious circle"? Can a spiral be vicious, in the sense that it

always comes back to the same point? Surely it advances as it
revolves?' He would read on, mystified and perhaps annoyed.
Yet a reader of poetry confronted with the couplet:

> War's vicious spiral
> Of mad reprisal . . .

would lay his book down for a moment. He would think: 'Yes,
if in war both belligerents wage a secondary war of reprisals for
some original act of wantonness, a vicious circle results, and not
so much a vicious circle as a vicious spiral: as hysteria mounts,
the first punishment returns in ever heightened form to the
punisher—so that the conflict is prolonged to a point of common exhaustion that could hardly have been reached had either side shown restraint at the outset.' This reflection is the
prose equivalent of the poetic couplet.

There should be two main objects in ordinary prose writing:
to convey a message, and to include in it nothing that will
distract the reader's attention or check his habitual pace of
reading—he should feel that he is seated at ease in a taxi, not
riding a temperamental horse through traffic. But there is a
form of prose called, at different times, 'the conceited style', 'the
grand style', 'prose-poetry' and 'aesthetic prose', the aim of
which is to divert leisured readers by ingenious or graceful feats
with language. It originated in Graeco-Roman schools of forensic oratory where young men learned the art of dressing up an
argument for the benefit of a judge or jury so that it might seem
stronger than it really was. In this sort of prose, correspondences
of sound and meaning are exploited, rhythms are imposed on
the sense rather than created naturally by it, and the reader is
amused by literary references, witty turns of language and far-
fetched metaphors.

There were three sorts of prose in Latin while it was still a
living language: the plain, the polished and the florid. Plain-
ness of language was a virtue under the early Republic, but
after the conquest of Greece the Romans became embarrassed
by their lack of culture and took to polishing their speeches and
letters. By the time of the Early Empire, the plain style was
held pedestrian and boorish and the polished also had gone out

of fashion: Cicero's admired works, which had been composed on careful rhythmic principles, now seemed pompous and boring. Then, as orators and historians found less and less to say, original thinking being dangerous under the Empire, every sort of bright decoration—'tropes' as they were called in the schools—was used to enliven the safe but threadbare themes. At English universities, where from the Middle Ages until late Victorian times the chief ostensible aim of education was to make the boys fluent public speakers in Latin, the polished and the florid styles were taught. In general, the plain style, as found in the works of Caesar and Sallust, was reserved for grammar-school boys. In the next chapters we shall show how strong an effect oratorical education had on English prose: for several centuries few writers who had been to the University refrained from decorating their work with Senecan flourishes and flowers or from cultivating a sonorous Ciceronian grace.

Rhetoric is meant to be spoken, or at least read with an attentive mental ear. Though speeches and sermons are still publicly delivered and the radio has even enlarged their audiences, no novelist or historian now expects his work to be read aloud as in Classical times. It is obviously futile to use rhetorical devices which are meant for the ear and expect them to catch the eye—especially an eye that reads three times faster than ordinary talking-pace. We are confident that few of our readers noticed a trick played on them on line 12 of page 36, where we introduced into ordinary prose a highly stylized sentence connected by a complex system of interlaced alliterations: they were reading for sense, not style. A company report or a newspaper leader might be published in blank verse and, so long as the lay-out was a prose one, nobody would notice the metre. A sentence in a late Georgian mathematical work ran something like this:

'It may at first seem unlikely that the pull of gravity will depress the centre of a light cord, held horizontally at a high lateral tension; and yet no force, however great, can stretch a cord, however fine, into a horizontal line that shall be absolutely straight.'

It was years before someone discovered that the second part of the sentence was a perfect *In Memoriam* rhymed stanza.

We have no quarrel with rhetoric: it is a legitimate and honoured pastime like acrostics or card-play. But since English by its simplicity of structure permits a greater mobility of thought than other languages, and so can express subtler insinuations and more powerful thrusts of meaning, an English writer with something to say needs no rhetorical art. That the hurry of modern life has put both the florid and the polished styles out of fashion, except for very special audiences, is not to be deplored if this leads to a more general appreciation of the capacity of the plain style. By 'plain' we do not mean bald (as, say, the style of the *Anglo-Saxon Chronicle* is bald), but simple and neat. For example, neither rhythmic repetition, adjectival profusion, nor quaintness of metaphor will convince a reader nearly so easily that such and such a house was disgustingly dirty and its proprietor an old wretch, as a simple, unemphatic anecdote of what happened early one Monday morning between the kitchen and the backdoor.

Towards the end of the nineteenth century Samuel Butler recorded in his notebook as a private eccentricity that, unlike his contemporaries Pater and Ruskin, he had never cultivated his literary style but tried instead to make his handwriting as clear as possible. Nowadays it is difficult to read Pater or Ruskin at all, because the information and ideas (many of them valuable) that they have to offer are so overlaid with painfully cultivated styles as to confuse rather than enchant; whereas Butler, who carried his aim of simple clarity past handwriting into prose, is still a modern.

Where is good English to be found? Not among those who might be expected to write well professionally. Schoolmasters seldom write well: it is difficult for any teacher to avoid either pomposity or, in the effort not to be pompous, a jocular conversational looseness. The clergy suffer from much the same occupational disability: they can seldom decide whether to use 'the language of the market-place' or Biblical rhetoric. Men of letters usually feel impelled to cultivate an individual style—less because they feel sure of themselves as individuals than because they wish to carve a niche for themselves in literature; and nowadays an individual style usually means merely a peculiar range of inaccuracies, ambiguities, logical weaknesses and stylistic extravagancies. Trained journalists use a flat, over-simplified style, based on a study of what sells a paper and what does not, which is inadequate for most literary purposes.

As a rule, the best English is written by people without literary pretensions, who have responsible executive jobs in which the use of official language is not compulsory; and, as a rule, the better at their jobs they are, the better they write. Some command a much larger vocabulary than others, are more eloquent and more aware of historic precedent in the use of words; but faults in English prose derive not so much from lack of knowledge, intelligence or art as from lack of thought, patience or goodwill. Though often letters, speeches and reports must be written in a hurry and, because of the countless considerations that clear writing involves, are bound in some way to fall short of the full intended meaning, conscientious people will aways regret this necessity and arrange their affairs as far as possible to avoid it. Arnold Bennett in his *Literary Taste* pointed out that faults of style are largely faults of character.

'How often has it been said that Carlyle's matter is marred by the harshness and eccentricities of his style? But Carlyle's matter is harsh and eccentric to precisely the same degree as his style. His behaviour was frequently ridiculous, if not abominable.'

The writing of good English is thus a moral matter, as the Romans held that the writing of good Latin was. And the British people, though at times it recognizes and applauds the first-rate in art, literature, statesmanship, technical achievement, social conduct and so on, is always overindulgent of the second-, third- or fourth-rate and often taken in by the simply bad. The national instinct is towards what is good, but there is a long-standing aversion to laying down standards in too final a way—cheats, scoundrels, careerists and dunces have profited greatly from this in politics, business, society, art and literature—and though it is generally assumed that there is good and bad writing in the present, as well as in the past, it is felt that nobody should be either hardy enough to define the difference or ill-mannered enough to make a detailed study of the short-comings of his fellow-writers. In fact, a leading trait of the British character is not only to suspend judgement on values but never to think further than is absolutely necessary, and to put off radical change of behaviour or policy until compelled by an acute crisis. We regard the present crisis as acute enough to excuse this book.

The short-term view of writing and public speaking held between 1919 and 1939 corresponded closely with the short-term view of clothes, household belongings and vehicles as temporary conveniences, soon out of date, not worth making well enough to last a lifetime. It was argued that almost every speech was wholly forgotten after three weeks and almost every book after three years. 'Why then trouble to write really well? Would anyone but a fool make a motor-car to be admired by posterity? The most economical car is the one built to run well and look smart only for the length of time that a car remains up-to-date mechanically—three to five years. The same is true of books.'

The consequent tendency of English—even of the dignified language spoken in Parliament—to become loose, confused and ungraceful was first officially recognized, and condoned, in 1924. Stanley Baldwin, political leader of the business class which had gradually taken over the direction of national affairs from the impoverished land-owning class, then made a statement of appalling frankness to the Cambridge Union, admitting the anti-literary prejudice of his associates, and even glorying in it:

'If there is one thing which those who have been in any other profession than the Bar distrust more than another, it is the eloquent man. In the business world . . . the man who has the power of talking is not the man who gets promotion. To be able to express oneself, in business, is always to be written down as not quite first class . . . it is not necessarily the man most fluent of speech to whom we should entrust the destinies of the country.'

This was a curious reversion to a view which had been held in the Middle Ages by the land-owning class, but was already by Stuart times abandoned in all but a few backward counties. Richard Pace wrote of it in his Latin *De Fructu*, 1517:

'One of those whom we call gentlemen, who aways carry a horn slung at their backs as though they would hunt during dinner, said: "I swear by God's Body I would rather that my son should hang than study literature. It behoves the sons of gentlemen to blow the horn tunefully, to hunt skilfully, to train a hawk well and carry it elegantly. But the study of literature should be left to rustics." '

When the policies of the anti-literary business party were finally discredited after a few months of the Second World War, and an all-party government was formed, the only Prime Minister acceptable to the Labour leaders was Winston Churchill, who had long been distrusted by the Baldwinian business members and 'written down as being not quite first class' because he was the most Classically eloquent member of the House, and who, shortly after his appointment, expressed his impatience with confused, unfluent business English in a strong memorandum to all Government departments.

An unsteady course was followed by English prose through the centuries. Every social and political change was marked by a corresponding change in the character of prose; and it may be assumed that the change in British life which follows the Second World War will be as pronounced as the one that followed the First World War. We hope, but cannot prophesy, that the style of prose best suited to the new conditions will be:

Cleared of encumbrances for quick reading: that is, without unnecessary ornament, irrelevancy, illogicality, ambiguity, repetition, circumlocution, obscurity of reference.

Properly laid out: that is, with each sentence a single step and each paragraph a complete stage in the argument or narrative; with each idea in its right place in the sequence, and none missing; with all connections properly made.

Written in the first place for silent reading, but with consideration for euphony if read aloud.

Consistent in use of language; considerate of the possible
limitations of the reader's knowledge; with no indulgence of
personal caprice nor any attempt to improve on sincere statement by rhetorical artifice.

Such a style has no chance of immediate adoption in public
life, even in contexts where it is realized that officialese is un-
suitable and that a simpler, more intimate English must be
used. The following Government announcement, which appeared in all the London and provincial daily newspapers on
June 1st, 1941, and which combines the technique of the politi-
cian with that of the advertising man, is an interesting example
of the effect on prose of present social and economic conditions.

'RATIONING OF CLOTHING, CLOTH AND FOOTWEAR
FROM JUNE 1ST, 1941

'There is enough for all if we share and share alike. Rationing is the way to get fair shares. *Fair shares*—when workers are producing bombs and aeroplanes and guns instead of
frocks, suits and shoes. *Fair shares*—when ships must run the
gauntlet with munitions and food rather than with wool and
cotton. *Fair shares*—when movements of population outrun
local supplies. Rationing is not the same as shortage. Rationing, or *fair shares*, is the way to *prevent* a shortage without
interfering with full war production.
So, from now on (June 1st, 1941) you will have to present
coupons to buy clothing, cloth, footwear and knitting-wool.
At present the coupons to be used are the Margarine Coupons in your Food Ration Book. (You don't need these for
margarine and it is a great saving of paper to use this page
for the clothing ration.) There are 26 coupons on the margarine page. The numbers printed on them are to be ignored;
each coupon counts 1 only. 'You will receive 40 more coupons making 66 to last you *for a full year.*'

This is not good prose. Indeed, it caused confusion for a day or
two, in some districts. Many people were under the impression
that to the 'guns or butter?' choice, which had been semi-offi-

cially put before them some months before, a new choice was now added: 'clothing or margarine?' Some clothiers had to explain that they could not give a customer a pair of socks, say, in exchange for three coupons' worth of margarine; and grocers that they were not authorized to give extra margarine to customers who had enough clothing for the whole of the ensuing year. Yet if the advertisement had been written in better prose it would not have served the Government's purpose so well. It was the work of a skilled advertising man, whose business it was to 'sell' the rationing scheme to the public. Advertising men admit that they can rarely afford either to tell the truth or count on the intelligence of the public. The appeal must largely be to the passions. Whether the passions appealed to are mean or generous depends on the nature of the goods advertised; but in either case the style will necessarily be loose.

If the Government had not decided to introduce clothes-rationing gently to the unintelligent masses, but had instead given a practical summary of the situation which made rationing necessary, something like the following might have been issued:

'RATIONING OF CLOTHING, CLOTH AND FOOTWEAR
FROM JUNE 1ST, 1941

'Many of the ships which once brought us wool, cotton and hides from overseas have been sunk; others are now carrying food and munitions instead. And many of the workers who used these raw materials for making frocks, suits, shoes, etc. have been called up to do more important war work. Far fewer of these goods are therefore being manufactured, which has caused inconvenient local shortages—for example, in country districts crowded with evacuees—and selfish hoarding. Since nobody must go short of these goods while others have more than enough, we have decided to ration them.

So, from to-day, if you want to buy cloth, knitting-wool, clothes, boots, shoes, etc.—let us call this "Clothing, etc."—you will have to give up coupons. The first twenty-six coupons for you to use are those on page 10 of your ration book. They are headed "Margarine" and have numbers printed on them. Cross out the word "Margarine", writing instead

"Clothing, etc.", and pay no attention to the numbers, since all the coupons are of the same value and can be used whenever you please. You will continue to get your usual ration of margarine from the coupons on page 11. Later, each of you will be given a sheet of forty more coupons for "Clothing, etc.", making 66 in all, to last you until June 1st, 1942.'

In this slightly longer version several important points left out from the original are restored: that some workers are still producing clothing and footwear, and some ships still importing the raw materials; that there is a national shortage, as well as local shortages, of clothing and footwear, the inconveniences of which can be mitigated by rationing; that there has been some hoarding; that the term 'Clothing' includes cloth and footwear; that the so-called 'margarine coupons' are now to be used for clothing, not margarine; that 'this page' means the Margarine Page and not the page of the newspaper on which the advertisement appears; that the margarine ration can be got as usual with the help of another page of coupons; that the numbers printed on the so-called Margarine Coupons do not limit the time during which these can be used for buying 'Clothing, etc.'

Yet, despite its greater clarity as prose, this version would be regarded as 'bad advertising'. The theory of advertising, which has been gradually deduced from a practical analysis of sales-statistics, is that most people do not read carefully, and to sell them popular commodities in a competitive world one must take advantage of their carelessness: one must give them not careful prose, but prose that has the effect of conversational haste and catches the eye with one or two alluring phrases. In this case, the Government copy-writer did his job well enough. He avoided telling unpalatable truths, namely that there was a national clothing shortage, that the evacuation-scheme had caused serious local shortages, that many ships had been sunk, and that there had been hoarding. This would have had a depressing effect, ranged popular feeling against evacuees, and encouraged the hoarding of still uncontrolled goods. He politically refrained from saying even that the Government had decided to ration clothing; to do so might have made people grumble at the Government. He wrote instead in a way suggesting that fate and the public themselves were jointly responsible for the scheme. By the elementary tricks of repeating and italicizing *fair shares*, mentioning the saving of paper, and focusing attention of the ships that gallantly ran the gauntlet, he made his point: that justice, gratitude and economy alike required that the nation should cheerfully submit to further rationing inconveniences. The sketchiness of the instructions about the use of coupons did not matter much: broadcast explanations of the scheme and detailed instructions issued to clothiers and grocers would be sufficient to clear up any serious misunderstanding. By the middle of the week, indeed, even the stupidest people had got the idea into their heads and the scheme was working well.

4

The Use and Abuse
of Official English

In the course of their work, Government officials have to use the
formal phraseology which has been called 'Whitehallese' but is
by no means restricted to the Ministries of Whitehall. All the
lesser Government establishments use variants of it—post-offices, police-stations, income-tax offices, municipal councils and
education authorities. So also do such semi-official bodies as
Corporations and Royal Institutes. Nor can any clear distinction be drawn between the Government style and other official
styles—any society, club, or trade union that has committee
meetings, minutes and memoranda uses an official style in discussing and recording its business. These official styles shade off
into the business style. What is generally meant by 'the business
style' is the phraseology perpetuated in the signs of Pitman's
shorthand—'We are in receipt of your favour of the 4th ult.'
etc.—but such phrases, which are regarded as ungenteel by the
Civil Service, cover only the shopping side of business. The
management of a large firm has complicated matters of policy
to discuss and decide upon. However chatty the preliminary
discussions may be, final decisions are always worded officially.
The larger the firm, and the more corporation-minded its management, the more official-looking does this language become.
There is no great difference of technique between running a
huge monopolistic concern and running a Government Department; naturally therefore, there is no great difference of language.

The Civil Service has the most official-looking of styles.
When a Principal Assistant-Secretary drafts an official document, it is not he who is supposed to be speaking: it is a Department of the Crown. Or, if the document contains instructions to

the public, it is not even a Department speaking, but His Majesty's Government with the backing of the Law and the sanction of Parliament. The style must therefore be dignified and impersonal and in keeping with the formal traditions of Parliamentary and legal language.

Parliament has several traditional languages. One of them is the rhetorical. Mr. Churchill's methods of rousing and persuading his hearers are much the same as those of Gladstone and Burke; and this tradition is likely to hold so long as speeches are delivered in a raised voice across the floor of the House, not spoken conversationally into a microphone, as in some European Parliamentary chambers; and so long as there are survivors of the landed gentry who a generation ago formed the bulk of the British ruling classes. This style is sometimes known as the Republican, because under the Roman Republic the Senate was composed of men closely corresponding in rank, wealth and attainments with members of the British Parliament in the eighteenth and nineteenth centuries, and the procedure and language were strikingly similar. Mr. Churchill seems to think almost habitually in the Republican style, and in his historical writings indulges in such flights as this, from his *World Crisis*:

'There is nothing on which policy, however wise, can build; no foothold can be found for virtue or for valour, no authority or impetus for a rescuing genius. The mighty framework of German Imperial Power, which a few days before had overshadowed the nations, shivered suddenly into a thousand individually disintegrating fragments. All her Allies, whom she had so long sustained, fell down, broken and ruined, begging separately for peace. The faithful armies were beaten at the front and demoralized from the rear. The proud, efficient navy mutinied. Revolution exploded in the most disciplined of States. The Supreme War Lord fled.

Such a spectacle appals mankind; and a knell rang in the ears of the victors, even in their hours of triumph.'

But the landed gentry have gradually been ousted from Parliament by Labour representatives and men of business, and the pure Republican style is now attempted by few members.

The rest tend to use the official style even in debates where general principles of government are raised. And the greater part of Parliamentary proceedings does not lend itself to rhetorical treatment. When Bills are debated point by point in Committee, or when questions on departmental matters are put to Ministers, this is done in pure Civil Service style. For Question Time, for instance, the question is printed beforehand on the Order Paper for the Day; the answer is then composed by the senior officials of the Government Department concerned and read out by the Minister. A question was asked early in 1941 on the employment, in auxiliary Army services, of aliens from the Balkans. It ran:

> 'In view of the fact that the Bulgarian Government has pursued a course of action very deleterious to this country, ought not applications from Bulgarians to be treated with the greatest reserve?'

The questioner was Philip Noel Baker, an acute critic of Government Departments, yet his question was as well-veiled as any Government statement and there were reasons why it should be so. 'In view of the fact that' is a purposely loose phrase implying that because the Bulgarians have done *x* the British Government should do *y*; but it avoids making British action hinge too definitely on Bulgarian action. His Majesty's Government is presumed to be above any small-minded policy of reprisals; it moves independently, keeping the facts large-mindedly 'in view', and leaves historians to work out the relationship between them and its course of action—*post hoc* is not necessarily *propter hoc*. 'Pursued a course of action'—a course of action and its pursuit suggests a deliberate purpose: all kinds of sinister calculations are thus politely imputed to the Bulgarians. 'Deleterious' is a euphemism for 'bad for us'; there may be setbacks, diffculties, obstacles, misfortunes, but it is always presumed that the Government is powerful enough to overcome them. Granted, 'deleterious' is originally a very strong word taken over from the Greek (*'deleterios'*, destructive), but it has somehow been softened (perhaps by use in advertisements for patent medicines) into meaning 'unfavourable in the long run'.

Finally, 'treated with the greatest reserve'. This is the official equivalent of 'not trusted an inch', and has the advantage of concealing beneath the cloak of diplomatic courtesy the most active forms of distrust: it can mean either taking no notice, or giving the lie direct, or even putting through the third degree. It is almost as useful a covering phrase as 'taking the appropriate steps'.

When a supplementary question is tacked on, *ex tempore*, to a tabled question, it is nearly always officially phrased; and is answered, *ex tempore*, in the same style—even by Ministers who in debate are natural orators. Here is Mr. Churchill himself answering a supplementary question by Mr. Alfred Edwards, tacked on to a tabled question about the desirability of taking steps to have all Acts of Parliament translated into Basic English:

'Mr. Edwards: Does the Prime Minister not think it would be a great economy of the time of this House and a saving of money if the language of the official draughtsmen, after they have done their best or their worst with Bills, were translated into more understandable English? Will he contemplate the calamity that might befall us if these draughtsmen translated his speeches into official language?

Mr. Churchill: There is a great deal of official jargon, but it is not with a view to causing inconvenience, but because those who are entrusted with expressing the decisions of this House in a statutory form have found that to be the most convenient and precise method. With regard to the idea that we should try to describe everything in Basic English, that is a very fanciful idea. I would call Mr. Edwards's attention to the fact that the word "basic", like its neighbour "basal", are both under great suspicion at the present time—(laughter)—in the way in which they are used.'

It will be noticed that Mr. Churchill, fumbling for his answer, has used several stereotypes of expression very loosely connected: 'but it is not with a view to', 'with regard to the idea that', 'I would call Mr. Edwards's attention to the fact that'.

The style commonly derided as 'officialese' is really 'legalese'.

Parliament passes hundreds of Bills, and Government Departments issue thousands of regulations, all of which have to be phrased in the technical language that gives them currency in courts of law. They are full of back-references to previous laws and to the definitions contained in them, and stylistically they must fit into the existing body of legislation. An Act is an inclusive statement which has to apply to thousands of particular cases, and is characterized by two chief devices: first, the listing of particulars, as in 'any box, chest, case, coffer, casket or other receptacle', and second, the repetition of qualifying clauses. The following is an example of repetition from an Act enabling local authorities to start repairs quickly when buildings are damaged by air-raids:

> 'Where under the said Section One a local authority serves on the person having control of a building a notice of their intention to execute works at the expiration of the period specified in the notice and within that period the said person gives to the authority notice in writing that he does not object to the execution by the authority of the works specified in the notice the authority may execute those works before the expiration of the said period.'

First there are block phrases setting out the circumstance: 'the person having control of a building', 'the intention to execute works', 'at the expiration of the period specified'; then follows the new regulation, the block phrases repeated in order to make quite clear from the legal point of view that everything remains the same in the second context, except the obligation to wait until a formal time-limit has expired. A very small change at a great expense of words. In a recent *London Gazette* a column and a half was used to order a simple decrease of half an inch in the width of a medal-ribbon.

In the lower departments of Ministries and in their branch offices, such as post-offices, labour-exchanges, registry offices, most business is conducted in this legalistic language, with the help of set forms: someone wants to apply for a job, or a pension, or a contract, or a licence; and without a word Form J 16 or 272 A is handed to him to fill in. Where set forms are inadequate to the occasion, stereotyped phrases are fished out from the pool and strung together to suit the context. Thinking comes to be done in the same stereotypes.

Court evidence given by police-officers is an example of such thinking. A constable is not allowed to submit evidence in ordinary English: the desk-sergeant 'gorblimeys' it for him, leaving in their natural state only the words attributed to the accused persons or to witnesses.

'On the fifth inst. at nine p.m. approximately, when on duty, I was approaching the western outskirts of Sutton Porcorum, when I observed accused behaving in a suspicious manner in the company of the female witness. There was a light haze at the time. Accused was seated in a squatting posture on a branch of a municipal plane-tree adjoining no. 3 Pelham Place, at about ten feet from ground level, and the female witness, who was in a recumbent position on the municipal bench under the said tree was inciting accused to make an entry into the premises. The words she used were: "Go on, Alf, go on in, have a bit of pluck! No one won't see you." The female witness appeared to be under the influence of drink: she spoke these words in a highly jocular manner. The impression she conveyed was that she was sky-larking.'

The official style in the higher departments of a Ministry is comparatively free from cumbrous legalistic devices, because its ordinary records and announcements are not called into question in courts of law. It is much less complex in structure and correspondingly less definite in meaning. The subjects about which higher Government officials have to write are, for the most part, concerned with policy and the appropriate application of policy. Policy itself is not expressed in legal terms, but kept fluid until particular circumstances crystallize it into precedents. The relationship between various aspects and items of policy is thus undefined until some departmental annalist relates them in retrospect; so the day-to-day style of a Government Department is full of ambiguous phrases and loosely related clauses—nobody can be quite sure how things will turn out and nobody wishes to commit himself. The following are

quotations from more than usually vague minutes (1934-7) circulated in a large Ministry:

> 'While the 80% can be used as a guide, other general con-
> ditions must be taken into account, and in particular we
> should not approve allowances for any particular force much
> in excess of the allowances at present paid in the generality of
> forces where circumstances are parallel.'

> 'I am rather doubtful whether there is much to be gained
> by taking these representations too seriously. On the whole I
> think the next step, if any, might be to make further enquir-
> ies.'

> 'This is a border line case, but not, I think, very far over
> the border: I agree that in this case and in somewhat similar
> cases an interview at H.O. may save us trouble.'

And here is a peremptory reminder from the Stationery Office:

> 'Dear Sir,
>   I have to call attention to communications from this De-
> partment of 3.4.34, 17.4.34 ("refer" and "hastener") and
> 26.5.34 (letter under above reference) respecting . . . in view
> of the fact that no reply has yet been received to any of them.
>   The matter is now urgent to the extent pointed out in the
> third paragraph of my letter of 26th ultimo.
>   Yours faithfully'

These quotations raise another point: the non-committal
timorousness of the official style. A Department does not give
away the details of its work: sometimes because they are so
complex that no one person fully understands them, sometimes
because they are confidential, but more often because of the
tradition of anonymous silence observed by the Civil Service in
all its contacts with the outside world. Government officials, like
members of the British Medical Association, are not allowed to
advertise themselves, nor to get into trouble in the newspapers
nor to defend themselves if they do. The Minister is briefed to
answer for his Department if it is criticized in Parliament and

no one else may do so in any other way—except in recent years the Public Relations Officer, who is allowed to write letters to *The Times* in defence of his Department, provided that he does not touch on major matters of policy. One of the effects of this rule is to make officials afraid of publicity. To avoid it they will publish the most indefinite generalities phrased with the most face-saving ingenuity; and when a Department needs to explain something to the public in order to persuade them to some co-operative action, it has to employ professional publicity-men untainted by the habit of official reticence.

In theory His Majesty's Government is One, collectively responsible for the actions of any part of it, and in practice most of its decisions are collectively made, no single person being actually responsible. This constitutional doctrine is applied within Departments and within the departmental committees. The Minister is allowed by courtesy to write 'I have decided', but all departmental officials must use the passive voice: 'it is considered desirable', 'it was felt necessary', 'in this connexion it might be pointed out'. The official always speaks in the name of his Minister, the Minister in the name of the Cabinet, the Cabinet in the name of the King. This ceremonial practice makes for extreme indecisiveness. When a great many officials have to be consulted on a complicated matter the circumstances may have changed entirely before they manage to agree. The delays so caused are fancifully ascribed to 'red tape'. Any interim announcement of such deliberations is sure to be even more indefinite than usual, for the draft of it will have gone through many hands to ensure that all signs of disagreement are well covered up. Even the frankest committee minutes on the most hotly contested questions are rarely more explicit than: 'There appeared to be considerable divergence of opinion regarding the line to be adopted in the event of . . .'

The official style is at once humble, polite, curt and disagreeable: it derives partly from that used in Byzantine times by the eunuch slave-secretariat, writing stiffly in the name of His Sacred Majesty, whose confidence they enjoyed, to their fellow-slaves outside the palace-precincts—for the Emperor had summary power over everyone; and partly from the style used by the cleric-bureaucracy of the Middle Ages, writing stiffly in the

name of the feudal lords to their serfs and, though cautious of
offending their employers, protected from injury by being servants of the Church, not of the Crown, and so subject to canon,
not feudal, law. The official style of civil servants, so far as it
recalls its Byzantine derivation, is written by slaves to fellow-
slaves of a fictitious tyrant; and, so far as it recalls its mediaeval
derivation, is written by members of a quasi-ecclesiastical body,
on behalf of quasi-feudal ministers (who, being politicians,
come under a different code of behaviour from theirs) to a serf-
like public. Permanent civil servants are sacrosanct, for they
cannot be dismissed from their employment by a Minister of
the Crown, but only transferred to another Department; yet
they fear his displeasure, if juniors, because of his influence with
their departmental chiefs.

Here is a typical official announcement:

> 'As regards the slaughter of sound cattle and sheep it must
> be recognized that by reason of the inevitable fluctuation in
> the supplies both from overseas and from home sources and
> the limited capacity of cold stores the maintenance of the
> meat ration presents problems of exceptional difficulty, and
> the Minister of Agriculture is anxious that farmers should do
> their utmost within the limits imposed by war-time feeding
> conditions to assist in maintaining a regular supply of fat
> stock for slaughter.'

This paragraph has suffered from collective authorship; no single person could possibly have written so confusedly by himself.
The first phrase is the official way of introducing a new aspect
of a subject without stating its connexion with what goes before
or follows. After 'as regards' comes 'it must be recognized', a
frequent form of official exhortation, put in the passive voice
because officials are never quite sure whether they are exhorting themselves, other officials, the public in general, or some
unspecified section of the public. Here it appears, but not until
the fifth line, that they are exhorting farmers. When 'by reason
of' follows such a phrase it can be assumed that the Department is about to offer excuses about the 'difficulties of the present situation', yet carefully avoid blaming anyone in

particular. 'Presents problems of exceptional difficulty' is the formula used here. This is how the situation appears to officials who know something of the details that make up the problem; but when addressing the public they forget that some people will know nothing of the details and others will be all too intimately acquainted with them, and that both will be inclined to regard general talk about 'problems' as a cover for muddle and lack of understanding. Now comes the real point, the instructions which farmers are to follow: they are to send their beasts regularly to slaughter. But since the necessary orders for ensuring such regularity would be impossibly complicated and vexatious, recourse is had to the voluntary principle. The farmers are told politely that the Minister is 'anxious' and that they 'should do their utmost to assist in maintaining a regular supply'. The paragraph reads absurdly because the official style, when used in addresses to the public, should be reserved for orders—a plea for co-operation should be written in the simple, catchy style of good advertisement copy. There is no excuse here for such heavily veiled language.

The chief trouble with the official style is that it spreads far beyond the formal contexts to which it is suited. Most civil servants, having learned to write in this way, cannot throw off the habit. The obscurity of their public announcements largely accounts for the disrepute into which Departmental activities have fallen: for the public naturally supposes that Departments are as muddled and stodgy as their announcements.

The habit of obscurity is partly caused by a settled disinclination among public servants to give a definite refusal even where assent is out of the question; or to convey a vigorous rebuke even where, in private correspondence, any person with self-respect would feel bound to do so. This mood is conveyed by a polite and emasculated style—polite because, when writing to a member of the public, the public servant is, in theory at least, addressing one of his collective employers; emasculated because, as a cog in the Government machine, he must make his phrases look as mechanical as possible by stripping them of all personal feeling and opinion. One of the common emasculating devices is to convey decisions in the conditional tense. They are thus translated from the ordinary world of practice into a region of unfulfilled hypothesis:

'The suggestion contained in your letter of 10th August regarding the terms of Clause 7 of the   and (Wartime) Regulations Act has received the fullest consideration, but the Minister would scarcely agree that they might under normal conditions be regarded as in any way offensive in tendency.'

This means that the departmental chief does not consider the wording of Clause 7 to be rude. The correspondent must not be bluntly told so, lest he should think his complaint had not been considered at all, but at the same time he must be gently reproached for having attributed offensive intentions to the authors of the Act. This is achieved by the conditional tense and the subjunctive which follows it; the complaint is thus turned into an hypothesis which, it is implied, should never have been proposed. Another example of this stylistic emasculation: a junior official had written a Minute, the purport of which was 'a byelaw on the subject is not necessary', but a senior amended it to 'a byelaw on the subject is not in the present circumstances considered necessary'; and so threw doubt on the view expressed, though it was permanently settled.

There are many ways of delicately suggesting that a correspondent should not have troubled His Majesty's Government. For instance:

'It would appear, however, that in the conditions prevailing this contention could hardly be regarded as justifiable . . .'

rather than:

'No, we disagree. Why don't you trust us? We are in a far better position than you to know all the facts and precedents.'

Or:

'The Minister is not aware that any undertaking of this character has been entered into, and for your information I

am instructed to remind you that the point in question was
made abundantly clear to the satisfaction of all parties in our
letter of May 17th, 1939.'

rather than:

'We took good care to promise nothing in 1939. Why bring
the matter up again, you fools?'

Such cloaked phrasing is not reserved for the negative side of
public business: official requests are often as emasculated as
refusals or denials:

'I am instructed by the Minister to make enquiries with a
view to obtaining information as to whether . . .'

'We want to know' would have been simpler; but an official
must not stupidly admit to ignorance. He avoids doing so by
making 'information' the chief word in the sentence: even officials can legitimately ask for 'information', as general medical
practitioners can ask for a 'second opinion', without seeming
incompetent. But having got 'information' into the sentence,
the official's problem is how to connect it with the machinery of
his Department and with the facts he wants to know. Hence
'with a view to obtaining' and 'as to whether': both are valuable means of introducing an appearance of relationship into a
difficult succession of abstract nouns.

We have mentioned a disagreeable quality mixed with the
politeness of official letters. The official himself often finds it
tedious to write such letters, and his tedium is communicated to
his style. But a more positive kind of disagreeableness is caused
rather by the contradiction inherent in all official writing: the
public approaches, or is approached by, temperamental individuals who are paid to disguise themselves as anonymous parts
of a vast and unerring mechanism. A member of the public
may know that he is in communication with a particular official, but can never identity him if he wishes to call him personally to account. He feels the same fear and distaste as when
meeting bats in a dark room—not sure whether they are mere

bats or, as their menacingly evasive gyrations suggest, creatures far more powerful and uncanny.

This sense is strengthened by the standing instructions that all letters from the public should be addressed to the Permanent Under-Secretary, and not to any named official. Officials make a habit of signing their names so illegibly that no one can decipher their signature and so be tempted to by-pass the 'proper channels' by starting a personal correspondence. Even announcements of changes in the staff at Ministries are usually made in terms of machinery. A junior official once drafted a public announcement beginning: 'The Minister has decided to appoint a statistical officer.' This was amended by one of his seniors to: 'The Minister has decided to inaugurate a statistical section.' It was then pointed out to the senior by an official more senior still that the appointment of one officer scarcely constituted a section. He wisely concurred and altered the draft again: 'The Minister has decided to inaugurate the nucleus of a statistical section.' The traditions of the machine were thus preserved at the cost of three unnecessary words.

Temporary civil servants, particularly women, feel uncomfortable in their use of the official style. It goes against their consciences to write something which conveys no precise meaning, but only the general impression 'we could say more'. Yet they feel obliged to conform to this style, because they are seldom lawyers and, when applying rules which they do not understand, do not wish to commit themselves to a precise opinion on any doubtful point. Often they have to write a letter like the following:

Dear Madam,

I am directed to refer to your letter no. 1 of the 3rd instant and to state that the circumstances of your case are not covered by any provision in the relevant sub-section of section 10 of the Railway Passengers' Insurance (Consolidation) Act 1918 and that therefore it would appear that you are not entitled to compensation under the Act.

I am, Madam,

your obedient servant

They long to write instead:

Dear Mrs. Smith,

So far as I can make out, the Railway Insurance Act, as it applies to your case, is shamefully unfair; but that is not my fault. I prefer not to go into the exact reasons why we cannot see that you get paid compensation for the damage you suffered from no fault of your own; the fact is, nobody here in this office is quite sure of the legal implications of the various sub-sections which come into question and if I gave you a summary of what *I* think they are, somebody important might read it and disagree and put me on the mat. I feel very badly about your case, really I do, and nothing would give me greater pleasure than to be able to write to you in the same warm way that the Chancellor of the Exchequer uses in the Personal Column of *The Times* when he acknowledges anonymous gifts to the Treasury; but all my letters have to begin "I am directed to refer to your letter no.——of——and to state that ——" and that makes too chilly a start for any pleasantness. Anyhow, charity begins at home, and it's as much as my job is worth to press for your getting compensation. So you won't get it. Please don't argue about this, because it will waste hours of your time and ours. Most of the other people in the office agree with me that the wording of the Act is against you; and only Parliament can amend Acts.

Yours sincerely, etc.

It is only very rarely that frankness and humour are admitted into official correspondence; however, they would be likely to occur in a confidential report, supposedly written by the Prime Minister to the King—for example, on the progress of a Government Bill—but in fact drafted by a high Treasury official. It might contain such phrases as:

'It was before a very thin and jaded house that the Bill was presented for its Third Reading—and the Government Whips had some difficulty in keeping sufficient of their flock on the right side of the wicketgate to assure its passing—truancy was particularly rife in the back benches. . . .'

The official style is generally used in public announcements by business firms and corporations; the only exceptions being occasional announcements in humorous form released by their advertising departments. Even informal announcements addressed vaguely to 'you', instead of beginning 'The public is requested', remain hopelessly official; often with fawning and snarling in the same sentence.

The following is a notice posted in 1940-41 in all the coaches of a West Country Bus Company:

> 'It is our desire to give you good travel service where most needed. If you experience inconvenience especially during the busy summer months we would ask your kind forbearance in the national interest which imposes economy in fuel and man-power. It will be our endeavour, as always, to serve your best interests.'

It will be noticed that the principal subject, the war, is omitted; that the phrase 'we would ask your kind forbearance in the national interest' has the disagreeable implication that it is unpatriotic to complain when buses are late or full; that 'to serve your best interests' is patronizing as well as repetitive; that no apologies are offered. What is probably meant is:

> 'Your interests are still our closest concern, as in peacetime. We will give you the best possible bus-service, consistent with necessary war economies in men and fuel. So please bear patiently the inconveniences which, to our deep regret, you are likely to suffer especially during the busy summer months.'

It would be foolish to quarrel with any of the dialects of officialese. Army officers are privileged to write: 'At the conclusion of the tactical exercise officers, warrant officers and n.c.o's will stand fast; other ranks will proceed in an orderly manner to their respective hutments'—instead of: 'After the manœuvres all private soldiers will return quietly to their huts; the rest of the battalion will stand fast'. And business men are privileged to write: 'Reference your esteemed advice undated' instead of

'Thank you for this morning's letter.' These are the styles that suit full-dress military uniform or formal business-dress. So long as such an impersonal dialect is written plainly according to its own rules, the only objection that one can raise is to an inappropriate extension of its use. For example, when a business man who has bought a country estate sends round an intimidating circular to a tenantry long accustomed to the direct personal language of generations of squires:

'The Loamshire Investment Company Limited wish it to be clearly understood that in future all applications for repair of roofs, window fitments, etc. will be made in writing direct to the Estate office and not communicated by word of mouth to individual employees concerned with such work.'

Or when B.B.C. bulletins containing good news are written in the same flat style that is found serviceable in lessening the impact of bad.

To many business men the official style is a proof-armour that they assume, often ridiculously, in every contact with their subordinates: managing directors of large stores and of public utility corporations are caricatured as using it even to their wives and children. The manager of a large advertising agency was obliged in 1938 to dismiss three of his copy-writers because an important customer-firm had given notice that they were withdrawing their account. He did not wish the reason for his decision to be known and was so nervous and embarrassed when he gave the three copy-writers their notice of dismissal that he forgot himself: he shook hands with one of them and said how sorry he was to lose him.

This encouraged the copy-writer to ask: 'In that case, sir, why are you getting rid of me?'

The manager grew red, fumbled round for a suitable stereotype and finally stammered . . . 'A highly improper question . . . highly improper! Let me remind you of the fact that *this is neither the time nor the place* to ask such a highly improper question!'

The following shrewd and valuable remarks were circulated, about 1930, in one of the larger Ministries by a senior Civil Service official; we have edited them here and there:

'I find myself involved in daily drudgery with letters and minutes referred to me, forced to correct glaring errors in spelling, grammar and punctuation. For the most part these errors arise from thoughtlessness rather than miseducation. For example:

A letter begins by "acknowledging" a report received weeks earlier, formal acknowledgement having already been made.

A Municipal Council is "reminded" of an opinion not previously communicated to it, or has something obvious "explained" to it, or has something not obvious introduced to it with the phrase "of course".

The second sentence of a two-page letter begins with "I am to add"—a phrase which is nearly always needless and only justified when it occurs in the final paragraph.

A careless abbreviation has been used—"Bye-laws concerned with h.w.c."—which the typist misreads as "height of water-closets" when what is meant is "the housing of the working classes".

The Minister is said to "regret" that he cannot intervene in some affair when there is no reason for such regret, and even sometimes when the Courts are dealing with the person so addressed. Regret must not be allowed to creep in as "common form" but should be kept for deserving cases. Or the Minister is said to be "glad" or "happy" to intervene. The words, like "regret", may suggest more than is meant; and it is therefore better to use colourless but practical words, such as "ready", "prepared" or "willing", or merely "will intervene"—unless any real encouragement is intended.

An Act of Parliament or bye-law is said to be "to the following effect", and then the relevant sub-section is quoted. This suggests that the quotation is merely a paraphrase.

We must try to write our letters with an eye to the recipient. To take two small examples: we ought to know that the request to "submit" drafts, observations and so on irritates some Local Authorities because of its suggestion that they are in a subservient position—"send" or "show" are shorter and better words. And we ought to know that Local Authorities will be exasperated to have their proposals rejected on the ground that to implement them "would be contrary to the practice of the Department". The tactful phrasing is: "The Minister cannot properly implement these proposals because . . ."

Unless a person who writes to us seems to be asking for a snub by putting on airs or being deliberately rude we must not frame our answer in a way to make him feel that he has made a fool of himself or taken a liberty in writing to us: for example, we must not begin by saying that we do not understand his letter, unless we literally do not. If there is some obscure phrase or reference contained in it, we can ask him, in the second or third sentence, to elucidate this; but must not discourage him by throwing it back at him at the outset.

In writing to outsiders about letters, sent on to us from other Departments of Government, which do not, however, concern us, we must not answer crudely:

"I am directed to advert to your letter forwarded from the Board of Trade and to state that the Minister has no jurisdiction . . ."

It will give the recipient a better impression of the Service if we answer:

"Your letter was forwarded to us by the President of the Board of Trade, who has himself no jurisdiction, to ascertain whether the Minister could help you. He regrets, however (if regrets are appropriate), that he is not in a position to do so, and, so far as he is aware, the matter does not fall within the powers of any Department of Government."

I have nothing to say against the old style of drafting letters, clauses, and so on, where the object is to be complete and precise, or (occasionally) when for practical reasons an air of portentousness has to be assumed. But in this style unnecessary words are often used merely from a habit of circumlocution. For example:

"As regards the suggestion in your letter I am to say that the Minister agrees to the course suggested."

Why not: "The Minister agrees to the course suggested in your letter"?

Or: "It is not clear from the terms of your letter whether the Council have had under consideration the question whether the fact that, in pursuance of Section 5, they are required to do A, renders B unnecessary."

Why not: "It is not clear from your letter whether or not the Council have considered that because Section 5 requires them to do A, it will be unnecessary for them also to do B"?

Or: "With respect to your letter relative to the desirability of the adoption in the case of an urban district of a regulation restricting the fouling of pavements by dogs, I am to state . . ."

Why not: "In answer to your enquiry, whether it is desirable for an urban district to adopt a regulation restricting the fouling of pavements by dogs, I am to state . . ."?

We must not let a letter be ambiguous because the question it answers has been ambiguously phrased. Recently a Local Authority asked whether an enactment, which they cited, authorised expenditure "in connexion with" a certain object. We answered this loose question with an equally loose answer "Yes", whereas the enactment authorised only certain specified categories of expenditure which, though "in connexion with" the object named, did not fall within the authorised categories; it was challenged and Branch X complained, justly, that we had put them in a difficulty. If we had quoted the enactment this difficulty would never have arisen.'

These remarks are admirable, but there are not many officials who have the knowledge, taste, time and patience to give their subordinates similar lessons in logic and manners. What perhaps is needed in every Department of Government is a trained Minute-master, charged to read through samples of Minutes by junior officials, carefully checking and explaining all infringements of the official decencies. Moreover, an example of discrimination in use of official language should be set by the Civil Service in general. Though the official style may continue in internal use in the Departments, ordinary straightforward English should be used for all external purposes. Similarly, crystallized legal language, though it may be retained for security's sake in the framing of laws and regulations, should not appear in notices posted on the public boards in church porches or in the vestibules of town halls. Or not unless glosses are provided in understandable—and we do not mean Basic—English for all whom they may concern.

5

The Principles
of Clear Statement—I

We here record our own principles for writing prose. They are concerned partly with the secure conveyance of information and partly with its decent, or graceful, conveyance, and have been suggested by our recent examination of a great mass of miscellaneous writing. Our practice was to pick up every book or paper we found lying about and, whenever our reading pace was checked by some difficulty of expression, to note the cause. Eventually we formulated our principles after cataloguing the difficulties under forty-one general headings—twenty-five concerned with clarity of statement, and sixteen with grace of expression.

The ancient Greeks, in working out their principles for prose, found that they could not confine themselves to Orthology (a study of the proper formation of words), Accidence (a study of the grammatical relation of words) and Syntax (a study of the grammatical relation of phrases and sentences): they had to include Logic, which is the study of the proper relation of ideas. We have found the same. Logic concerns the secure conveyance of information: information containing a contradiction or an absurdity is as puzzling to the recipient as one from which relevant facts are omitted or in which ambiguities or grammatical faults occur.

We are aware that the formulation of these principles invites the objection that Principle Nine contains Principles One to Seven (those that apply most practically to the writing of messages and narratives); that Principle Twenty-Three contains Principles Seventeen to Twenty-Five, and that Principle Eight contains the whole series; but look into any carpenter's tool-bag and see how many different hammers, chisels, planes and screw-drivers he keeps there—not for ostentation or luxury, but for different sorts of jobs.

The twenty-five numbered principles which we formulate for clarity of statement are contained in Chapters Five, Six and Seven; the sixteen lettered principles which concern the graces of expression are contained in Chapter Eight.

Principle One

It should always be made clear who is addressing whom, and on the subject of whom.

We shall begin with the word 'we'. Throughout this book 'we' means Robert Graves and Alan Hodge, and nobody else. The casual use of 'we' is often extremely confusing. It may mean 'we', members of a nation identifying themselves with their Government or armed forces ('we are doing very well against Italy'); or 'we', the common people protesting against the Government; or 'we', the thinking people ('we can see that this argument is invalidated by etc.'); or 'we', the writer and the particular public he addresses; or 'we', a committee or other collaborative body; or 'we', the participants in certain recorded events; or we, the Editor. Each of these uses is legitimate so long as the 'we' is clearly defined, and remains constant in sense throughout the passage in which it occurs. Every writer should be clear *who he is* for the purpose of writing—whether himself, or the representative of a point of view, or the spokesman of a particular group. Similarly with 'you'. Every writer should envisage his potential public—which may be twenty people, two hundred, twenty thousand, or the whole wide world—and should write nothing either above or below its supposed capacity.

Religious writers are particularly capricious in their use of 'we'. Sometimes 'we' means the priesthood, sometimes the Church, sometimes sinners. If a preacher says: 'My brethren, we are all worshippers of the Devil and of Mammon,' he obviously expects his congregation to understand this as a formal expression of Christian self-abasement, not as a definition of

Church policy; yet in some contexts it is not at all clear whether he is speaking as priest or as sinner.

The following is from an essay on the Elizabethan playwright, John Marston, by T. S. Eliot; he is discussing *The Tragedy of Sophonisba*:

> 'We may be asked to account, in giving this play such high place, for the fact that neither contemporary popularity nor the criticism of posterity yields any support. Well; it may be modestly suggested that in our judgements of Elizabethan plays in general we are very much influenced by Elizabethan standards. The fact that Shakespeare transcended all other poets and dramatists of the time, imposes a Shakespearean standard: whatever is of the same kind of drama as Shakespeare's, whatever may be measured by Shakespeare, however inferior to Shakespeare's it may be, is assumed to be better than whatever is of a different kind. However catholic-minded we may be in general, the moment we enter the Elizabethan period we praise or condemn plays [etc. etc.].'

The first 'we' is Mr. Eliot's editorial 'we'; the 'we' in the second sentence and the 'we' in the last means all critics *except* Mr. Eliot—who gives high place to *The Tragedy of Sophonisba* because, as he goes on to say, it is not Shakespearean but 'Senecal'.

Many writers avoid the direct attribution of acts or words to their authors, wherever this might possibly cause trouble or heart-burning. This often makes a passage read mysteriously. In a recent 'Sermon on Silence', by the aged Bishop of Norwich (who writes in the overterse style of Seneca), it is not clear who first made the remark about the Silent Column hinted at in the second sentence; who misapprehended or exaggerated the remark; whose good sense subsequently restored proportion; and so on throughout the passage:

> 'We hear little now of the silent column. What was first said seems to have been misapprehended or exaggerated. Good sense has subsequently restored proportion. Such good sense often leads to a wholesome reversal or disuse of formal declarations which came to be felt mistaken or out of place.

The practice of law and the formulation of Church system supply examples of discarding the obsolete. No one desires to discountenance thoughtful criticism directed to quicker winning of the war or to silence anyone who has something worth hearing to say. The upshot of the discussion seems to be "Think before you speak". This will protect you from folly and regret.

Once a word has been spoken it is out of control. A plan when disclosed invites criticism and ceases to be the property of the originator. Silence often gives to authority a greater weight than the spoken word. Reserve need involve nothing unfriendly or disagreeable.'

A more outspoken writer would have put:

'Mr. Duff Cooper, the Minister of Information, who first coined the phrase "The Silent Column", has now perhaps realized that when he recommended the public so urgently to silence he had lost his sense of proportion. Perhaps he has reasoned with himself: "Must people be silenced who have something worth while to say, especially about quicker ways of winning the war than those already tried?—I should not want that to happen." At any rate, we now hear little about the Silent Column; and this is another of the many cases in which Ministerial exhortations have wisely been either withdrawn or allowed to become a dead letter. (Representatives of the Law and the Church frequently do the same thing with obsolete or mistaken formulas.)

My own conclusion about silence is that people ought always to think before they speak and thus avoid saying anything regrettable: for once a word has been spoken, though it may be withdrawn, it cannot be unsaid.

Silence is particularly becoming in a person who is responsible for making important decisions. If he discloses a plan before the proper time, he invites criticisms which may prevent its being carried out as he intended. Often, the less a person in authority says, the more respect he earns. A reserved person is not necessarily considered unfriendly or disagreeable.'

A very frequent cause of misunderstanding is careless use of the word 'he'. The convention about 'he' or 'him' is that it refers to the person most recently mentioned, unless this happens to be someone of so little importance in the sentence that the person of most importance is obviously the 'he' in the writer's mind. For example: 'Pankerton picked up the meal sack, which happened to belong to his brother Fred; he staggered with it through the hall and disappeared in the shrubbery.' Obviously the 'he' who staggered out was Pankerton himself, not his brother Fred. But who are the different 'he's' in this passage from a pulp novel?

> 'Dave ruminated. The Lynchburg Kid was up to his old tricks, eh? He would see to it that the district was set ablaze. He couldn't afford to let him get away with that—so there'd be dirty work at the cross-roads before the night was much older.'

The best way out of difficulty would have been to write:

> 'Dave ruminated. He would see to it that the district was set ablaze now that the Lynchburg Kid was up to his old tricks. The Kid couldn't afford to let him get away with that, so there'd be dirty work at the cross-roads before the night was much older.'

Here are two other examples in which a regard for Principle One would have made for clearer prose. H. G. Wells in a newspaper article:

> 'Within recorded time there is no such thing as complete natural man. He climps himself, he cuts himself about, he hacks bits off himself. He tattoos himself, and sticks things through his ears and nose, he wraps skins and fabrics about himself.'

Who is this 'he'? Nobody has yet been mentioned except 'a complete natural man', and even his existence has been denied. It cannot even be 'man' in general: Mr. Wells's readers, for example, do not stick things through their ears and noses. 'Atticus', the Sunday columnist:

> 'So far none of the offspring of our Premiers have [*sic*] looked like emulating the younger Pitt.'

He goes on to discuss the sons of Bonar Law, Baldwin, Lloyd George, Ramsay MacDonald, but without explaining the Pitt reference. Since he does not mention Miss Megan Lloyd George or Miss Ishbel MacDonald, it may be concluded that by 'offspring' he means 'sons', and since he goes back no further in date than Lloyd George, he probably means 'our recent Premiers', not 'all our Premiers since Pitt'. The sentence would have been clearer if writtern:

> 'So far no son of any recent British Premier has looked like succeding his father, as the younger Pitt succeeded his.'

Principle Two

It should always be made clear which of two or more things already mentioned is being discussed.

The following are examples of a failure to be clear in this sense.

From a newspaper short-story:

> 'Mr. Rattray used morosely to couple Charley and young Herb with Hitler and Goering, saying that he did not know which he disliked the more.'

What did Mr. Rattray not know? Whether he disliked Charley more than young Herb (or contrariwise)? Or whether he disliked Charley and young Herb as a pair more than Hitler and Goering as a pair (or contrariwise)?

From Roger Coxon's Biography, *Chesterfield and His Critics*:

> 'Criticism at its worst may hinder, and at its best hasten the rejection of a bad or the acceptance of a good trend in

art; but beyond this fourfold function in the light of history
criticism seems to have done little more, so far as broad
movements are concerned.'

Which four functions are these? If he is writing about the functions of criticism in supplying history with movements, then
there are eight, not four, such functions; but if about the moral
functions of criticism, then there are four but a different four
from those he specifies. For criticism at its worst not only hinders the rejection of a bad trend and the acceptance of a good,
but hastens the rejection of a good trend and the acceptance of
a bad; at its best it not only hastens the rejection of a bad trend
and the acceptance of a good, but hinders the acceptance of a
bad trend and the rejection of a good. If Mr. Coxon is writing
about the moral functions of criticism, it is likely that the four
he intends are: the hindering of the rejection of a good trend;
the hindering of the acceptance of a bad; the hastening of the
acceptance of a good; the hastening of the rejection of a bad.

An interesting example of a writer making an effort to distinguish which from which, and failing in consequence to get
things straight, is found in Miss L. Susan Stebbing's critique of
political thought, *Thinking to Some Purpose*:

> 'It is instructive to compare this [analogy of Sir Arthur
> Eddington's] with the analogy quoted from Professor An-
> drade at the beginning of this chapter. Eddington does not
> use his analogy purely for the sake of illustration; he uses it in
> order to draw conclusions with regard to the nature of the
> external world and the nature of our knowledge about the
> external world.'

Miss Stebbing conscientiously repeats 'external world' perhaps
because the phrase 'our knowledge about it' (which would be
grammatically irreproachable, as referring to the most recently
named object) might be misunderstood. She has not been quite
conscientious enough. She has left out an element in her argument, by a failure to distinguish between 'knowledge of the
external world' (which an animal might have) and 'knowledge
of the nature of the external world' (which a thinking person

might have). She probably felt, as she wrote, that 'nature of the knowledge of the nature of the external world' was an impossibly cumbersome phrase; so compromised with 'the nature of our knowledge about the external world' which reads more easily, but is not adequate to the context.

An easy way out would have been:

> 'It is instructive to compare this analogy [of Sir Arthur Eddington's] with that quoted from Professor Andrade at the beginning of this chapter. Eddington does not use his analogy for the sake of illustration, so much as for drawing conclusions with regard to the nature of the external world and to that of our knowledge of this nature.'

Principle Three

Every unfamiliar subject or concept should be clearly defined; and neither discussed as if the reader knew all about it already nor stylistically disguised.

It is a common defect of English critical writing that terms are not immediately defined, but alter in meaning during the argument. Art-critics, for example, write about 'significant form' in painting without explaining what the form is supposed to signify, and use it in the same context equally for 'representational' and 'abstract' pictures. They also introduce musical metaphor into their descriptions of painting—'Mr. Duncan Grant's delicious contrapuntal effects', 'the shrill arpeggios of Guevara'— without defining the extremely tenous relation of music to painting. Literary critics use the word 'romantic' as though it had only one meaning rather than a thousand shades of meaning lying between the concepts 'derived from the Latin' and 'emotional'. Theorists of political economy are equally slipshod: they will, for example, build financial arguments on the assumption that there is only one sort of statistically recognized ton, though actually there are nine or ten. This is done less in ignorance than in self-defence: not to turn a blind eye to the difference between the ton-measure used in various sets of statistics would involve them in so much mathematical drudgery that they would fall behindhand in their theorizing. Similarly, they prefer to use 'value' as though it had a simple, evident, invariable meaning, rather than define the criterion of evaluation in each context.

The evasive use of language in official writing has been commented on in Chapter Four. Such evasion is not confined to official contexts. For example, in the following letter to the Press (1940), the Principal of Webster's College, Aberdeen, seems incapacitated by the official style from stating his case simply. (Or is he using it as a cloak for writing in what might be thought an unrealistic or even 'defeatist' strain?)

'Sir—The immediate issue in regard to "reprisals" would appear to be indiscriminate bombing v. objective bombing. . . . So long as our brave lads are sent out to bomb objectives, and thus cripple the enemy at the source, so long will they perform their duties with zeal and enthusiasm. . . .'

What he probably means is:

'Sir: I trust that the Government will not order immoral counter-measures to the recent air raids. So long as our brave Scottish airmen are sent out to cripple the enemy by dropping bombs on military objectives, rather than to take reprisals against his civil population by an indiscriminate bombing of residential districts, they will perform their duties with zeal. . . .'

Modern stylistic disguises of sense are innumerable. They range from the neo-Euphuistic novel-style to the smart-aleck style of football reporting. To take a midway example: a well-informed American professor, Louis Gottschalk, writing in modern academic style on the literary origins of the French Revolution:

'As for Raynal, it is Lamartine who is responsible for the statement that Marat was chiefly under his intellectual sway.

Lamartine in this case as in others has allowed his poetic imagination to run away with his historical judgement. There is more cause to consider the influence of Beccaria. Though the great Italian criminologist received but scanty mention in the voluminous writings of Marat, the latter's *Plan de Législation Criminelle* resembles the former's *Traité des Délits et des Peines* to such an extent as to have led to the accusation of plagiarism by later writers—a charge which was nevertheless not justified. But another and perhaps greater source of inspiration and knowledge for this work must certainly have been Montesquieu's *Esprit des Lois*.'

The best schooling for historians of this sort would be to make them write out their paragraphs as if they were to be cabled at a shilling a word, and then put back the 'and's' and 'the's' and other unimportant but comforting parts of speech. Thus:

'LARMARTINE UNTRUSTWORTHY HISTORIAN WHEN RHETORI-
CAL FIRST STATED MARATS WRITING OVERINFLUENCED BY RAY-
NAL STOP LATER WRITERS UNJUSTIFIABLY ACCUSE MARAT PLA-
GIARIZING BECCARIA ITALIAN CRIMINOLOGIST HARDLY
MENTIONED IN MARATS WORKS STOP PLAUSIBE BECAUSE RESEM-
BLANCE MARATS PLAN LEGISLATION BECCARIAS TRAITE DELITS
STOP ANYHOW PLAN OWES MOST MONTESQUIEUS ESPRIT LOIS.'

which would ease out again to:

'It was Lamartine, an untrustworthy historian when he was writing rhetorically, who first said that Marat's work was over-influenced by Raynal. Later writers, also, accuse Marat of plagiarizing Beccaria, the Italian criminologist, whom he hardly mentions in all his many writings. This is unjustified, though more plausible since there is a certain resemblance between Marat's *Plan de Législation Criminelle* and Beccaria's *Traité des Délits et des Peines*. In any case, Marat's *Plan* owes more to Montesquieu's *Esprit des Lois* than to any other work.'

A common stylistic disguise of sense is irony. Great care should be taken to let the reader know just when the ironical note is sounded and just when it ceases. An example from a letter by an evacuee girl:

> 'The old cat was on to me yesterday about being careful with my crusts. I bet she's careful enough with hers, the old devil. . . . I don't suppose she'd give one to a beggar-child, not if it was starving. I must waste not and want not and put everything in the savings bank for safety. I must bow down to her as if she was a little tin image. I must get out of this place before I go potty.'

The three 'I must's' here are not parallel. The first is the reported advice of the Old Cat; the second is the writer's ironical deduction from the tones that the Old Cat has used in giving advice; the third is the writer's practical decision, given without irony.

Here is an example of the amusing hit-or-miss style used by highly paid columnists, in this case by Viscount Castlerosse (now the Earl of Kenmare):

> 'After the advertising interlude Dick Daintree returned to his old love, the City, and then when this war broke out he joined the Navy again and served under Captain Vivian, who may or may not, I am not quite sure, have served in the same term as myself at Osborne.'

Of what was Lord Castlerosse not quite sure? Whether it was perhaps a different Captain Vivian? Or whether it was perhaps a different term? Or whether it was perhaps not Osborne, but Sandhurst, or even West Point?

Here is an example of failure to work out a descriptive sentence in sufficient detail for a reader to understand it immediately. It is by Lt.-Col. G. Val Myer, F.R.I.B.A., architect to the B.B.C.:

> '[At the outset it was thought that the ideal arrangement would be to place all the studios on one floor at the top of the building.] The site of Broadcasting House, however, though picturesque in form, is irregular, which fact would have caused the studios so grouped to be of awkward shape.'

The obscurity of the second sentence is due to the following errors in expression:

'The site, though picturesque in form. . . .'

A site cannot have picturesque *form*: picturesque form is three-dimensional.

'. . . though picturesque in form . . . would have caused the studios . . . to be of awkward shape.'

Here a false contrast is suggested between the picturesque form of the site and the awkward shape of the studios.

'. . . which fact would have caused . . .'

This is an unnecessary restatement of the subject.

Furthermore, Col. Myer has not made it clear that the studios were to be of a certain size. By building them small enough he could have made them what shape he liked. And even if he had built them of the right size, one or two of them at least could have been made the right shape. He means perhaps:

[At the outset it was thought that the ideal arrangement would be to place all the studios on one floor at the top of the building.] But though the irregularity of the site suggested a picturesque form for Broadcasting House, it prevented me from fitting enough studios of the right size into a single storey, unless I gave some of them awkward shapes.

Principle Four

There should never be any doubt left as to where something happened or is expected to happen.

A great many generalizations in books and newspapers are untrue because the limited locality to which they refer is not mentioned. For example:

'Everyone this autumn is wearing amusing antelope-skin gloves.'

This may have been true in 1934 of every woman, or almost every woman, of a certain income level in certain London districts; elsewhere it was demonstrably untrue. Fashion notes of this sort were not, however, confined to the expensive shiny-paper magazines but appeared in newspapers of the widest circulation; historians will find them most misleading.

Or:

'Nobody has any confidence left in astrologers'

—a generalization of still more restricted application.

Or:

'You will find bee-orchids almost anywhere in Devon'

—meaning perhaps in a few fields in several parishes in the Torbay district of South Devon.

A typical example of failure to make a geographical situation clear occurs in a despatch from the war-correspondent of a London daily paper (March, 1941):—

'For over three weeks the armies of the Sudan have been sitting here on the last stretch of the Eritrean plain with what seemed to be an insurmountable obstacle before them. There, confronting them, towered a ridge of solid rock tousands of feet high—a high ridge that rose from the plain at an angle of 90 deg. and was crowned by a succession of arrow-head peaks. The only road up those peaks, and to Keren hidden between them, had been blasted out of existence by the Italians, now expert in the art of demolition. . . .

Under the light of the moon shortly afterwards I moved in with our forward troops, creeping up the last stretch of passable road leading to the escarpment . . . while behind the guns rumbled up the gradients.'

This is a very confused account. We shall comment on it
point by point:—

> '. . . a succession of arrow-head peaks. The only road up
> those peaks, and to Keren hidden between them. . . .'

Keren may have been hidden from the British forces by a
row of peaks; or from the British forces by one row and from the
Italian reserves at Asmara by another; or may have lain between two peaks of a row, or of a succession; but could not have
been 'hidden between a succession of peaks'. And from where
did the road run? Did it merely switchback up and down the
peaks of the ridge-top before eventually turning east towards
Keren? Probably what is meant is 'up the cliff crowned by
those peaks', though 'a succession of peaks' suggests that they
were arranged in depth, which would imply a succession of
ridges, not one ridge.

> 'There . . . towered a ridge of rock thousands of feet
> high. . . .'

The next paragraph makes it clear that where the plain
ended an escarpment began. An escarpment is a stretch of high
land separated from low by a steep cliff. This cliff may be
crowned with a ridge but cannot be a ridge itself, because the
nature of an escarpment is that the ground-level on one side is
much higher than that on the other; whereas a ridge slopes
away more or less equally on both sides.

> '. . . a high ridge which rose from the plain at an angle of
> 90 degrees and was crowned by a succession of . . . peaks.
> The only road up those peaks . . . had been blasted out of
> existence by the Italians. . . .'
> '. . . creeping up the last stretch of passable road. . . .'
> '. . . while behind the guns rumbled up the gradient.'

If, as seems possible, 'up these peaks' means 'up the cliff
crowned by the peaks', what about 'blasted away'? The cliff
rose vertically from the plain, and since the guns 'rumbled up
the gradient' of 'the last stretch of passable road', this must
have been cut slantwise up the face of the cliff. The road cannot
therefore have been 'blasted out of existence'.

Probably the correspondent meant:—

'For over three weeks our army from the Sudan had been encamped at the edge of the plain from which I write this despatch, with what seemed an insurmountable obstacle towering before them—the buttress of the Eritrean escarpment. It is a cliff of solid rock, thousands of feet high, and in parts sheer precipice, crowned with a row of peaks like stone arrow-heads. These form a ridge behind which lies Keren. The only road to Keren from the plain used to slant across the cliff face (?), but the Italians, experts in demolition, blasted it away some time ago. . . .

A screen of skirmishers began to climb the cliff by moonlight . . . We moved cautiously up the last passable stretch of road that mounted from the plain to the base of the cliff. Behind us rumbled the field artillery.'

Principle Five

There should never be any doubt left as to **when.**

History is almost valueless without dates or other indications of time. Historical novelists who begin: 'The Tartar chief quaffed his cup of blue-white *kavasse* and bounded into his saddle' or: 'Petronella knelt by the Western door of St. Peter's Cathedral with a cold shaft of golden light slanting upon her white neck' ought to give indications before the first chapter is finished of the approximate year, or at least the century, in which these events are supposed to have taken place.

Even where dates do not much matter, the proper sequence of events remains important. Bad reporting or bad detective-story writing consists largely in muddling the sequence of events.

The following are examples of various misleading indications of time.

From a novel by Francis Brett Young:

'The cruising liner swayed to her moorings alongside the quay at Naples. For ten days turbines had driven her throbbing hull, with the short respite of calls at Gibraltar and Algiers, out of the Atlantic swell into a paler, glassier sea.'

This suggests that the liner took ten days to go from, say, Cadiz to Algiers; and, to anyone weak in geography, that she met an Atlantic swell off the Algerian coast.

From an article by J. Wentworth Day:

'Queen Elizabeth, that wise woman who saw future truths centuries before their birth, said that London was too big.'

If Queen Elizabeth's remark was not true until nearly four centuries later, it was not a wise one. Mr. Day probably meant:

'Queen Elizabeth, in a fit of petulance, anticipated by nearly four centuries the present complaint: "London is too big." '

From an article (1940) by F. G. S. Salisbury, the war-correspondent:

'More intensive bombing of Germany and an increasingly effective discouragement of day and night raiders over this country take us confidently into November—three months after Hitler's advertised conquest of Britain.'

Since this conquest had not taken place, it should have been made plain whether November was three months after the date supposed to have been assigned by Hitler to the conquest of Britain, or three months after the date on which he advertised his intention of conquering it.

From a newspaper article (Nov. 1939):

'Tension between states is so great that all are arming to the teeth for a conflict which as has long been known might come at any moment, which really indeed began in Spain in 1936, and has certainly begun now.'

Come, come, when *did* it begin? The sentence probably means: 'International tension had long prepared us for the European war, for which Franco's successful insurrection in Spain was the prelude, and which, with all nations arming to the teeth, has now at last begun in earnest.'

From a recent biography of Earl Granville, by Ethel Colbourn Mayne:

> 'There is a ballad by Sydney Dobell in which a young man is reminded, over and over again, that he comes of a doomed race: "O Keith of Ravelston, the sorrows of thy line!" Reading the *Private Correspondence of Lord Granville Leveson Gower (afterwards Earl Granville)*, we seem to hear a kindred refrain, more cheerfully worded indeed but in the early letters no less charged with foreboding. "O Granville Leveson Gower, the glories of thy line!" For though this young man was reminded that his race was illustrious, Granville's family and friends were almost as gloomily presageful as Keith of Ravelston's apostrophist was to be.'

This is very confusing, especially the 'was to be', because it introduces two time levels, the historic and the fictional. Granted, Sydney Dobell was a poet of the Eighteen-Fifties and Earl Granville was a Regency diplomatist; but Dobell's apostrophe was supposed to have been written in mediaeval times, and the reader has perhaps already fixed it hypothetically in the early fifteenth century—for all he knows there may have been a historical Keith of Ravelston.

From 'Parochial Memories' in a West Country newspaper:

> 'A fat man eating whelks at a barrow. An opening window shining with its panes into my eyes. The dull murmur of the sea. The whine of the hurdy-gurdy man. Sand in my shoes. Earlier than 1873, when there was no railway in the little town, manners were simple. Fishing was the main industry and nets were spread where Woolworth's emporium now stands.'

Here the writer should have dated the memories of the first five short sentences, to show whether they go back before the year 1873.

Principle Six

There should never be any doubt left as to how much, or how long.

Most recorded quantities and durations are necessarily approximate. English is a tricky language to use for approximations, because illogical conversational usage can be confused with prose usage, which is, or should be, logical. 'Infinitesimal', for example, is an adjective properly applied to the difference between the quantities 99.9 and 100—even in journalistic prose it should not be applied to the size of a grain of dust that has stopped a watch from ticking; 'microscopic' would also be an exaggeration in this context, for though the watch-mender used a magnifying glass to examine the works, he would probably be able to see the grain without. However, there is a popular scale of emotional approximation (not to be found in any dictionary or table of measures) for estimating the comparative degrees of success in, say, catching a train. It may be legitimately used in prose and goes something like this:

Not nearly, nearly, almost, not quite, all but, just not, within an ace, within a hair's breadth—oh! by the skin of my teeth, *just*, only just, with a bit of a rush, comfortably, easily, with plenty to spare.

It could perhaps be phrased mathematically, with a scale of minutes and seconds—the ideal zero being the half-second at which the coaches begin moving out of the station too fast for even an athlete to scramble into a compartment.

Similarly, there is a popular measure of proportion, with approximate percentages as follows:

(100%) Mr. Jordan's fortune consisted wholly of bar-gold.

(99%) Practically all his fortune consisted of bar-gold.

(95%) His fortune consisted almost entirely of bar-gold.

(90%) Nearly all his fortune consisted of bar-gold.

(80%) By far the greater part of his fortune consisted of bar-gold.

(70%) The greater part of his fortune consisted of bar-gold.

(60%) More than half his fortune consisted of bar-gold

(55%) Rather more than half his fortune consisted of bar-gold.

(50%) Half his fortune consisted of bar-gold.

(45%) Nearly half his fortune consisted of bar-gold.

(40%) A large part of his fortune consisted of bar-gold.

(35%) Quite a large part of his fortune consisted of bar-gold.

(30%) A considerable part of his fortune consisted of bar-gold.

(25%) Part of his fortune consisted of bar-gold.

(15%) A small part of his fortune consisted of bar-gold.

(10%) Not much of his fortune consisted of bar-gold.

(5%) A very small part of his fortune consisted of bar-gold.

(1%) An inconsiderable part of his fortune consisted of bar-gold.

(0%) None of his fortune consisted of bar-gold.

This simple, generally accepted, scale is confused by writers who, for dramatic effect, try to make 5% seem more than it is. For example, the late Earl of Birkenhead twice uses the same forensic trick in the following autobiographical passage:

> 'No inconsiderable part of my reading leisure has been spent in the company of swash-bucklers and pirates. . . . Before I was of age I had read all Scott's novels more than once. I had galloped as often with *The Three Musketeers* from Boulogne, and dived with the Count of Monte Cristo from the Chateau d'If into the midnight sea; and I cannot but believe, in reference to my own career, that no inconsiderable portion of any success which I may have achieved derives from the impulse of these magicians and the example and emulation of their heroes.'

Perhaps he means that 5% of his reading leisure was spent in the company of fictional swashbucklers and pirates, and 2% of his success was derived from his reading of Scott, Dumas and the rest. He had used this negative formula because he cannot in either case conscientiously write 'quite a large part'; and yet, remembering his novel about a swashbuckler named Ralph

Rashleigh, is pretty sure that it was more than 1%. Similarly with 'more than once': he is aware that he read very few of the Waverley Novels through more than twice—perhaps only *Ivanhoe;* but 'more than once' sounds far more than 'at least twice'. In the next sentence 'as often as more than once' is a hard quantity to estimate. Perhaps it means simply 'twice'.

The following blurred sentence is from Dr. C. Alington's *A Schoolmaster's Apology*. He is writing about the learning of poems by heart:

> 'We no longer impose on our youth the gigantic tasks which an earlier generation performed with success, and it may well be that the verbal memories of our pupils suffer in proportion.'

If, say, one-third of the gigantic tasks were now imposed, the verbal memories might be said to suffer 'in proportion'. But since these tasks are no longer imposed at all, the verbal memories cannot suffer 'in proportion'—unless by being totally destroyed. The sentence should have run something like this:

> 'We do not impose on the present generation of schoolboys nearly such gigantic tasks as we once successfully performed, and perhaps, therefore, their verbal memories are proportionately weaker than ours.'

Principle Seven

There should never be any doubt left as to how many.

English has many traditional figures of speech for estimating number, which have now lost their original connotations. From an early level of national experience, a 'legion' seemed a huge number of armed men. But when a speaker now says: 'The mothers who ungrudgingly do without sleep themselves, if their babies are sleepless, are a credit to the country—their name is legion', he means there are 'millions of mothers like that'. Yet a Roman legion consisted of four or five thousand men only. Similarly: 'There are a myriad grains of sand on this beach'—

but a myriad is only ten thousand, and probably 'tens of millions' is intended. It is wiser to avoid such rhetorical use of numbers. The phrase 'as the stars of the sky', for example, either may mean ten thousand, which is the approximate number of stars visible to the naked eye of a person with very good sight; or it may mean the hundreds of thousands of stars seen through telescopes or registered at observatories; or it may even mean the many hundreds of millions of stars now computed by advanced physicists to be in existence.

The scale of approximate counting is: 'one or two, two or three, a few, several, a dozen or so, a score or so, a dozen or two, a score or two, a few dozen, dozens, a hundred or so, a few score, scores, a hundred or two, a few hundred, hundreds, a thousand or so, etc.'

If the impression of number is still vaguer, one uses 'many, a good many, a large number' and so on, according to the context. But there are disingenuous measures of number that ought to be avoided in writing: for example, 'handful' when not applied to nuts, blackberries, coffeebeans and similar small objects. Here are three instances of its use. From a newspaper article:

'Few as women M.P.s have been—a handful in comparison with their male colleagues—they have often made their mark in the House of Commons.'

If a comparison had here been made between a handful and a bucketful, it would have meant something. As a matter of fact the number of women M.P.s was then fourteen—a number which corresponds pretty well with A. L. Rowse's assessment of 'handful' in a monthly journal:

'Pasteur, Debussy, Degas, Pierre Curie, Mallarmé, Bergson, the two Charcots, Alexis Carrel, André Citroën, Blériot, Père de Foucauld, Sainte Thérèse of Lisieux, Madame de Noailles, Sarah Bernhardt, Gaston Paris, Littré, Le Corbusier, a handful of names taken almost at random reveals the variety of talents or of genius that modern France has bred or provided a home for.'

But Mr. Rowse's handful is taken from millions, which suggests that for him a handful is not a number proportioned to a total sum as, in the M.P. context, a handful of fourteen was to six hundred. And when Mr. Mallory Browne, European Editorial Manager of the *Christian Science Monitor*, wrote (1940):

> 'Lord Lothian has been in all but a handful of the forty-eight States of the Union . . .'

it was difficult for his readers to guess whether Lord Lothian had missed out merely, say, Montana, Nebraska, and Nevada, or whole sections of the South-West and North-West amounting to twenty States or more.

G. D. H. Cole wrote in the autumn of 1939:

> 'In this spirit, presumably, Mr. Chamberlain gave the unqualified British guarantee to the Polish Government, and one forgets how many other European Governments, which he was powerless to help without Soviet aid.'

The suggestion was that Mr. Chamberlain had given so many guarantees that people lost count. In fact, guarantees were given to three countries only: to Poland, Roumania, and Greece. Mr. Cole was being disingenuous.

From a letter to the Press by John Gielgud, on the subject of Sunday theatres:

> 'Quite apart from the fact that a week of matinee performances might help to balance the Budget and encourage enterprise and employment, it seems a great pity that actors should not be allowed to serve the public at the times when the greatest majority of them are likely to have a little leisure and inclination for the theatre.'

How many is the 'greatest majority' of forty-six million people? Where there is no comparison between recorded majorities, one should say no more than 'the majority' or, by a conversational licence, 'a large majority'.

6

The Principles
of Clear Statement—II

Principle Eight

Every word or phrase should be appropriate
to its context.

This is a counsel of perfection. No writer of English can be sure
of using exactly the right words even in a simple context, and
even after twenty or thirty years of self-education. But he
should at least act on the assumption that there is always an
exactly right word, or combination of words, for his purpose—
which he will gratefully recognize as such if it happens to occur
to him; and that, though he may not always find the right
word, he can at least learn by experience to avoid the quite
wrong ones, and even the not quite wrong.

The chief trouble with English is the vastness of the vocabulary, and the lack of a dictionary that, instead of presenting
closely related words as roughly synonymous, clearly distin-
guishes them from one another. Laura Riding has written of
the puzzlement of a student who wishes, for example, to find
out the meaning of the word 'modify'. The dictionary gives
'alter, change'. He then turns to 'alter' and is told that it means
'change, modify'; and to 'change', and is told that it means
'alter, modify'. Until an authoritative dictionary of related
meanings is published, each writer must painfully build one in
his own head from his casual experience of words. The big
Oxford English Dictionary now helps him in this task with the
precedents it gives for the usages of words. He will, for instance,
gather from it that 'change' is the more general word; that

'modify' is used of change in detail, usually made in answer to some objection; and that 'alter' is a more wholesale form of change than 'modify'. But there has been so much careless writing by well-known, as well as by anonymous and little-known, writers that precedents for almost any stupid choice of words can be found—as it were, screw-drivers used for chisels, and contrariwise.

Take, for example, the word 'protagonist'. It first meant, 'the leading actor in a Greek drama'. Originally the Greek *dramatis personae* consisted merely of this leading actor and a 'chorus' with whom he exchanged confidences. After a time a *deuteragonist* (or second actor), a *tritagonist* (or third actor), and so on, were added. The 'protagonist' remained the leading actor. The word was first adopted into English in the seventeenth century and is still a useful one. For example:

'In Milton's *Paradise Lost*, as in the classical religious dramas of Spain, the Devil is the protagonist.'

But in the late nineteenth century, perhaps from a misreading of John Morley's much-quoted remark (1877): 'If social equity is not a chimaera, Marie Antoinette was the protagonist of the most execrable of causes', 'protagonist' came to mean 'leading spokesman or spokeswoman'. In the last few years it has come to be used as a pompous equivalent of 'champion':

'Miss Christable Pankhurst will be remembered as one of the leading protagonists of the Women's Suffrage Movement.'

This is absurd, because either she was the protagonist, or else she played a secondary part; but this usage (which would allow twenty Princes of Denmark to appear in *Hamlet*) seems already too firmly established to be shaken. For the blunting of a useful word and the addition of an unnecessary synonym for 'champion' the 'handy dictionaries' are responsible: they give 'leading actor, spokesman', as the meaning of 'protagonist' instead of 'the leading actor or spokesman'.

Prospectuses of some Correspondence Schools of English promise richness of vocabulary, but chiefly in terms of synonyms: students, they say, will learn to speak of a strange event as an 'unusual occurrence', or a 'remarkable happening', or an 'extraordinary incident'. But students are not promised any instruction in the difference between these phrases, or even allowed to suspect that there is any difference.

A great many misuses of words arise from ignorance. An example from a novel by James Hilton:

'When he had been at Millstead a little while he would, he decided, import some furniture from home . . . For the immediate present a few photographs on the mantelpiece, Medici prints on the wall, a few cushions, books of course, and his innumerable undergraduate pipes and tobacco-jars, would wreak a sufficiently pleasant transformation.'

Probably Mr. Hilton believed 'wreak' to be the present infinitive of 'wrought'; but the correct form is 'work'. One may wreak harm, wrong, vengeance and similarly unpleasant things, but nothing pleasant at all.

From a novel (1937) by Dr. A. J. Cronin:

'The din [of the restaurant] rose and fell like a transpontine college yell.'

By 'transpontine' he probably meant 'American'; and would perhaps have written 'trans-Atlantic' if this had not been too closely associated in his mind with liners—so, as we reconstruct the story, he consulted the Thesaurus and caught at the word 'transpontine'. He evidently thought that, since *pontus* is Latin for 'sea', 'trans-pontine' must mean 'from over the sea'. It does not—it means 'over the bridges', and is derived from *pons* not *pontus*. Its only familiar usage in English is the theatrical one: it means 'on the Surrey side of the Thames from London' and, therefore, from the style of drama in vogue at the Surrey-side theatres in the middle of the nineteenth century, 'melodramatic'.

From an article by an American journalist, Paul Manning:

'It's when dinner is over that the real conference of the day begins. Churchill and his key dinner guests sit around in an atmosphere of heavy cigar smoke and beat and mould Britain's policy into a malleable form.'

The dictionary definition of 'malleable' is 'capable of being beaten into shape' (e.g. brass is malleable); it is a companion-word to 'fictile' which means 'capable of being moulded' (e.g. clay is fictile) and 'ductile' which means 'capable of being drawn out thin' (e.g. tin or pure gold is ductile). Since one cannot therefore be said to mould a policy into a malleable form, still less beat it into one, perhaps he means merely 'easily managed'.

Leading American politicians have added numerous precedents to the language from ignorance of the correct forms. President Harding coined 'normalcy' from ignorance of 'normality'. The form sub-normalcy has recently been added. Wendell Willkie wrote:

'My grandparents left Germany ninety years ago, because they were Protestants against autocracy.'

—as though a Prostestant were one who made a *protest* rather than a *protestation* (or declaration on oath). The word *protestant* as a rare variant of *protester* has a small *p*. Senator Gibson of Vermont demanded the

'. . . expulsion of the diplomatic and consular staff of Germany, Italy, and the French Vichy Government, . . . on the ground that behind the cloak of diplomatic immunity they are conniving for our downfall.'

He apparently thought that 'connivance' was the equivalent of 'conspiracy'—perhaps because a foreman or night-watchman who 'connives', that is to say winks at, a theft or other felony committed on the premises for which he is responsible, is liable to be tried for 'conspiracy'. But to conspire for the downfall of the United States is not to 'connive' for it. Perhaps the Senator meant 'contriving our downfall'.

Thoughtlessness, rather than ignorance, accounts for the following passages. From a parish magazine:

> 'None of us is very perfect, none of us is very Christian. We are all very subject to human errancy, very dead in spirit, very lost to grace.'

The writer should have considered that there are no degrees in perfection, Christianity, subjection, death or loss. He and his fellows may be not nearly perfect, not really Christian, fully subject to errancy, long dead, or hopelessly lost; but not 'very' any of these things.

From an article by Hilaire Belloc:

> 'We see it exemplified in the cumulative effect of raids upon urban populations and of physical destruction, especially in things that cannot be quickly replaced. It is true that a corresponding attrition is going on against the enemy, and particularly in his air army.'

In the first sentence, does he mean 'in things' or 'of things'? Can one be said to witness physical destruction *in* things— surely only physical decay or break-down? In the second sentence, can attrition go on *against* the enemy? 'Attrition' is a word like 'erosion'—one could hardly say that erosion was going on against a cliff. And can attrition be said to 'go on in his air army'? Surely only a process of attrition could do so? And what is an air army? Is it air-borne troops, or airmen?

From an article by the Managing Director of *The Farmer and Stockbreeder* (1941):

> 'No industry has worked greater miracles than dairy farming. It emerged from an unusually severe winter with scarcely a ripple in the continuous flow of milk to the consumer . . .'

A ripple does not necessarily imply a snag, and a sluggish

stream does not ripple so much as a fast one; so that the absence of ripples does not suggest either that there was no hitch
in the milk supply, or that it flowed particularly fast.

There is a class of error that is merely grammatical. Here, for
example, is an extract from the minutes of a Parish Council:

> 'Resolved that the Clerk writes to the proprietors as fol-
> lows: "The Council undertakes that we shall show no dispo-
> sition to take precipitate action nor to object to them
> arranging the matter in their own way so long as it has been
> speedily arranged." '

Here 'writes' should, grammatically, be 'write' (with the word
'shall' understood). And 'we shall' should be 'we will', because
the future tense goes: 'I shall, thou wilt, he will, we shall, you
will, they will'—except in the case of a resolve, threat or undertaking, in which case it goes: 'I will, thou shalt, he shall, we
will, you shall, they shall'. And 'nor' should be 'or', unless the
word 'to' is omitted, because a simple alternative ruled by a
negative does not need 'nor' for 'or'. And 'object to them arranging the matter' should be 'object to their arranging the
matter', the hypothetic objection being not to the people, but to
the arrangement. And 'so long as it has been speedily arranged'
should be 'so long as it be speedily arranged', because 'so long
as' imposes a condition and therefore in formal language demands a present subjunctive—not, in any case, a perfect indicative. And 'the Council undertakes that we' is an absurd
change from the third person singular to the first person plural.

Emphatic words natural to conversation often lose their significance in prose. For example, Captain Liddell Hart writes in
a newspaper article (November, 1940):

> 'The occupation of Roumania may prove of invaluable
> help in improving Germany's own petrol supplies.'

'Invaluable help' means help that is powerful or timely but not
assessable in terms of financial or other value. The element of
doubt in the phrase makes it inappropriate for use after 'may
prove', which already denotes doubt. It would have been better
to write: 'is likely to prove of great value in improving. . . .'

Many words have been so debased by conversational use that they cannot be safely used in serious poetry or prose. Nathaniel Hawthorne could write in 1862, 'however awfully holy the subject'; Thomas Hood in 1845, 'Spring . . . bitter blighter'; and Tennyson in *The Princess*, 1847, 'Wan was her cheek, her blooming mantle torn'. None of these usages would be possible now. One would have to write: 'however awesomely holy the subject', 'Spring . . . bitterly blighting', 'Wan was her cheek, her flowering mantle torn'.

When the word 'dole', as a synonym for 'Unemployment Insurance Benefit', crept into Bank of England publications in the 'Thirties, a sensitive bank-official pointed out to the authorities that this was 'illiterate': 'dole', a catch-word first introduced by the *Daily Mail* in June, 1919, to mean 'Unemployed Insurance Benefit', really denoted 'charitable gifts sparingly dealt out by patrons to clients', and seemed inapplicable to payments made under an insurance scheme. The word 'illiterate' had the desired result: 'dole' was ejected. As a matter of fact, the Bank of England could have made out a good case for 'dole' as originally meaning 'a portion, especially one that belongs by right to the recipient'—in fact, 'a square deal', *deal* and *dole* being originally the same word.

Principle Nine

No word or phrase should be ambiguous.

The most frequent cause of lost battles, political strife, and domestic misunderstanding is ambiguity of terms in reports, orders or requests. Recrimination of the following sort has its parallel at General Head-Quarters after most lost battles, and at Party Head-Quarters after most lost elections:

Girl: Why didn't you meet me in the break, as I told you?
Boy: You weren't there, darling.
Girl: I was. I waited five minutes.
Boy: That's funny. Didn't you say outside Woolworth's?
Girl: Yes, and you weren't there.
Boy: But I was.

Girl: What? Don't tell me you were fool enough to stand outside Woolworth's when you knew I was getting my toffees at Littlewood's?

Boy: Well, you said Woolworth's. You've just said you said it. Littlewood's isn't Woolworth's.

Girl: It's the same sort of place and you know I always go there for my toffees, stupid. And if you were there, as you say, why didn't you see me as I came out of the Works? I go right past Woolworth's.

Boy: I don't know. Why didn't *you* see *me*? I was there at eleven o'clock sharp.

Girl: Eleven o'clock—no wonder! What a man!

Boy: But you said you'd nip out in your eleven o'clock.

Girl: Oh, you prize-fool! Haven't I told you and told you that in summer-time we have our eleven-o'clock at ten-thirty?

The disastrous charge of the Light Brigade at Balaclava in the Crimean War was made because of a carelessly worded order to 'charge for the guns'—meaning that some British guns which were in an exposed position should be hauled out of reach of the enemy, not that the Russian batteries should be charged. But even in the calmest times it is often very difficult to compose an English sentence that cannot possibly be misunderstood.

From the Minutes of a Borough Council Meeting:

Councillor Trafford took exception to the proposed notice at the entrance of South Park: 'No dogs must be brought to this Park except on a lead.' He pointed out that this order would not prevent an owner from releasing his pets, or pet, from a lead when once safely inside the Park.

The Chairman (Colonel Vine): What alternative wording would you propose, Councillor?

Councillor Trafford: 'Dogs are not allowed in this Park without leads.'

Councillor Hogg: Mr. Chairman, I object. The order should be addressed to the owners, not to the dogs.

Councillor Trafford: That is a nice point. Very well then: 'Owners of dogs are not allowed in this Park unless they keep them on leads.'

Councillor Hogg: Mr. Chairman, I object. Strictly speaking, this would prevent me as a dog-owner from leaving my dog in the backgarden at home and walking with Mrs. Hogg across the Park.

Councillor Trafford: Mr. Chairman, I suggest that our legalistic friend be asked to redraft the notice himself.

Councillor Hogg: Mr. Chairman, since Councillor Trafford finds it so difficult to improve on my original wording, I accept. 'Nobody without his dog on a lead is allowed in this Park.'

Councillor Trafford: Mr. Chairman, I object. Strictly speaking, this notice would prevent me, as a citizen who owns no dog, from walking in the Park without first acquiring one.

Councillor Hogg (with some warmth): Very simply, then: 'Dogs must be led in this Park.'

Councillor Trafford: Mr. Chairman, I object: this reads as if it were a general injunction to the Borough to lead their dogs into the Park.

Councillor Hogg interposed a remark for which he was called to order; upon his withdrawing it, it was directed to be expunged from the Minutes.

The Chairman: Councillor Trafford, Councillor Hogg has had three tries; you have had only two . . .

Councillor Trafford: 'All dogs must be kept on leads in this Park.'

The Chairman: I see Councillor Hogg rising quite rightly to raise another objection. May I anticipate him with another amendment: 'All dogs in this Park must be kept on the lead.'

This draft was put to the vote and carried unanimously, with two abstentions.

From a travel book by Ethel Mannin, 1934:

'The Socialist authorities in Vienna built cheap modern flats for the workers.'

Were they cheap to build? Or cheap to live in? Or both?

From a despatch to a London newspaper:

> 'An official circular, which fell into the hands of the Polish Government in London, orders the encouragement of improper literature. Dr. Goebbels hopes probably that such literature will help to break morale. It would be rather comic if there were not other methods towards the same goal.'

This probably does not mean 'If someone told me that this was the only way of breaking Polish morale, I should laugh' but 'That is not so comic as it seems at first sight, since the Germans use other, more brutal, means of breaking Polish morale.'

In a country village a certain Mr. Hill wrote to Mrs. Sanders, a neighbour:

> 'Dear Mrs. Sanders:
> Will you kindly tell my daughter how much water-glass is a lb, as I bought mine last year and I cannot remember, and I am pickling eggs to-night for the Vicarage? And have you any apples?
>
> Yours
K. Hill.'

Mrs. Sanders wrote back:

> 'Dear Mrs. Hill:
> A lb of water-glass is about as much as will go into the jam-jar I send you with my little boy. Yes, thank you, I have enough apples to last me through the winter.
>
> Yours,
P. Sanders.'

But what Mrs. Hill had meant was: 'How much does water-glass cost a pound? I have some left over from last year and don't want to charge the Vicarage an unreasonable price. And may I buy some of your apples?' This is the sort of thing that starts a village feud.

Many cases of ambiguity are due to coincidence: words to

whose appropriateness in a sentence no objection could otherwise be raised form accidental misalliances with words placed
near to them, and so seem to mean something entirely different.
Here is an example from a pamphlet by Professor Dennis Sau-
rat, Director of the *Institut Français* in London:

> 'In the animal races those in which the *female bears* in pain
> give the greater care to their young, and those races in which
> birth is painless show, as a rule, no affection for their off-
> spring.'

It would have read less grotesquely as: 'the female suffers pain
during parturition.'

From a *Countryman's Diary* in a newspaper:

> 'The hedges now seem less bare with the young male cat-
> kins already showing palest yellow and the elder coming into
> leaf.'

Since 'the elder' seems to mean 'the elder male catkins', the
word 'elder-bushes' should have been used.

From a newspaper account of Red Cross work:

> 'Parcels had been sent on several days before this.'

This would explain itself if written either as:

> 'Parcels had been sent on several occasions before this.'

or as:

> 'Parcels had been sent on, several days before this.'

Ambiguity occasionally arises from a difficulty, in prose, of ren-
dering vocal inflexions; even italicizing is often insufficient. A
house-owner hears the sound of breaking glass and rushes out to
catch whoever threw the stone. 'Who threw that stone?' he asks
a big boy who is lounging not far off. 'I can't say, sir', the boy
answers. The tone may be offhand and so convey genuine or

affected ignorance, or it may be guarded and solemn and so convey an unwillingness to give evidence against another boy. Probably the householder will understand, but there is no typographical device for indicating the different tones in print. Or a girl says to an airman who has just baled out into her father's garden: 'You may see me again'. There is no typographical device for showing whether she means, 'You have my permission to call again at our house,' or simply, 'Who knows but that we may meet again?'—though the airman will probably understand. This sort of ambiguity occurs occasionally in newspaper reports from police-courts. For example:

> 'Summoned at Tunbridge Wells yesterday for speeding at 53 miles an hour through a main street of the town, John Shorter of Brightlington Road, Crofton Park, S.E.4, wrote: "A clear road and a pretty girl waiting at the other end proved too great a temptation for me."
>
> Shorter, who has since joined the R.A.F., was fined £1, the Mayor (Alderman C. E. Westbrook) remarking: "In the circumstances we cannot be too drastic." '

Since the fine does not appear either very heavy or very light, the reader will not know whether the Mayor meant 'In these atrocious circumstances, even the heaviest fine I might impose would not be undeserved': or, 'So charming an excuse disarms me: I cannot impose so heavy a fine as I usually do.'

Principle Ten

Every word or phrase should be in its right place in the sentence.

Perhaps the most frequently misplaced word in English is 'only'. In conversation the speaker's accent would make it perfectly plain, for example, what was meant by:

> 'The Council are only warned to do their own repairs.'

When written, this may mean either: 'The Council are only

warned (not instructed) to do their own repairs' or 'The Council are given no advice except the warning that they must do
their own repairs.' But what is meant is perhaps: 'The Council
are warned to do only their own repairs (not repairs for which
they are not legally responsible).'

'Either' is another word frequently misplaced. From a written commentary (1941) by Raymond Gram Swing:

> 'The Atlantic, as far as Iceland, either will be left alone by
> Axis warships, or the United States will be in the shooting
> war. . . .'

It should have been:

> 'Either the Atlantic as far as Iceland will be left alone by
> Axis warships, or the United States will be in the shooting
> war. . . .'

Here are other miscellaneous examples of misplaced words or
phrases.

From a newspaper 'short':

> 'Latest reports show that 28,306 children do not go to
> school in England. More than 4½ million are getting full-
> time instruction, 72,505 are receiving part-time schooling.'

Far more than 28,306 children do not go to school in England;
but in England 28,306 children do not go to school.

From Captain Anthony Cotterell's *It's Nice to be in the Army:*

> 'About 15 p.c. of men will delay reporting sick too long.
> Sergeant-majors usually arrive to report sick feet first.'

This means:

> 'About 15 p.c. of men will delay too long before reporting
> sick. Sergeant-majors usually arrive feet first to report sick.'

From a newspaper leader:

> 'Mussolini accused the Fuehrer of having lost the war by attacking unnecessarily Soviet Russia.'

Was Russia unnecessarily Soviet?

From a despatch to a London newspaper:

> 'Señor Suñer was not convinced that even the German people believed in the success of German arms, but were dejected under the Nazi regime.'

He means:

> 'Señor Suñer was convinced that even the German people did not believe in the success of German arms and were dejected under the Nazi regime.'

Principle Eleven

No unintentional contrast between two ideas should be allowed to suggest itself.

Unintentional contrasts are often due to elegant variation of a descriptive phrase.

The following is from a newspaper report:

> 'Mrs. Gwendolen Foster, a member of the theatrical profession, prayed for the dissolution of her marriage with Mr. Basil Foster, an actor.'

This falsely suggests that Mrs. Foster was not an actress, but a dresser, a programme-girl, a prompter, or the like.

From a despatch by the New York correspondent of a London weekly:

> 'Writers favouring Mr. Willkie crossed swords with authors who are for Roosevelt.'

Since the word 'author' is somewhat grander than 'writer' the suggestion is that the more successful writers were Democrats.

From an Exchange Telegraph report (1926):

> 'On entering the Guildhall, Mr. Lloyd George was enthusiastically cheered, while Lord Oxford was accorded a great ovation.'

The reader wonders which of the two received the louder applause.

From a novel by Ernest Raymond:

> 'Soon Clara Shepherd appeared, but he could not have stated the details of her dress, his awareness of his wife's clothes being always in inverse ration to his consciousness of his own.'

The apparent contrasts between 'Clara Shepherd' and 'his wife' and between 'awareness' and 'consciousness' could both have been avoided.

> 'Soon his wife, Clara, appeared, but he could not have described her dress offhand: the more conscious he was of his own clothes the less he always was of hers.'

The phrases 'in inverse ratio to' and 'varying inversely with' are unnecessary and cumbersome in any except mathematical contexts. The rhyme:

> 'A wise old bird sat on an oak;
> The more he heard the less he spoke;
> The less he spoke the more he heard.
> Let us not joke at that old bird'

does not read more precisely when changed to:

> 'Upon an oak sat a wise old bird;
> What he spoke was in inverse ratio to what he heard;

What he heard varied inversely with what he spoke.
At that wise bird let us not joke.'

Principle Twelve

***Unless for rhetorical emphasis, or necessary recapitulation,
no idea should be presented more than
once in the same prose passage.***

Rhetoricians often use a key-word or phrase three times to
make it seem holy, important or indisputably true. But, apart
from this hoary device, repetitiveness is nowadays considered a
sign of pauperdom in oratory, and of feeble-mindedness in narrative.

Undisguised repetition needs no illustration; but here are
various examples of conceled repetition. From a published
speech by Neville Chamberlain:

'We want to see established an international order based
upon mutual understanding and mutual confidence, and we
cannot build such an order unless it conforms to certain principles which are essential to the establishment of confidence
and trust.'

When we remove the repeated ideas, this passage reduces to:

'The international order that we wish to establish must
conform to certain principles of mutual understanding and
trust.'

From an article by J. Wentworth Day, the agricultural expert:

'To-day, the difficulties of defending . . . Greater London
have taught us the lesson that to defend the Capital, we must
go to the lengths and expense of defence and strategy enough
to defend a small country, let alone a great city. . . . That is
merely one example of many which I could multiply.'

This reduces to:

'We have now learned that the defence of Greater London

raises strategic and financial problems that suggest a small country rather than a city. . . . I could quote many such examples.'

From a leader (1941) by J. A. Spender:

'We are to Russia, as she is to us, one of the imponderables which cannot be weighed in the ordinary diplomatic scales.'

This reduces either to:

'Russia is to us, as we are to her, an imponderable diplomatic problem.'

Or to:

'Russia cannot weigh us, nor we her, in the ordinary diplomatic scales.'

From '*The Sleeping Beauty* at the London Alhambra', by Sacheverell Sitwell:

'. . . But the prospect of five scenes and three hundred dresses by Leon Bakst was in thrilling anticipation for me.'

Here, 'was in thrilling anticipation for me' should have been merely 'thrilled me'.

From a novel by Norah James:

' "Yes, sir, I'll see to it," she answered and put another gleaming plate on the pile that was rising at her side in a shining mound.'

This reduces to:

' "Yes, sir, I'll see to it." And she added another plate to the gleaming pile at her side.'

From G. K. Chesterton's *Sketch of Dickens*:

'But it is true to say that his whole soul was seldom in anything about which he was wholly serious.'

This reduces to:

'But he was seldom wholly serious about anything.'

Principle Thirteen

No statement should be self-evident.

Platitudes, such as 'all flesh is grass'; 'all men are liars'; 'the Law is an ass'—must be distinguished from 'tautological', or self-evident, statements, such as 'every mortal man must die', 'No liars speak the truth', 'Foolish old men often do foolish things'.

A typical example of tautology is a Departmental Minute (1930):

'Minutes are not to be written in illegitimate places.'

i.e. 'Minutes must not be written in places where they must not be written'. What was perhaps meant was: 'Minutes are not to be written on odd slips of paper, or anywhere but on the Minute sheets provided.'

From a book-review in a Church newspaper:

'In the contents of *Bells and Grass* (Faber, 7s. 6d.) the best of old and new are an expression of spontaneous delight in things that are of inestimable value, but have no price.'

All things with no price in this metaphorical sense are of inestimable value.

Principle Fourteen

No important detail should be omitted from any phrase, sentence or paragraph.

The common sense or the knowledge of the prospective reader must be accurately gauged. It would not be enough, for example, to tell a semi-educated audience that in 1825 the journey from Rome to Venice took from a week to ten days, without reminding them that railways had not yet been built in Italy. Even an educated audience would expect to be told (or reminded) what was the distance by road from Rome to Venice, what was the normal means of conveyance—coach all the way? or horseback for part of it?—and what natural obstacles lay between the two cities.

The following are miscellaneous examples of the omission of relevant detail, a fault usually due to the writer's impatience to get something down on paper.

From a gardening handbook:

> 'Light soils—i.e. soils light to the spade and not in colour—quickly lose their moisture.'

But soil may be both light to the spade and light in colour. The word 'necessarily' should have been inserted after 'not'.

From a newspaper article:

> 'Fires in workshops and factories operating for the Reich are everyday affairs. By one means or another, the output has been brought down in many cases from 40 to 60 per cent.'

The omission of the word 'by' before 'from 40 to 60 per cent' makes nonsense of the second sentence.

From a novel by Edith Bagnold:

> 'Round and round went the horses, and the rain down Velvet's neck.'

This means: 'and the rain went down Velvet's neck.' The rain did not go round and round down Velvet's neck.

From a statement by Admiral of the Fleet Lord Chatfield (1941):

'The longer the war lasts, the more certain it will be that the land forces will be essential for ultimate victory, quite apart from our imperial dangers now.'

This probably means:

'We need a strong army now for imperial defence, and the longer the war lasts the more evident it will be that ultimate victory can only be won by attacking the enemy on the Continent of Europe with a very strong army indeed.'

From a newspaper article:

'. . . Everywhere the town is a magnet to young people, and the drift from the land in many parts of the world is a problem for farmers and for governments.'

The problem is incompletely stated: 'the drift from the land' is not a problem, but a fact. The problem may be how it is caused, or how it is to be checked, or how many young people who have already drifted away are to be recalled. Such incomplete statements are influenced by newspaper headings: e.g. 'The Drift from the Land—Problem for Farmers'. (Note also the misplaced phrase. The last clause should have run: 'and the drift from the land is a problem for farmers, and for governments, in many parts of the world.')

From a newspaper leader (1940):

'The friendly onlooker is confident that whatever they have to endure the British will . . . find the way of turning the tables on their enemy. He anticipates what the Prime Minister said on Tuesday.'

This probably means:

'. . . He anticipates that the prophecy made by the Prime Minister on Tuesday will be fulfilled.'

From a newspaper item:

'Antique lace, much of it of great value and dating back to

the early seventeenth century, which has been collected to go to America, was on view in London yesterday. A party is to be given at the British Embassy in Washington in November to show the lace. It will afterwards be sold free of expense in the principal American stores.'

Free of expense to whom? The donors, the stores, or the customers?

Principle Fifteen

No phrase should be allowed to raise expectations that are not fulfilled.

Writers often begin a sentence with, say, 'Turning to cheese', or 'When we come to consider cheese,' and then, leaving this phrase in the air, continue with 'the protein content varies considerably from sample to sample', or, more grotesquely, with 'Professor Queso has listed over a thousand distinct European varieties of the cream cheese'.

From a fishmonger's letters:

'Referring to your kind enquiry, you may expect the lobsters by the first delivery on the 15th instant.'

and

'Referring to your further kind enquiry, the lobsters will arrive by the first delivery on the 16th instant.'

In the first case, it is the person addressed who seems to be referring to the enquiry; in the second case, it seems to be the lobsters.

From a novel by Somerset Maugham:

'Bathing as they did three or four times a day, he could not get his hair to stay down, and the moment it was dry it spread over his head in unruly curls.'

The 'they' is two boys and a man called Tom. Perhaps what is meant is:

> 'It is hard for anyone who bathes, as they did, three or four times a day, and has unruly hair, to get it to stay down. Tom couldn't, and the moment it was dry, it spread over his head in curls.'

From a travel pamphlet:

> 'Kenya is a land of contrasts. On the one hand you meet with the highest refinements of educated English society, and the next moment you find yourself confronted with a picturesque savage whose chief pleasures in life are to hunt lions with a spear and feed on raw flesh.'

Here the reader will not perhaps realize that the contrast has already been made, and will expect an 'On the other hand' in a later sentence.

The following is from Field-Marshal Lord Birdwood's memoirs, *Khaki and Gown*:

> 'So far from being a stern and unsympathetic man of the kind repellent to children, I well remember how, when our son was a small boy of about five, we were at a Garden Party at Viceregal Lodge in Simla, when suddenly there was a large crash. This frightened Chris, who at once ran up to Lord Kitchener, seizing his hand and standing close to him for protection—a gesture which evidently pleased him enormously at the time.'

Rejecting the possibility that either Lord Birdwood himself or 'our son' is the subject of 'So far from being an unsympathetic man', one reads on, in search of a suitable subject—until the sentence ends disappointingly with 'a large crash'.

Lord Birdwood should have written something of this sort:

> 'Lord Kitchener was by no means a stern and unsympathetic man of the kind repellent to children, as the following incident proves. At a Garden Party at Viceregal Lodge in

Simla, when our son Chris was about five, there was a sudden loud crash . . . etc.'

Principle Sixteen

No theme should be suddenly abandoned.

We separate this Principle from Principle Fourteen, 'No important detail should be omitted from any phrase, sentence or paragraph', because disappointed anticipation may cause readers who would not baulk at a simple omission to lose track of an argument or narrative.

From a boys' adventure story:

'There were five of us in the long boat—Henri, Allen, Sophocles, Big Otter and myself. Well, I needn't describe myself—you'll soon see the sort of man I was in those days. But at any rate Henri was a big square-jawed argumentative French-Canadian, weighing about two hundred pounds, Sophocles was a fat, greasy little Greek cook with a genius for savoury rice dishes, and Big Otter was a Seminole Indian, the bravest man I ever met. We shipped a lot of water the first day, for the sea was still a bit rough.'

What about Allen? Until the boy reading the story has Allen securely placed he will feel the same sort of discontent as when he knows, by an unsatisfied feeling in his mouth, that he did not quite finish eating his apple and yet cannot remember where he has laid it down.

From a literary article in a provincial paper:

'The change in Foster's mentality is to be seen, as we read these letters of the years 1881-93, both in the literary composition and in the handwriting. The sprawling "a's" and "u's", the grotesque capitals, the hobbledehoy loops to the "g's" and the "y's", give place to a neat and clerkly script, with the capitals modelled exactly on those of contemporary copperplate. In 1894 he married Letitia Fareham.'

What about Foster's literary composition?

7

The Principles
of Clear Statement—III

Principle Seventeen

**Sentences and paragraphs should be linked together
logically and intelligibly.**

It should always be clear whether a sentence explains, amplifies
or limits the statement that it follows; or whether it introduces
either a new subject, or a new heading of the original subject.

From a newspaper feature, *All the Year Round in Your Garden*:

> 'Picking over seed-potatoes in the potting shed is a pleas-
> ant job. You will find many with ugly blotches and scabs and
> not be sure whether they will favour your prospects of a good
> crop. . . .'

The connection between these two sentences is blurred. Either
the second should begin a new paragraph, to show that the
gardener's anxieties about his crop do not illustrate the pleasantness of the job; or else it should be introduced with a 'But'.

From memoirs published in a provincial paper:

> 'On leaving the hospital of Saint Antoine, I remember, the
> Empress Eugénie was carried almost to her carriage by the
> crowd, who eagerly pressed around her, weeping, kissing her
> hands and heaping blessings on her head. But the most comi-
> cal event of the day was when a coal-black negro from Daho-
> mey presented himself at the Palace with a basket of freshly
> caught fish. . . .'

Here the 'But' is illogical, because it suggests that the simple enthusiasm of the crowd was also comical.

From a book-review by Basil de Sélincourt:

> 'Having loved Ruskin unsubdued, he [Sydney Cockerell] was ready to love and be loved by everybody; as the girl friend who later became a nun wrote to him from her novice cell: "You do seem to have a remarkable capacity for meeting distinguished people." That is it; they are all here; Hardy, Doughty, Lawrence, Blunt, Mrs. Hardy, Lady Burne-Jones, Charlotte Mew. . . .'

The phrase 'as the girl friend wrote' purports to justify the statement that Sydney Cockerell was ready to love and be loved by *everyone*; but all that it provides is a (possibly ironical) reference to his being ready to love and be loved by distinguished people.

Here is part of an article by Admiral C. J. Eyres:

> 'The Germans in the last war, in the use of lethal gas and unrestricted submarine warfare, acted disgracefully and immorally, just because the German Government had formally, by Treaty, denounced their use, and were dishonouring their bond.'

The 'just because' should be 'for' or 'since'. Either of these words would explain why the Admiral considered the Germans to have acted 'disgracefully and immorally'. The 'because' suggests that the motive for the Germans' disgraceful and immoral actions was merely to flout a previous renunciation by their Government of the use of certain weapons. (He probably means 'renounced', not 'denounced'.)

From an address to the University of Oxford by Viscount Halifax, its Chancellor:

> 'What has, for example, been the driving force behind the Nazi movement in Germany? It has been German youth. . . . Their point of view stands in stark opposition to yours. They

do not understand your way of thinking. Your ideals mean nothing to them. . . .

The real conflict, therefore, to-day is not between age and youth, but between youth and youth. . . .'

The 'therefore' is illogical, unless Lord Halifax is washing his hands of the conflict on the ground that it is not of his making.

Principle Eighteen

Punctuation should be consistent and should denote quality of connexion, rather than length of pause, between sentences or parts of sentences.

There is a widespread ignorance among writers of English as to the use and usages of punctuation. Many of them leave their commas, semi-colons, and the rest of the more difficult signs, to be corrected by their typists, or by the printers. The trouble is that there are two conventions for English punctuation, which contradict each other. The older convention is that punctuation-marks denote duration of pause between parts of a sentence or paragraph. This was stated as follows by J. Mason in his *Elocution* (1748): 'A comma stops the voice while we may privately tell one, a semi-colon, two; a colon three; and a period four.' (Here 'period' means 'full stop'.) The more sensible and·more modern convention, which we recommend, is that all punctuation-marks that do not (like the question and the exclamation mark) merely denote tone of voice, show in what relation to one another sentences, or parts of a sentence, are intended by the writer to stand.

The Comma

The original meaning of 'comma' is not the tadpole-like comma-sign, but a distinct part of a sentence, which should be cut off from the other parts by comma-signs. If the part to be cut off comes in the middle of a sentence, as in this one, a pair of comma-signs is put to show how much is being cut off. But a part cut off from the beginning or end of a sentence has only one comma sign, as in this case. The cutting-off of part of a sentence prevents two or more parts from running together in a way that might disturb the sense.

The commonest example of sense being disturbed by the omission of a comma is a sentence containing 'because'. 'I did not go to the party, because I was not wanted' means that I did not go, and that my reason for not going was that I was not wanted. But 'I did not go to the party because I was not wanted' means that I *did* go, but that my reason for going was not that I wished to spite the people there who did not want me to go.

Here is a rather complicated example of a 'because' sentence, taken from J. W. N. Sullivan's *Bases of Modern Science*, 1928:

> 'Our aesthetic and religious experiences need not lose the significance they appear to have merely because they are not taken into account in the scientific scheme.'

This might mean:

> 'Our aesthetic and religious experiences need not have their apparent significance cancelled by the mere failure of Science to include them in its scheme.'

Or, less probably, it might mean:

> 'Our aesthetic and religious experiences need not lose the appearance of significance which is given them by the mere failure of Science to include them in its scheme.'

If Mr. Sullivan, wishing to prevent his readers from taking the second of these two alternatives, had put a comma at 'have', then he would have offered them a third and still more improbable meaning:

> 'Why our religious and aesthetic experiences need not lose their apparent significance is merely that Science has failed to include them in its scheme.'

How, then, should he have punctuated the sentence? He should have written it along the lines of one or the other of our first two alternative versions.

Here is a typical example of under-punctuation from a newspaper:

> 'Harton Miners' Lodge have sent a protest to the Durham Miners' Association because a number of ex-miners transferred a month ago to Harton Collieries from vital war work under the Government back to the pit scheme and since drawing the guaranteed wage of £3 9s. without having any work to do were given fourteen days' notice immediately they were put on the pay-roll.

To help the reader to pick his way through this long but well constructed sentence there should have been commas after 'ex-miners' and 'work to do', and 'back to the pit' should have been 'back-to-the-pit'.

Here is an example of over-punctuation, which is far less often found, from a leader by Edward Hulton in his *Picture Post*:

> 'The world has long, in fact, been, whether we like it or no, not really a series of countries, but one country in a state of grave disharmony.'

Each of these commas can be justified, but when a sentence comes so thickly studded as this it should be rewritten in a simpler way. For example:

> 'Whether we like it or no, the world has in fact long been a single country in a state of grave disharmony, not an aggregate of mutually hostile countries.'

The Long Dash

In some cases, comma-signs are not quite strong enough to mark the cutting-off of part of a sentence from the remainder.

Where a very strong separation has to be made between a part and the main body of the sentence, the long dash can be used. Take, for example, the news-item:

'Only one house in the row was left standing with all its windows intact.'

The sense of the context in which this sentence occurred proved that it meant:

'Only one house in the row was left standing, but this was undamaged: it even had all its windows intact.'

not:

'Only one house, of those left standing in the row, had its windows intact.'

A comma after 'standing', in the original version, would not have done justice to this freak occurrence. Instead, a long dash was needed, thus:

'Only one house in the row was left standing—with all its windows intact.'

Here is another news item, which at first sight reads mysteriously:

'Ex-Sergt. Oliver Brooks, v.c., hero of Loos, who has died at Windsor, aged 51, was decorated by King George V, who was in bed in a train following the accident when he fell from his horse in France.'

No, the train was not following Sergt. Brooks' accidental tumble from his horse in France; neither was King George V. The facts were: that King George was in bed in a hospital train as the result of falling from his horse while reviewing troops in France, and that he called Sergt. Brooks to his bedside for a decoration ceremony. But it would not be enough to put a comma after 'train': a long dash is needed to show that the rest of the sentence is another story tacked on to the account of the bedside decoration.

The long dash is also used to join together short sentences of headings which do not quite deserve a full stop. For example:

'I have been in such trouble lately—Mrs. Purdell calling about the little shoes—not done, of course— and then a load of soot falls down the chimney, bang on top of the muffins warming in the grate—how the lodger carried on!—and I lost my wedding ring, washing—it was twenty-two carat gold—and now this!'

The Parenthesis

Another substitute for the comma is the parenthesis. Parenthesis-signs are always used in pairs. They denote an explanatory comment or aside of such a sort that, in speaking, one would naturally lower one's voice slightly to show that the comment was not part of the main argument of the sentence. Where the explanatory comment does not need this lowering of the voice, it is customarily put between long dashes. Thus:

'Mr. Hollins (always "Mr." to me, even when he was an Earl) nodded to us in his friendly way.'

But:

'Mr. Hollins—generous, open-hearted Mr. Hollins!— nodded at us in his friendly way.'

Parenthesis-signs are curved, brackets are rectangular. Brackets are used for critical interpolations: that is, for explanatory or corrective remarks inserted by an author in a passage quoted from someone else's work or from previous work of his own. Thus:

'Young William Hunter wrote: "It is easy to be a Company man" [this was while the East India Company still ruled in Calcutta] "and yet be superior to the common run; but it is impossible to be first class and fritter your evenings away in walking cuadrills [sic] and consuming ices".'

When one parenthetical remark occurs within another, brackets are sometimes used to prevent the reader getting confused between them; but this practice is not to be recommended, because the brackets then seem to be enclosing a critical interpolation. If one has to put one parenthetical remark within another (for example, in the present—admittedly rather clumsy—instance) it is more safely enclosed between long dashes, as here.

The Full-Stop

A full-stop, also called a 'period', ends a sentence. (If the sentence does not end, what seems to be a full-stop is merely a single dot. We will discuss the dot separately.) There are degrees in the value of full-stops. Sentences end with full-stops; but when paragraphs end with full-stops the rest of the line is left blank—the next paragraph beginning on the following line, after a slight space (or 'indentation') which indicates that this is a new paragraph. A paragraph should concern only one phase of a narrative or argument. This phase may be large or small, but must be self-contained. In a novel, for example, a paragraph may contain either a brief summary of the heroine's early life (or declining years), or merely perhaps a complete account of her reflections as she passed on some occasion from the music-room to the conservatory. In a critical work, it may contain, for example, a concise account of Shakespearean forgeries in the eighteenth century, or merely, perhaps, one self-contained part of an argument intended to prove that Ireland, one of the forgers, possessed a copy of the *Hamlet* First Quarto.

The newspaper practice of trying to brighten an article by printing ordinary sentences as if they were paragraphs often confuses the reader: he does not know where one subject ends and another begins. The following is an example of false, or journalistic, paragraphing (1941):

'According to the Nazi High Command, German forces, driving from Gomel across the Desna River and from the Dnieper on both sides of Kremenchug, have met at a point 130 miles east of Kiev. The Germans say that four Soviet armies have been caught between the arms of these giant pincers.

Even if the German claim is true, it will take them weeks to mop up the Russians in the huge area enclosed in the pincers. Already their advance had been slow, painful and costly in the extreme.

This is shown in the Berlin admission that at many points the Russians are still launching fierce counter-attacks across the Dnieper and in a Moscow report that a German troop-train with ammunition was blown up by Russian bombers near Dniepropetrovsk.

Meanwhile, Marshal Timoshenko's victories at Yelnya and Yartsevo in the Smolensk region have removed, at least temporarily, the direct German threat to Moscow.

In one sector alone his forces have destroyed 60 Nazi tanks in the last four days, and during eight days' fighting the Nazis lost 10,000 dead and wounded.'

The impropriety of the paragraphing here is seen in the fifth sentence. Because it begins a paragraph, 'This is shown' seems at first sight to relate to the prophecy made in the third sentence, that the Germans will take weeks to mop up the Kiev armies—rather than to the historical comment, made in the fourth sentence, that they have been meeting with great difficulties in their Ukraine offensive considered as a whole. With proper paragraphing the passage would have read as follows:

'According to the Nazi High Command, German forces, driving from Gomel across the Desna River and from the Dnieper on both sides of Kremenchug, have met at a point 130 miles east of Kiev. The Germans say that four Soviet armies have been caught between the arms of these giant pincers. Even if their claim is true, it will take weeks to mop up the Russians in the huge area enclosed by the pincers.

Already their general advance in the Ukraine has been

slow, painful and costly in the extreme. This is shown in the Berlin admission that at many points the Russians are still launching fierce counter-attacks across to the west bank of the Dnieper, and in a Moscow report that a German troop train with ammunition was blown up by Russian bombers near Dniepropetrovsk.

Meanwhile, Marshal Timoshenko's victories at Yelnya and Yartsevo in the Smolensk region have removed, at least temporarily, the direct German threat to Moscow. In one sector alone his forces have destroyed 60 Nazi tanks in four days and during eight days' fighting the Nazis lost 10,000 dead and wounded.'

It is sometimes said that one should never start a sentence with 'And' or 'But'—that these conjunctions are only for internal use. This is not so. One may start a sentence with 'But' if to tack it on to the previous sentence after a semi-colon would not be appropriate. For example:

'Uther ap Mathonwy was King of Thulë. According to Gandolph the Jongleur he lived in a palace wholly paved with gilt gingerbread and hard plum-cake. But this is not the Thulë of Heine's ballad: it is situated rather within the confines of fabulous Cockagne.'

Here it would have been wrong to tack on the third sentence to the second, since the 'But' refers back to the first.

Similarly:

'Uther died of grief in his palace after the loss of his daughter Reynardine who accidentally swallowed fern-seed and disappeared from mortal gaze. (According to Gandolph, the fern-seed had been brought in on a careless page's hunting-shoes and trodden into the gingerbread and plum-cake.) And that was the end of the Royal House of Thulë.'

Here it would have been wrong to tack the third sentence on to the second, not only because there are already two 'and's in the last seven words, but because 'And that was the end' refers to Uther's death, not to the page's carelessness. And the word 'And' could not be omitted without a loss of narrative grace. One should not, however, begin a paragraph with an 'And' or a 'But'. If one did, it would mean that the preceding paragraph was not a complete one.

The Asterisk

A row of asterisks implies an omission. It may be an omission that cannot be avoided—as, for example, in the following passage:

'The letter as it survived the fire was only decipherable in places. It ran:

Dear Godf * * * have you really broken off * * * coming as it does between the first squalid app * * * but never mind— all will be well, when all is forgotten.

Your loving Sally.

P.S. The kitten swall * * *'

Or it may be a deliberate omission, especially where intimate narrative details are left for the reader to supply. For example:

' "It is our marriage-night," he mumbled in confusion.

Very deliberately she came over to him, kissed him dispassionately, sat on the edge of the poor iron bedstead, and began briskly to unlace her shoes.

*   *   *

The Dot

Single dots are used to mark the end of an abbreviated word, such as 'Mr.', 'etc.', 'Ltd.'. A row of dots has two legitimate significances: either that the person who is supposed to be speaking is hesitating with 'er . . . um . . . er', or that it would be tedious or irrelevant for the writer to write out the sentence or paragraph in full.

For example:

' "Let me see . . .", Mr. Quennell remarked, "it would be

. . . yes . . . seventeen . . . no! exactly eighteen shillings! Thank you, Madam, I'm sure!" '

Or:

'The law provided that: "any person found guilty under the aforesaid Act of killing or maiming any domestic animal, to wit, horse, mare, gelding, mule, hinny . . . hound or dog, shall be mulcted of fifteen marks, unless aforesaid person be a knight of the shire, burgess, pot-walloper . . . or yeoman worth £10, and shall be confined to the stocks for the space of thirty-six hours, where the beadle shall be at pains . . ." '

The Exclamation Mark

Exclamation marks, also called 'notes of admiration', should be sparingly used. Queen Victoria used so many of them in her letters that a sentence by her that ends with a mere full-stop seems hardly worth reading. Exclamation marks do not necessarily close a sentence, as a full stop does.

For example:

'And then, horror! in marched Mrs. Blackstone with the little corpse held out accusingly between the pincers of the kitchen fire-tongs!'

The Question Mark

A question mark, similarly, can appear in the middle of a sentence without necessarily ending it. For example:

'That she had asked herself, was he really there? or was she imagining things? now troubled her conscience.'

The Semi-Colon and the Colon

A sentence joined only with commas (or the equivalent of commas in parenthesis-signs, brackets, long dashes and the like) is a single sentence. But sentences are often twins, triplets or even quintuplets, sextuplets and septuplets—semi-colons and colons make them so. A 'colon' originally meant a separate limb of a sentence, as a 'comma' was a piece cut off from the limb or trunk.

In modern usage, a semi-colon is no longer a pause of the time-value of half a colon—or two-thirds, as Mason suggested: it has an entirely different function. The chief modern distinction between a semi-colon and a colon is that parallel statements, if united in the same sentence to show their close connection, are (as in this sentence) separated with a semi-colon; whereas two statements, the second of which is looked forward to by the first, are separated with a colon. Examples:

> 'Mr. Jones went laughing up the hill; Mrs. Jones, in tears, down to the mill-pond. The dew was heavy on the grass of Farmer Turvey's four-acre field; above her head no stars were visible; somewhere an owl hooted. An idea entered Mrs. Jones' puzzled pate: she would refresh herself with a few drops of old and mild. She called out: "Child, child, run home and fetch me a pot of beer!" But it was not a child after all, as it proved: it was only the village pump!'

Care should be taken, when using colons and semi-colons in the same sentence, that the reader understands how far the force of each sign carries. Take, for example, the following sentence:

> 'It was as I anticipated: the *Friendship* came up with the rest of the feet at about six bells; the privateer then thought better of it and sheered off, lying about two leagues to windward.'

Here the reader would not know whether the narrator had anticipated merely that the *Friendship* would come up with the rest of the fleet, or also that the privateer would then sheer off. A full stop at 'six bells' would make things clear.

A long dash may be put after a colon, for emphasis. For example:

> 'The Captain arose and said: "Come, Antonio, amuse the men, and tell them one of your favourite stories!" Antonio

arose, rolled the quid from side to side in his coarse mouth
and, after a pause, began thus:—

"About the year 1874, in Lisbon . . ." '

Commas may do the work of colons and semi-colons in very
short sentences. For example:

'He ran off, I followed. He stumbled and fell, I overtook
him. He cried, "Are you mad?" I assured him, "Certainly I
am not." '

In each of the first two of these sentences the comma should,
strictly, have been a semi-colon; in each of the last two, it
should have been a colon. (In German no such relaxation is
permitted; the colons and semi-colons would have to be used.)

The Hyphen

The hyphen is used to link words which, if separated, might
possibly have some other meaning than the one intended, or
confuse the reader's eye.

The following is an example of an obvious lack of hyphens,
from an American antique-dealers' journal:

'High prices are still paid for pre-Christian Seltzer Pennsylvania Dutch chests, if painted with flowers in the *fractur*
style.'

These were not pre-Christian Dutch chests. Christian Seltzer
was a late-eighteenth-century painter of chests, fire-boards and
such-like for the 'Dutch', or Germans, of Pennsylvania. The
sentence should therefore have run:

'High prices are still paid for pre-Christian-Seltzer Penn-
sylvania-Dutch chests, if painted with flowers in the *fractur*
style.'

The accidental omission or insertion of a hyphen often makes
nonsense of a passage:

'In the Southern States slave-owners of property were expected to give their masters a proportion of its yield.'

Here 'slave-owners' should be 'slave owners'—i.e. slaves who were owners of property.

'A child photographer yesterday celebrated his silver wedding at Herne Bay: he was Mr. John Tulse, one of the first to specialize in the use of gauze filters.'

Mr. Tulse was really a child-photographer.

Adjectives should not be joined to their nouns with hyphens except in such special cases as blue-book, large-black pig, French-polisher, small-sword—where to omit the hyphen would be to endanger the sense.

Principle Nineteen

The order of ideas in a sentence or paragraph should be such that the reader need not rearrange them in his mind.

The natural arrangement of ideas in critical argument is:

Statement of problem.

Marshalling of evidence, first on main points, then on subsidiary ones—the same sequence kept throughout the argument.

Credibility of evidence examined.

Statement of possible implications of all evidence not wholly rejected.

The weighing of conflicting evidence in the scale of probability.

Verdict.

The natural arrangement of ideas in historical writing is the one recommended in *Alice in Wonderland* by the King of Hearts to the White Rabbit:

'Begin at the beginning, and go on till you come to the end: then stop.'

The natural arrangement of ideas in familiar correspondence—unless some all-important news pushes its way forward
to the first place—is:

> Acknowledgement of previous letter.
> Comment on the points raised in it, in order of impor-
> tance—the recipient's interests being given priority.
> New information in order of importance—the recipient's
> interests being given priority.
> Questions.
> Postscript.

It would take up too much space to analyse a mishandled
argument in full. But readers will be familiar with the sort of
argument that, if it ever commits itself to a statement of the
problem, does not do so until a mass of jumbled evidence on
subsidiary points has been adduced, after which it gives the
verdict, and then evidence on the principal point, and then an
irrelevant report on 'what the soldier's wife said', and then
contradictory statements about evidence on subsidiary points,
and then perhaps a reconsideration of the verdict, and then
fresh evidence, and finally a restatement of the verdict. Doubts
are cast by modern mathematicians on the universal validity of
the conclusions reached by Euclid in his propositions; but at
least he knew how to handle an argument, and always wound
up with 'This conclusion should be tested by practical experi-
ment.'

We shall, however, quote part of a carelessly constructed
argument by Major-Gen. Sir Andrew McCulloch. It is from his
answer to an editorial question (October 1941): 'Do you think
that any form of British invasion of Europe would be possible
during the next weeks or months?'

> 'I think it feasible to force an entry into Europe. This
> opinion, however, is of little value, because I do not know
> what force is available. If I knew as much as Mr. Churchill
> or the Chiefs of Staff my views might be of value. As it is, my
> opinions are in the realm of dreams. For this reason I shall
> take a purely imaginative situation, and on this premiss shall

discuss the relative merits of landing at various places on the coast of Europe.'

The logical order of ideas in this passage is:

1 If I knew as well as Mr. Churchill or the Chiefs of Staff
2 what forces are available
3 my views might be of value;
4 but I do not know,
5 and, when, therefore,
6 after discussing the comparative merits of various landing-places,
7 I pronounce it feasible to force an entry into Europe,
8 my premisses
9 must be recognized as no less imaginative
10 than if I had dreamed them.

The order in the original is 7, 4, 2, 1, 3, 10, 5, 9, 8, 6.

Readers are familiar with the long badly arranged family letter—everything jumbled together so confusedly that they have to read it through several times to find their way about it. No need to quote an example here. We shall, however, quote examples of newspaper reporting in which, because the historic order of events does not correspond with the order of what is held to be their dramatic importance, the reader's sense of what happened is distracted. Here is part of a report by Joan Slocombe of her experiences in Unoccupied France:

'But Vichy is dreary beyond words. I preferred Marseilles. In Vichy there is no plump madame of the green-grocery store for ever remarking on my accent. She asked, "Are you English?" and then drew me into the inner room, where over twenty people were listening to the B.B.C. French broadcast.

That happened to me in a cheerful, sunny little street in Marseilles one evening.'

The natural order of events is:

1 Marseilles was dreary enough
2 But a plump madame who kept a green-grocery store

3 in a cheerful little street
4 was always remarking on my foreign accent and one
5 sunny evening
6 asked me: 'Are you English?'
7 When I said 'Yes' she
8 drew me into an inner room where over twenty people
   were listening to the B.B.C. French broadcast.
9 There was none like her in Vichy,
10 which is dreary beyond words.

The order in the original is: 10, 1, 9, 2, 4, 6, 8, 3, 5 (with 7 omitted). The length of the two versions is the same.

But confused sequence of ideas is not confined to journalistic writing. Here is a hasty sentence from Rose Macaulay's essay on Virginia Woolf:

'With her conversation was a flashing, many-faceted stream, now running swiftly, now slowing into still pools that shimmered with a hundred changing lights, shades and reflections, wherein sudden coloured fishes continually darted and stirred, now flowing between deep banks, now chuckling over sharp pebbles.'

To suit the antiqueness of 'still pools that shimmered', 'a hundred changing lights', and 'wherein sudden coloured fishes', as well as to show the reader his way about the sentence, a conventional eighteenth-century treatment would have been appropriate here. Miss Macaulay might well have told with antithetical care how the water ran alternately deep and shallow, fast and slow, wide and narrow, through level fields, down rocky inclines. The principal imaginative figure, the pools of coloured fish, should have been placed at the end: this would have avoided the suggestion that the sudden coloured fish chuckled over the pebbles. Thus:

'With her, conversation resembled a changeable bright stream that now widening, chuckled over sharp pebbles, and now narrowing, flowed smoothly between steep banks; now it cascaded over rocks; now it lagged and deepened into still pools (shimmering with a hundred reflected lights and shades) wherein coloured fishes suddenly appeared, slowly swimming, and as suddenly darted from view.'

The exact position of subordinate clauses in relation to the main body of a sentence has never been fixed in English. However, there is this difference between modern English and Classical Latin usage: that, in Latin, subordinate clauses are put before the main body of the sentence, though sometimes the first of them may be artfully designed to hold the chief meaning of the sentence—even so complicated a writer as Cicero observes this general rule; whereas in English the rule is exactly reversed. We will show what we mean by rewriting the foregoing sentence in the Latin style:

'This, however, that in Latin, exactly in reverse manner to English usage, unless some subordinate clause, being artfully designed to hold the chief meaning of the sentence, comes first, all subordinate clauses—such is the general rule observed by even so complicated a writer as Cicero—are put before the main body of the sentence: this, I say, is a difference between modern English and classical Latin.'

It will be noted that this version recalls the prose of Milton, who tried to impose Latin syntax on English.

Principle Twenty

No unnecessary idea, phrase or word should be included in a sentence.

This does not mean that one should write with as much compression as if one were sending a cable, when short of cash, and scheming how to make one word do the work of three—for the reader will take far longer to get the sense of a skeleton message than that of the same message written out in full: it means that irrelevancies, at least, should be cut out. It is difficult to define what an 'irrelevancy' is in narrative, because most British readers enjoy almost any sort of incidental anecdote or reflection, tacked on to a story with only the feeblest excuse; but there are certain proprieties to be observed. For example, the following sentence from a recent history of Peter the Great of Russia seems to us improper:

> 'In his progress through this province Peter may have passed through the little town where, some two centuries later, his successor the Czar Nicholas II was to be murdered. We wonder what Peter's feelings would have been had he been granted prevision of this dastardly crime! Arrived back at his Capital . . .'

Since it is not even certain that Peter passed through the town, his hypothetic feelings do not seem relevant to the story, especially as the author has made no attempt to reconstruct them.

From a Tobruk despatch by J. H. Hodson, a war correspondent (1941):

> 'After that we breakfasted on sardines, biscuits, and tea in an atmosphere that seemed (fictitiously, no doubt) as peaceful and quiet as a beach in Devon.'

The parenthetic 'fictitiously, no doubt' belongs to some other story—e.g.: 'our hosts told us (fictitiously, no doubt) that they often borrow the enemy's spoons to stir their tea-cups.'

From a novel by James Hilton:

> '. . . sometimes on these delectable Fridays he would cycle for miles along the flat fen roads with the wind behind him, and return in the afternoon by crawling romantic-looking branch-line trains which always managed to remind him of wild animals, so completely had the civilized thing been submerged in the atmosphere of what it had sought to civilize.'

The idea of white men 'going native' in remote savage districts which they came to civilize is irrelevantly superimposed on the idea of domesticated animals that escape from civilization and run wild.

From a newspaper article:

> 'That, plainly, is the only way open to us of dealing with

India, or with any other colony or mandated territory that is
capable of looking after its own affairs.'

The word 'other' is irrelevant: India is not either a colony or a
mandated territory of Britain.

In the following example, from Sir Walter Citrine's *My Finnish Diary*, the unnecessary words are due to geniality:

> 'The ice lay in patches somewhere about a dozen feet
> across in all sorts of shapes. The steamer made easy work of it
> and soon cut a channel through, guided by the red and green
> lights which we saw swinging out at us. There was a light-
> house beyond, shooting out its rays through the darkness.'

Since nobody expects ice to stand up on edge or to form in
geometrical figures, and since lighthouses do not usually flash in
daylight, this boils down to:

> 'Guided by red and green swinging lights the steamer eas-
> ily cut a channel through the patches of ice, which measured
> on an average two or three yards across. Beyond, a lighthouse
> flashed.'

From an article by the Marquess of Crewe:

> 'The British Empire is no parvenu creation. The Tudors
> justly claimed that even then the Crown of England was an
> Imperial Crown, for it ruled several nations.'

When was the 'even then' time to which the Tudors referred in
their claim that the Crown of England was an Imperial one?
None has been indicated. If 'even then' is omitted, this problem
does not arise.

Principle Twenty-One

All antitheses should be true ones.

This means that all antitheses, or contrasts, should be between
opposing ideas of the same order. Here is an example of an

antithesis between ideas of different orders, from *Hansard's* report of a speech by Mr. Arthur Greenwood, M.P. (Aug. 1939):

> 'Our spirit has not weakened; our spirit has deepened.'

Here 'has deepened' should have been 'has strengthened'.

An example, from a gardening book, of an antithesis between similar ideas of the same order:

> 'Good soil deserves digging, bad soil needs it.'

The antithesis should not have been between what bad soil needs and what good soils deserves. Both soils need digging; both deserve digging. The intended antithesis here is perhaps:

> 'Good soil needs digging, to get the best crops out of it; bad soil needs digging, to get any crops out of it at all.'

An example from an article by Negley Farson:

> 'Bevin has just made a startling, yet bold . . . speech when he declared that positions in the Diplomatic Corps should be thrown open to working-class boys.'

Bold speeches are usually startling.

From a book-review by Desmond MacCarthy:

> 'Certainly I have never come across a better letter-writer than Lady Wentworth either in envelopes or print.'

He means presumably: 'Certainly, I have seldom come across better letters, published or unpublished, than Lady Wentworth's.'

From a novel by Graham Greene:

> 'Drover was not reading; they spied on him through a little window the size of a postcard in the cell door. He was asleep upright on his chair, clenched hands hanging between his knees. He might have been sitting for his portrait in the grey loose unaccustomed clothes, seen at better advantage

than half hidden by a bus's hood, but in his dreams he seemed to be in a bus still; a foot pressed the floor, the hands opened a little and twisted.'

In the last sentence there are four sets of true antitheses telescoped into a single false one. The first is: 'he might have been sitting for his portrait, but he was asleep.' The second is: 'he was wearing grey loose clothes, unlike his busman's uniform.' The third is: 'sitting in this chair his figure showed to advantage; but when he drove a bus he was half hidden by the bus's hood.' The fourth is: 'he was asleep, but in a position suggesting that he was driving a bus in his dreams.'

Principle Twenty-Two

Over-emphasis of the illogical sort tolerated in conversation should be avoided in prose.

In conversation people say: 'There are dozens of octogenarians in our village' [meaning, nine] 'and hundreds of children who have never seen the sea' [meaning, fifty or sixty] 'and a parson who invariably goes to sleep while preaching' [meaning, 'who openly smothered a yawn last Sunday']. Yet, reading a prose study of *Our Village*, one would take such remarks literally and feel aggrieved if they turned out to be misleading.

Here are examples of conversational emphasis that we consider inadmissible in good prose.

From an editorial of the *British Medical Journal*:

'That food is more important in the preservation of health than housing was shown by the late Dr. M'Gonigle at B——, but this is by no means to say that housing is not of the first importance.'

If food is more important than housing, housing cannot be of the first importance.

From a book review by A. G. Macdonell:

'*The Voyage* seems to be an incomparably better book than *Sparkenbroke*. Mr. Morgan has cut out almost all the dead-wood which used to encumber his writing and make him so difficult to read. There is still the misty silvery atmosphere of spiritual exaltation which Mr. Morgan can evoke as no one else since Conrad, but now the men and women are clear and vigorous against the mist and silver.'

It was not an incomparably better book—as Mr. Macdonell proved by the comparisons in the two succeeding sentences.

From two newspaper reports:

'The route from America is now a more essential artery to us than it has ever been.'

'Sir Horace Wilson, head of the Civil Service, has circulated to all departments a demand for man-power economy by the stringent cutting-out of less essential work.'

There are no degrees in essentiality: a thing is either essential or unessential.

Here is a characteristic example of forensic over-emphasis in a newspaper leader:

'The outrages committed by the German forces in the present war are almost identical with those they committed in the last except that they are even more atrocious; the excuses with which they are accompanied are exactly similar except that they are even more shameless. Mr. Churchill, in a flash of genius, divined this when he declared the present war to be "a continuation" of the last.'

Here the over-emphatic 'almost identical' and 'exactly similar', by restricting the possible differences between German behaviour in the First World War and the Second, take the wind from the sails of 'even more atrocious' and 'even more shameless'. Also, 'a flash of genius' is praise which leads the reader to expect a satisfyingly original epigram from Mr. Churchill instead of a sensible commonplace.

Principle Twenty-Three

Ideas should not contradict one another,
or otherwise violate logic.

The practice of oratorical disputation in mediaeval schools, though it led to absurd logic-chopping, and though little attempt was made to verify the truth of the facts used in the arguments, did at least make people conscious of the logical consequences of what they said. A modified form of such disputation might usefully be revived in English education. School-children would soon be able to put their fingers on logical flaws and would gradually learn to avoid absurdities themselves.

From the Historical Introduction to the *Oxford English Dictionary*:

> 'In this way began the system of voluntary readers, without whose help the material for the Society's Dictionary could never have been collected at all, except at a prohibitive cost of time and money.'

But if the cost had been prohibitive, the material could not have been collected.

From a novel by John Masefield:

> 'Do you see him?
> There went the fox, indeed, a little red flashing thing, looking much smaller than he was, because he was already fully extended.'

If the fox was fully extended, it might possibly look larger than it really was—as a cat does when it puffs out its fur to frighten dogs or as a horse does when it 'goes full out'—but not smaller.

From the autobiography of David Kirkwood, M.P.:

> 'Sir William Joynson-Hicks had made a stupid blunder by instructing a raid on "Arcos", the headquarters in London of

the commercial section of the Russian Government, for the purpose of discovering an imaginary document which wasn't there.'

If the police knew that the document was not at 'Arcos' and indeed that it existed only in their imagination, their purpose could not have been to discover it. (But perhaps the passage is ironical.)

Principle Twenty-Four

The writer should not, without clear warning, change his standpoint in the course of a sentence or paragraph.

What grammarians call 'false sequence of tenses' (e.g. 'He would not have come if he *saw* me coming too') and 'false concord' (e.g. 'Common-sense and honesty *is* all I ask', or 'I gave the wether *her* feed') are becoming increasingly common in English. The Latin grammarians took a more serious view of false sequence than the Greeks: the famous Greek historian Thucydides, especially when quoting speeches, often started a sentence with one construction and finished it with another. The Latins were right to be strict, for the eye is always delayed by a false sequence or concord.

Here is a typical example of false concord from a notice issued by a Head Warden of 'Rural Areas F. Division'.

'A new organization has been formed and is known as the "Fire Guard". The object of this body is to recruit every available person to fight fires in their own homes.

A meeting will be held at the Galmpton Institute on Wednesday September 10th at 8 p.m., when the Chief Officer of the Totnes Rural District Fire Services will attend to fully explain the scheme. It is hoped that everyone who can will attend, even if they are already members of a stirrup-pump party.'

It should have been: '. . . every person to fight fires in his own home', 'everyone will attend, even if he is already a member'.

In English one may legitimately refer to a Council, a firm or a society as either 'they' or 'it'—as one may refer to Great Britain, or Germany, or The Church, or a ship, as either 'she' or 'it'—but whichever form is chosen should be consistently used. Here are examples of inconsistency.

From a report by the Committee of Convocation (1931):

> 'Further, we would stress the debt of the Church for this provision of some form of worship for her sons scattered over the seven seas in ships and lighthouses, on the Continent, in the Australian back-blocks, in Canadian clearings, in loneliness in tropical Africa, where the Church itself is unable to supply regular ministrations.'

Because of 'her sons' it should be 'the Church herself'.

From a leader by J. A. Spender:

> 'All eyes are on Great Britain, which has announced that she does not recognize partitions of territory carried through by violence in the middle of war.'

It should be 'who has announced', because of the 'she' that follows.

Here are typical examples of false sequence of tenses. From the American news-magazine *Time*—an account of Napoleon's Moscow campaign:

> 'Before his troops marched last week, Hitler may—and very likely did—pause to review this pertinent chapter of history.'

This should be 'may have paused and very likely did'.

From a newspaper article, in which the past and historic-present are improperly mixed:

> 'Now, while Marx's activist theory of knowledge curtailed

the view that human beings are continuously changing, when
he comes to treat them historically he conceives of them as
uniform.'

It should be 'came' . . . 'conceived'.

From *Why Britain Is at War*, by the Hon. Harold Nicolson, M.P.:

'Would it really mean for us a loss of prestige and power if
all our African colonies were placed under the mandatory
system and administered in the interests of the natives and of
humanity as a whole? That in fact is the system which we are
already adopting. We should notice little change.

And in return for this we should achieve a world which is
worth fighting for.'

The 'is' in the last sentence may be justified as a Thucydidean
usage which gives greater emphasis to the sentence. But, grammatically, 'would be' is correct.

Most changes of standpoint are due to the writer's forgetting
how his sentence started. (The grammatic term is 'anacolu-
thia'.)

From a book-review by Desmond MacCarthy:

'There are a few things in his letters which Time has made
to look more foolish and some more wise than they were
when uttered.'

This should have been either:

'Time has made a few things in his letters look more foolish, and a few wiser, than when they were first written.'

or:

'Some things in his letters now look more foolish, and some
wiser, than when they were first written.'

From an article in a gardening journal:

'These markings are caused partly by natural etiolation,

sometimes because of frost, but generally from a microscopic pest.'

This should be either 'partly . . . partly . . . mostly'; or 'sometimes . . . sometimes . . . most often'; or 'in some cases . . . in others . . . generally'. In each case it should have been 'by', not 'because of' or 'from'.

From a Ministry of Information advertisement:

'To-day, the fanaticism of the Nazis is matched by a faith that is stronger and more enduring than their own, . . .'

Either: 'matched with', or 'opposed by'.

From a parish notice:

'Scrap metal, tins, paper will be collected the first Monday of every month; refuse will also be collected on alternate Tuesdays of each week.'

Very few of the parishioners noticed anything unusual about this—until Tuesday.

From a novel by Agatha Christie:

'In his mind phrase after phrase succeeded each other.'

Either:

'. . . phrase succeeded phrase'

or:

'. . . many phrases succeeded one another'

From *The Long Week End,* by Robert Graves and Alan Hodge:

'Samuel Butler, a prophet before his time, had suggested in his *Note-Books* . . .'

Either 'a shrewd prophet' or 'who was in advance of his time'.

Admittedly, many prophets including (so Biblical scholars say) Jermiah have been prophets after their times—i.e. some of the prophecies credited to them were written after the events to which they referred—but this was not what we meant.

Principle Twenty-Five

In each list of people or things all the words used should belong to the same category of ideas.

For example, one does not write: 'Various sorts of animals—carnivorous, herbivorous, fructivorous, marsupial, rodent.' The first three sorts of animals are classified according to their diet, the fourth according to its order in natural history, the fifth according to its family.

An Oxford butcher advertises himself as 'Family, pork and general butcher.' 'Family' denotes a particular class of custom; 'pork' denotes a range of commodities sold; 'general' may denote either that he butchers all animals fit for human consumption or that he sells to casual buyers as well as to families. The correct description is: 'Family and General Butcher; Specialist in Pork'.

From a B.B.C. news bulletin:

'The combined operations in Libya were a notable example of land, air, and naval coöperation'.

This should have been 'land, air and sea coöperation'.

From a local paper:

'The hotels have been taken over by the military, the Navy and the R.A.F.'

In popular usage the initials 'R.A.F.' have no counterpart: for 'R.N.' is not used and the Army as a whole has no initials. Since 'the military' is in a category by itself—such forms as 'the naval' and 'the aerial' not being used—this sentence should have read:

'The hotels have been taken over by the Navy, Army and Air Force.'

The form 'by the Royal Navy, the Army and the Royal Air Force' calls unnecessary attention to the Army's lack of royal patronage despite its seniority to the Royal Air Force.

8

The Graces
of Prose

There is a Debatable Land between the region governed by our numbered principles, those concerned with the secure conveyance of information, and the region governed by our lettered principles, those concerned with its graceful conveyance. For example, most cases of the use of obscure references, discussed under Principle F, also come under Principle 3, which concerns general unintelligibility of expression; and most cases of the circumlocution discussed under Principle G also come under Principle 20, which concerns irrelevancies. That does not trouble us. We have separated the two classes of principles because a failure to conform with the lettered ones is an offence against sensibility, rather than sense; whereas with the numbered ones the offence is against sense, rather than sensibility.

Principle A

***Metaphors should not be mated in such a way
as to confuse or distract the reader.***

Metaphors are used more often in English than in most modern European languages, and far more often than in Latin or Greek. A metaphor is a condensed simile. Here are two similes:

'Marriage is like a lottery—with a great many blanks and very few prizes.'

'Our struggle against sin resembles a cricket-match. Just as the batsman strides out to the wicket, armed with pads, gloves and bat, and manfully stands up to demon bowling, with an adversary behind him always ready to stump him or catch him out . . . and when the sun sets, and stumps are drawn, he modestly carries his bat back to the pavilion, amid plaudits. So likewise the Christian . . . And when, finally, safe in the celestial pavilion, he lays aside the bat of the spirit, unbuckles the pads of faith, removes the gloves of doctrine and casts down the cap of sanctity upon the scoring-table,—lo, inside, is the name of The Maker!'

Examples of metaphors derived from these two similes are:

'Poor Edwin has indeed drawn a blank in the matrimonial lottery.'

'St. Paul, that great sportsman, faced the bowling manfully in the struggle against Paganism.'

When two unconnected similes are reduced to metaphors, and these are combined in the same sentence, the effect on the reader is to blur both of the mental pictures which the metaphors call up:

'Edwin's matrimonial record deserves our praise rather than our pity: he drew two blanks but on each occasion faced the bowling manfully.'

The mismating of metaphors is justified only in facetious contexts. For example, Mr. R. A. Butler, M.P., remarked in a Commons debate:

'The Hon. Member for East Wolverhampton is to be congratulated on producing a very tasty rehash of several questions which have been fully ventilated in this House up to date.'

Here, the unpleasant implications of the word 'ventilated' were sure of a laugh. The columnist 'Atticus' often makes genial use of the mismated metaphor. For example:

'Colonel Moore-Brabazon's predecessor, Sir John Reith, continues on his Gulliver's travels, and is now on his way to that distant land, the House of Lords, from whose bourne no traveller returns.'

But there is no facetiousness in this remark by Mr. Arthur Greenwood, M.P. (1939):

'While we strive for peace, we are leaving no stone un-turned to meet the situation should the fateful blow fall.'

In what conceivable circumstances could anyone turn up a stone to ward off a fateful blow? Mr. Greenwood meant:

'We who strive for peace are seeking every means of ward-ing off the fateful blow.'

The Archbishop of Canterbury in a pamphlet (1940):

'But just as truly pioneers of that far-off age are those who accept the common obligations of men and strive to live in the spirit of Christ as they discharge them.'

One may be the pioneer of a new route to some far-off land; one may be the herald or harbinger of a new age; one may be the prophet of a far-off age. But 'a pioneer of a far-off age' is a difficult conception.

From a letter to the Press by Eden Philpotts:

'Exorcize forever the vision of Germany as a bleeding mar-tyr who calls upon civilization to cut the cancer from her bosom; since Germany is herself the cancer. . . .
She penetrates web and woof, destroying the fabric of hu-man society, pouring her venom through every existing chan-nel of international relations, creating nests and pockets in the healthy tissue of her neighbours, fouling and destroying the forests of human kind that her own fungus breed alone shall inherit the earth and the fulness thereof . . .'

A ready test of the legitimacy of a metaphor is whether it can be illustrated even in fantastic caricature or diagram. Mr. Philpotts fails to pass the test here: it would puzzle the most ingenious and morbid-minded painter alive, even Salvador Dali, to show a seeming cancer, which is really a fungus in the world's bosom, pouring venom through channels in the universal cloth fabric, at the same time creating nests and pockets in the healthy tissues of her neighbour fungus-cancers (?), and destroying forests of mankind.

There are many nearly dead metaphors in English; but they are apt to revive when two or three are included in the same sentence.

From a newspaper article:

'The I.F.S. had held out the olive branch, but nothing of a concrete nature had come out of it.'

Principle B

Metaphors should not be piled on top of one another.

Constant change of metaphor is very tiring to the reader: the visualizing of metaphors requires a different sort of mental effort from that required for visualizing facts.

Here is an account from the American magazine *Time* of President Roosevelt's electoral campaign in 1940:

'No ivory tower held Candidate Roosevelt. He knew well that a candidacy should reach its crest on Election Day and not one moment before. But the Gallup Poll, giving him a terrific majority, left no option now but to go ahead and kill off Candidate Willkie, for any slip from that lead might still be fatal in a year as full of loose electricity as 1940. He decided to go ahead full steam.'

It would have been better to write this report in a simple sustained metaphor—for example, that of a boxer who has planned to win a match on points, intending not to go all out until the last round, but getting an unexpected chance to knock out his opponent in an early one. In the *Time* version the change from the electricity to the steam metaphor is particularly confusing.

'Atticus' sometimes overdoes his trick of mismating metaphors. An occasional mismating may be good fun, but an orgy disgusts.

> 'After a series of punishing defeats the Premier's son, Mr. Randolph Churchill, has won a bloodless victory and will now join the gallant six hundred at Westminster. No doubt he will have mellowed since the days when as a young politician he not only rode ahead of the hounds but in front of the fox.'

H. G. Wells is being solemn, not facetious, in this sentence from a newspaper article:

> 'And the raw material, that hairy ape, is so made over that it is only in some moment of crazy lust, panic, rage or bestial vitality that we realize he is still the core, the blood injection at the root of us all.'

Mr. Wells tends to take a scientific view of language—that words are tools, and those with the strongest pictorial associations have the keenest cutting edge: if he wishes to express himself trenchantly, why should he not use 'hairy ape', 'the core', 'blood injection', 'at the root of us all'? Because it is dangerous to play with edged tools.

Readers would understand and accept Mr. Wells's meaning far better if he had written:

> 'And the passionate material of which we all are made has been so carefully processed in the factory of our social habits that it is only an occasional crazy moment of lust, rage, or panic that suddenly recalls our bestial origin.'

Principle C

Metaphors should not be used in such close association with unmetaphorical language as to produce absurdity or confusion.

The principle is best illustrated by this short sentence from a melodramatic chapter in Graham Greene's novel *It's a Battlefield:*

> 'Kay Rimmer sat with her head in her hands and her eyes on the floor.'

And her teeth on the mantelpiece? A slip like this will break the spell of a novel for any intelligent reader.

In the following quotation from J. N. W. Sullivan's *The Bases of Modern Science* (1928), the fantastic metaphor in the first sentence is disconcertingly given an appearance of reality in the second and third sentences:

> 'The principle requires us to believe that, *to an observer mounted on such an electron*, a ray of light would pass the electron with the speed of 186,000 miles per second, whether the electron was moving in the direction of the ray or whether it was moving in the opposite direction. We have said "to a observer", but we do not intend to imply thereby that any merely psychological effect is involved. We may replace the observer by scientific apparatus making the necessary measurements automatically. What is essential is that the apparatus should be mounted on the electron.'

From the Minutes of a Municipal Council:

> 'The sub-committee have reported that though every avenue has been explored, no street in the central district bounded by Station Road on the North and High Street on the South could be used as a permanent parking-place for cars without incommoding tradesmen and/or impeding traffic.'

There were no avenues in the central district—only narrow streets lined with shops.

Principle D

Characteristically poetical expressions should not be used in prose.

Except, of course, in quotations. When Daphne du Maurier writes in a pamphlet:

> 'All that remained of the gallantry, the courage, the brotherhood and sacrifice, of four years in Flanders, were the graves of the fallen and the blown and scarlet poppies.'

the reader is entitled to make such burlesque variants on 'the blown and scarlet poppies' as 'the infant and chestnut foals', 'the adolescent and Red Indian'.

Our phrase 'poetical expressions' includes such conceits as these from a novel by Dr. A. J. Cronin:

> 'The force of the hurricane almost bowled him off his feet. The station was deserted. The young poplars planted in line at its entrance bent like bows, whistling and shivering at every blast. Overhead the stars were polished to a high glitter.'

Prose decency demands rather: 'Overhead, the stars glittered with such brilliance that he fancied them burnished by the force of the wind.' These are conceits in the French style. French is a less poetic language than English, since fewer liberties can be taken with it and possible meanings are therefore restricted. If, obeying the traditional rules of French, one attempts to write great poetry, the result, judged by English poetic standards, is at best merely magnificent verse. This is what André Gide meant when, asked who was the greatest French poet, he answered 'Victor Hugo —*hélas!*' Modern poets who are born French have despairingly cultivated an anarchic 'disorientation of the senses', following the example of Rimbaud, a true

poet. Such characteristically French movements as impressionism, symbolism, and surrealism all began from disorientation.
Impressionism is a hit-or-miss way of describing the general
appearance of things without consideration of details; symbolism is a way of describing things with conscious disregard of
how one intellectually knows them to be, for the purpose of
emphasizing their emotional significance; surrealism is the real-
istic expression of disturbingly anti-conventional fancies.

Many feelings and scenes are extremely difficult to describe
accurately in prose. Here, for example, is a description of a
'damnable room' by Rebecca West, in her novel *Harriet Hume*,
as it looked when one Arnold Condorex switched out all the
lamps but an alabaster urn on the chimney-piece:

> 'The fluted pilasters, their grooves black with shadow,
> looked like claw-nails drawn down the walls, and the gold
> convoluted capitals might have been the claws that traced
> them. The painted lunettes on the panels and ceiling were
> black oily smears from which shone only the whiter details of
> a universe lackadaisically falsified, swan necks bent by an-
> gelic meekness to re-entrant curves, profiles so tense with
> nobility that the breath must rush forth from the nostrils like
> the shriek of a police whistle, forearms like fins with languish-
> ment.'

This reads queerly, but then, the room was damnably queer;
and when one examines the words in detail there is not one to
which one could justly take exception, except 'like claw-nails
drawn' for 'as though claw-nails had been drawn': it is as intelligibly expressed as so difficult a scene could be. But in the same
novel occurs another passage:

> 'Tenderly he reflected that her little head, which was al-
> most egg-like in its oval blandness, was as full as an egg is of
> meat with the desire to please. But for that his shrewdness
> rebuked him. There must be much else besides. She had
> mastered the shining black leviathan that just behind her
> proclaimed Bechstein its parent. Like him she had crawled
> up the dark tunnel which leads from obscurity to the light,
> and had performed the feat more expeditiously.'

This does not seem written in the same sensitive syle as the
other passage. Some sort of 'ism' pervades it. The reader feels
that Rebecca West is trying to put something over on him,
some sort of verbal hypnotism. When he examines the words in
detail they do not answer for themselves in a commonsense
way. Blandness cannot be oval. 'But for that' is ambiguous.
'Shrewdness' cannot rebuke; though a 'shrewder self' can.
Bechstein was not a shining black leviathan who spawned other
black leviathans and crawled up dark tunnels rather less expe-
ditiously than Harriet.

Here is an example of impressionism from W. E. Woodward's
biography *George Washington*:

> 'Writers, historians, philosophers and men of that tribe
> have more inner life than they really need. On the other
> hand, there are many people who could take on a larger
> amount of inner life without being harmed at all.
>
> McMaster thought that Washington's inner life had never
> been understood and probably never would be.
>
> From him we get the impression of a great figure, sitting in
> dusky isolation, like a heroic statue in an empty plain. To
> reach it we must travel a road that has been worn so deep by
> McMaster, and Irving, and Sparks, and Wilson, and
> Lodge—and innumerable others—that we cannot see over its
> sides. It is cluttered with the prayer tablets of the pilgrims
> who have preceded us; and we are out of breath from climb-
> ing over the hurdles of reverence and fancy. We approach on
> tiptoe; we utter the sibilant whispers of awe.
>
> No wonder Washington's character appears elusive. Any-
> body's would under the circumstances. . . .
>
> The background of elusiveness has been painted in the
> picture by biographers who have looked into Washington's
> soul for the quivering inner life which they themselves pos-
> sessed. When they did not find it there they lost their bear-
> ings and ran round in circles.
>
> Washington's mind was the *business mind*.'

This is a plausible argument and a sensible conclusion; but it
would carry far more weight with the ordinary reader if written

more soberly. It is not merely that the metaphors are mis-mated—one does not expect to find hurdles across a well-worn road, or a three-dimensional statue melting into a two-dimensional background; nor merely that the contrast between the crudely facetious 'take on a large amount of inner life' and the rhetorical 'sitting in dusky isolation, like a heroic statue in an empty plain' is shocking. The worst is that the reader feels himself written *at*, not written *for*—especially in the de Quinceyesque: 'We approach on tiptoe; we utter the sibilant whispers of awe.'

Here is an impressionistic passage from a short-story by H. A. Manhood:

'They kissed, and happiness was a singing colour in the stillness. They lay down, and their passion was an exquisite winging of time and beyond reason, a glimpse of harmony at its uttermost source, a moment of immortal growth. And, having raced to rapture and savoured all creation, they came laughing back like guests to sleep where sleep was known, lying close in a gracious half-state that made the final waking less like bruising, gave them time to secure memory for ever. . . .

They never lost the first ecstasy. The richness and marvel of their oneness increased to a deep, sustained over-beat within them, a radiance which seemed larger even than death.'

These are wild words. How can a winging be a glimpse? How can a source be uttermost? How can harmony have even an original source? What is immortal growth? How can a glimpse be a growth? What is the meaning of even so apparently simple a phrase as 'like guests to sleep where sleep was known'?—is the first 'sleep' a verb or a noun? 'Half-smile', 'half-apple', or 'half-century', yes!—but what is a half-state?—does he mean 'intermediate state'?—if so between what extremes? How can an over-beat be a radiance, and how can a radiance seem larger than death?

Principle E

Except where the writer is being deliberately facetious, all phrases in a sentence, or sentences in a paragraph, should belong to the same vocabulary or level of language.

Scholars and clergymen are seldom able to keep their language all of a piece.

The following is from a newspaper sermon:

> 'It is one of the mysteries of that inner life of man (one so replete with mysteries hard to accept or solve) that some of us are clearly, as it were, freeborn citizens of grace, whilst others—alas! many others— can only at great price buy this freedom. Of this there can be no doubt. The Gospel appointed for to-day reports to us, in the words of our Lord Himself, a story at once simple and mystifying, about day-labourers in an Eastern vineyard. Some of them had worked a full day, whilst others had only "clocked in", so to speak, when it was nearly time to go. Yet each received from the employer the same flat rate of remuneration—a Roman penny. Our Lord said that was all right, which must be enough for us.'

It begins with ecclesiastical-scholarly language 'whilst others—alas! many others—can only at great price buy this freedom'; gradually presses through the apologetically modern, 'others had only "clocked in", so to speak, when it was nearly time to go', and the commercial, 'each received from the employer the same flat rate of remuneration'; descends to the downright vulgar, 'Our Lord said that was all right . . .'

Scholars are at their worst in translations, especially when trying to give antique work a modern flavour: over-attention to the Classics has blinded them to the moods of their own language. From Dr. Rouse's translation of Seneca's *Apocolocyntosis:*

> *'Citius mihi verum, ne tibi alogias excutiam.*
> Out with the truth and look sharp, or I'll knock your quips and quiddities out of you.

Contentus erit his interim convictoribus.
These boon-companions will satisfy him for the nonce.

Vosque in primis qui concusso
Magna parastis lucra fritillo.
And you, above all, who get rich quick
By the rattle of dice and the three-card trick.'

This is to dart about confusingly between the seventeenth and twentieth centuries.

The same uncertainty of language-level is found in Michael Heseltine's translation of Petronius's *Satyricon*. Here there is an attempt at brisk modernity:

' "*Oro te*," *inquit Echion centonarius*, "*melius loquere.*"
"Oh, don't be so gloomy," said Echion, the old-clothes dealer.'

But there are sad lapses into the antique:

'*In pinacothecam perveni vario genere tabularum mirabilem. Nam et Zeuxidos manus vidi nondum vetustatis injuria victas.*'

Mr. Heseltine's translation is:

'I came into a gallery hung with a wonderful collection of various pictures. I saw the works of Zeuxis not yet overcome by the defacement of time.'

This, to match the other quotation, should have read:

'I visited the gallery. The exhibition of paintings there was most representative and contained some fine old-masters, among which I even found a few Zeuxises that had kept their original tones surprisingly well.'

Principle F

No reference should be unnecessarily obscure.

If everyone had to write for the stupidest reader, as a regiment on the march accommodates itself to the pace of the slowest soldier, literature would be as tedious as a tenpenny nail,[1] and since the precise degree of literary and historical education with which one's public can be credited varies greatly with its estimated size, this principle is a difficult one to observe.

The Parliamentary Correspondent of a daily paper who writes: 'The "'ouse couldn't but do it" as Bunce remarked on a similar occasion' is. expecting too much of even his educated readers. A few of them will have read Trollope's *Phineas Finn*, but of those not all will remember the minor character Bunce and hardly one of those who do will be able to recall the 'similar occasion'.

From a detective novel by Dorothy Sayers:

> ' "I feel," said the lawyer, carefully stirring his coffee, "that . . . Mr. Arbuthnot is right in saying it may involve you in some —er—unpleasant publicity. Er—I . . . cannot feel that our religion demands that we should make ourselves conspicuous—in such very painful circumstances."
>
> Mr. Parker reminded himself of a dictum of Lord Melbourne. "Well, after all," said Mrs. Marchbanks, "as Helen so rightly says, does it matter? . . ." '

The particular dictum of Lord Melbourne appropriate to this context cannot be unerringly singled out by any of Miss Sayers's readers, who number hundreds of thousands, nor even guessed at by more than a dozen or so Melbourne experts— none of whom is necessarily a reader of Miss Sayers's novels. That Mr. Parker, a police inspector, could recall a dictum of Lord Melbourne's is not an indication, either, that he was an educated person: he might have come across it in a 'Great Thoughts' calendar or in a popular newspaper.

Malcom Muggeridge writes in his history, *The Thirties*:

> 'In the restless determination to extract ever more material satisfaction from life to compensate for other satisfactions which were lacking, ever heavier drafts were drawn on the future. Expense of shame in a waste of passion . . .'

---

[1] We use this to exemplify the sort of incidental expression that one should avoid. A 'tenpenny nail' is an old-fashioned school reading-book, but (except in Scotland) the phrase has been a hundred years out of fashion.

This crooked reference to the 129th sonnet of Shakespeare's which begins:

> 'Th' expence of spirit in a waste of shame
> Is lust in action . . .'

seems to us indefensible. The line is first inverted, then misquoted, and in its new form does not explain itself as prose.

Principle G

All ideas should be expressed concisely, but without discourteous abruptness.

Circumlocution is one of the few bad habits in writing that has gradually gone out of fashion since the daily newspapers first set an example of snappy reporting of events. Yet there is still plenty of verbosity left over from the leisured days before the First World War when it was often considered a sign not of pomposity but of ingenuity to make five words, without irrelevance or repetition, do the work of one. Pontifical critics, who wish to full up a column easily, politicians and retired Headmasters who wish to be regarded as men of letters, and officials who wish to be portentous for reasons of policy are, in general, the most verbose writers of to-day.

Victorian readers did not much mind having their time wasted; a few survivors still feel that they are not getting their money's-worth unless, say, an article on modern novels in the leading literary weekly begins in the leisurely expansive style of the following (1940):

> 'Nothing is vainer at the present time, of course, than prediction. But one broad conclusion seems reasonably safe. If, as is most likely, we come out after the war into rather a different sort of world, we shall almost certainly be getting a rather different sort of novel.
>
> English fiction of the past two years throws little light on precisely what differences may be expected. So far, that is,

the war has not stimulated any noticeable "new tendencies"
in the novel; there is nothing to indicate the birth of either
new ideals or new methods. But at the same time there is
evidence, admittedly slight and possibly unreliable except in
rough outline, of a deepening selectiveness among old ideals
and methods. For what it is worth this evidence may supple-
ment certain general deductions from the course of events
since the outbreak of war that concern much else besides
literature.'

This amounts to no more than:

'Though the style of English novels is likely to change after
the war is over, it is not safe to prophesy just how it will
change. Fiction published during this war has shown signs,
not of new ideals and methods, but only of what I, perhaps
mistakenly, judge to be a more conscientious choice of old
ones. I will relate this judgement to certain general deductions from events of the last two years.'

From the Minutes of a Debating Society:

'It was proposed by Mr. J. H. Dix and unanimously carried: that whereas discussions in this Society are not liable to
end in the breaking of furniture or fixtures, so long as they
are checked when they become too noisy; and whereas discussions unwisely conducted endanger the peacefulness of
this Society; and whereas discussions that go on under the
chairmanship of Mr. E. B. Silvoe sometimes end in the
breaking of furniture or fixtures; and whereas discussions in
this usually peaceful Society are, if wisely conducted, always
checked when they become too noisy—Mr. E. B. Silvoe be
not again appointed to take the chair at a meeting of this
Society.'

This can be reduced simply to:

'It was proposed by Mr. J. H. Dix and unanimously carried: that whereas, when Mr. E. B. Silvoe is appointed chairman, the discussions of this usually peaceful Society are not

always checked before furniture or fixtures are broken, he be not again appointed.'

Verbosity, as in the last example, is often due to over-conscientiousness; in the following instance, from a Head Warden's circular, it is due to embarrassment at having to point out something obvious:

> 'With the coming of the longer periods of darkness the possibility of enemy action is increasing and it is necessary that all steps should be taken by the civilian population to minimize the dangers attendant on the falling of bombs, by organizing themselves into stirrup-pump parties, and so face up to the war.'

This would have been put more simply as:

> 'As the nights draw out, civilians must face the increased danger of enemy bombing, by forming stirrup-pump parties.'

This, from Professor A. N. Whitehead's *Science and the Modern World* (1925), is probably also written in an embarrassment similarly caused.

> 'The inevitableness of destiny can only be illustrated in terms of human life by incidents which in fact involve unhappiness.'

Since destiny is by definition inevitable, this reduces to:

> 'Human destiny can be exemplified only with unhappy instances.'

Principle H

The descriptive title of a person or thing should not be varied merely for the sake of elegance.

Elegant variation of names and titles is a common French trick, derived from Latin verse. A Latin poet, writing about the God

Bacchus, for example, or the God Juppiter, would have thought meanly of himself if he could not present the God under ten or twelve aliases, each recording a part of his legendary history and attributes. The French novelist Balzac, similarly, used as many as six different descriptive identifications of the same person at the beginning of successive sentences. Mr. Philip Guedalla emulates Balzac. Here is a passage from his *Mr. Churchill: a Portrait:*

'. . . he prepared a discourse, learned it off, and established himself in his father's seat. His predecessor in debate was a Welsh Radical, a few years older than himself, who had been ten years in the House already, and, courageous in his criticism of the war, emulated Winston Churchill's escape from Pretoria in a Dutch pastor's hat by escaping from a hostile audience at Birmingham Town Hall in a policeman's helmet.

The black-haired orator resumed his seat, and Mr. Churchill followed Mr. Lloyd George. It was an unimpressive little speech . . . Though he managed to be loyal to the Government, the new member's tone about the Boers was a shade unusual. . . .

The ordeal was over; and when someone introduced him to Lloyd George, the fervent Welshman told him that he was "standing against the light". The Tory novice answered that his new friend seemed to "take a singularly detached view of the British Empire".'

Anyone who read this passage hurriedly would imagine that at least four or five people, not two, were involved in this historic meeting.

An official leaflet, E D L 66, circulated by the Ministry of Labour to women who registered under the 'Registration for Employment Order, 1941', contains this paragraph:

'Women are wanted for the work of supplying the Forces with aeroplanes, guns, shells, and all the munitions and equipment that they need. Large numbers are also required in the Women's Auxiliary Services—the W.R.N.S., the A.T.S., the W.A.A.F., . . . The Nursing Services also require a great many additional recruits. More women are wanted by the Women's Land Army and N.A.A.F.I. There are also many other essential industries and services which must be maintained.'

This constant change of formula is unnecessary, confusing and invidious. The paragraph would have read more persuasively as follows:

'Large numbers of women are needed in industry, especially in the factories that supply the Forces with aeroplanes, guns, tanks, ammunition and equipment. Large numbers are needed also in the W.R.N.S., the A.T.S., the W.A.A.F., in the Women's Land Army, in the N.A.A.F.I., in the Nursing Associations—these and many other vital services must be maintained.'

From an historical article on the American War of Independence:

'When news of the disaster came, Cornwallis sought to retrieve it by cutting off Morgan, but that general had dropped back with such celerity that the force sent out was too late, the troops being detained by torrents of rain which made the creeks almost impassable.'

'That general', 'that gentleman', 'that worthy' are never either neat or necessary substitutes for 'he'. The author should have written something of this sort:

'When news of the disaster came, Cornwallis sought to retrieve his position by cutting General Morgan's line of retreat. But Morgan moved quickly and the force that Cornwallis sent out arrived too late [at the Dan River], having been detained by torrential rain which made the intervening creeks almost impassable.'

Expressions such as 'the former, the latter', 'the first, the second', should be used as seldom as possible: they are invitations to the reader's eye to travel back—and it should be encouraged always to read straight on at an even pace.

An Air Ministry announcement was phrased:

> 'One of our fighters attacked and destroyed three enemy bombers in as many minutes.'

This is a device for avoiding the repetition of 'three'. But why trouble to avoid it? Why ask the reader to work out an equation sum—which is not even amusingly complex?

An American magazine takes this device a stage further into absurdity:

> 'For the second time in as many months the panic was on.'

Principle I

Sentences should not be so long that the reader loses his way in them.

A sentence may be as long as the writer pleases, provided that he confines it to a single connected range of ideas, and by careful punctuation prevents the reader from finding it either tedious or confusing. Modern journalists work on the principle that sentences should be as snappy as possible; they seldom, therefore, use colons or semi-colons. Historians and biographers have learned to be snappy too. Here is H. C. Armstrong writing about Mustapha Kemal Ataturk in his *Grey Wolf*:

> 'Enver was always inspired by great ideas, by far-flung schemes. The big idea absorbed him. He cared nothing for details, facts or figures.
>
> Mustafa Kemal was cautious. He was suspicious of brilliancy. Big, vague ideas did not rouse him. His objectives were limited, and undertaken only after long and careful consideration and calculation. He wanted exact facts and figures. He had no sympathy with and no ability at handling Arabs or any foreigners. He was a Turk, and proud of being a Turk. . . .'

A biographer of the old school would have fitted these ten sentences into a single one, connected by a semi-colon at the place where Mr. Armstrong has begun a new paragraph.

Sentences by eigthteenth-century authors sometimes continue for a page or more, yet are not allowed to get out of hand. Here, however, are a couple of modern instances where even a seven-line sentence is too long.

From an article by D. R. Gent, the sporting-journalist:

'I spent many hours dipping into Rugby books of all kinds, and two especially suggested lots of subjects that, I think, will interest my readers these days, when we can face up to the strenuous times we are living in, even more bravely when we can refresh ourselves occasionally with memories of great days behind us, and especially days on the Rugby field or watching glorious matches.'

This would have read better if he had broken it up into three sentences, in some such way as this:

'I spent many hours dipping into a variety of books about Rugby and two especially interested me. I think that they would have interested my readers too, for they concerned great events in the history of the game. In these strenuous times we can face up to our trials and responsibilities more bravely if we occasionally refresh ourselves with memories of the glorious matches which we have witnessed or in which we have been fortunate enough to take part ourselves.'

This is from an article by Ernest Newman, the music critic:

'Berlioz's faults as a composer are obvious, but not more so than those of many other composers who, however, had the good luck to have their misses counted as hits by umpires whose sense of values had been perverted by too long a toleration of bad art so long as it was bad in the orthodox way, whereas Berlioz's directest hits were often debited to him as misses.'

This is too long a sentence only because it is mismanaged. Commas are not enough to separate so many complex ideas into properly related parts of a single argument. We suggest this alternative version:

'Berlioz's faults are obvious to us modern listeners, as are those of many other composers who in their time fared far better with the critics than he did: their misses were often counted as hits, his most direct hits as misses—merely because musical standards had been perverted by a long toleration of work which, though bad, was not eccentrically so.'

This is from an article by Arthur Krock in a New York newspaper (1941):

'It is Morava-Varda that is the military stake for which Hitler is playing in his game of high-tension diplomacy with the Yugoslavs. Should he be confined to the Struma because of unwillingness or inability to add to his enemies the Yugoslavs massed against a Salonika front which would be the result if the people and their government fulfil the expectation noted above, Hitler's designs would be obstructed.'

The second sentence is too long only because too many ideas have been tied to one another in a bundle. They should have been separated in this sort of way:

'If the people and government of Yugoslavia, fulfilling my expectation of them noted above, decide to forbid Hitler the use of the Morava-Varda valleys, and if he is unwilling or unable to add them to his enemies, he will be unable to approach Salonica except by the Struma valley and his designs will thereby be obstructed.'

Principle J

No unnecessary strain should be put on the reader's memory.

Some writers think in far longer stretches than others: they start an essay or article with some unobtrusive point and, after introducing a whole new body of argument, slowly circle round and pick the point up again two or three pages later as if it had only just been made. They should remember that most people, though they may be expected to retain the general sense of any paragraph until the end of the chapter, will forget a particular phrase in it (unless heavily accentuated) after three sentences and a word (unless very remarkable) as soon as they have finished the sentence.

Here are examples, from two leaders by J. A. Spender, of excessive strain put on the reader's memory:

> 'There could, for example, be no better contribution to "Federal Union" than the pooling of resources for mutual defence recently achieved by the United States, Britain and Canada. Here, for the first time, is shown the way to break down the obstacle of "sovereignty" which worked so disastrously before the war to isolate and divide the smaller nations and leave them at the mercy of the Dictators. Lord Lothian, who has long been a student of this subject, brings back this sheaf with him on his visit to London.'

The phrase 'this subject' in the third sentence presumably refers to 'Federal Union'; and 'this sheaf' to 'the pooling of resources for mutual defence'. But because of the intervening sentence few readers will have been able to identify these references without a quick look-back to the first sentence.

> 'Our habit of taking the whole world into our confidence about our casualties and the damage done by German raiders to our buildings and property is, I am sure, well justified. A free and self-respecting people needs to be assured that nothing is being concealed from it, and that there will not some day be a sudden shock of discovery when concealment is no longer possible. Yet contrasted with the grim silence of the dictators about what is happening in their countries, it produces a one-sided psychological effect which needs to be corrected by some effort of imagination.'

Here, the 'it' of the third sentence is separated from the subject to which it refers by a longish sentence. Few readers will have been immediately able to identify the 'it' with 'our habit of taking the whole world into our confidence about our casualties and the damage done by German raiders to our buildings and property'.

The Archbishop of Canterbury writes in a pamphlet (1940):

> 'Especially we must remember that it is very hard to extract justice from strife. The passions evoked by war blind the vision and distort the judgement. We dare not hope to make our victory result in pure justice. We can, indeed, make it result in something far nearer justice than a Nazi domination; that alone would justify our fighting. But we must not ignore the perils inseparable from our enterprise; and we must steadfastly determine that we will resist, so far as by God's help we can, these corrupting influences, so that if He gives us victory we may be found faithful to the principles for which we have striven.'

Here, similarly, the 'corrupting influences' in the last sentence are not easily identified with 'the passions evoked by war' mentioned three sentences previously: most readers will be able to think back only as far as 'a Nazi domination'.

Principle K

The same word should not be so often used in the same sentence or paragraph that it becomes tedious.

For emphasis it is legitimate to go on using the same word or phrase time after time:

> 'The crow has been peculiarly my bird ever since I can remember. Indeed, my earliest recollection of childhood is a crow perched on my nursery window-sill. On my third birthday a crow came to my party and helped himself to my birthday cake. On my first journey to school I was accompanied by a crow. A crow perched on a tree outside the room

where I sat for my first successful examination. A crow was the cause of my meeting my first wife; a crow attended our wedding; a crow nested on the chimney of my first freehold house. Finally, a crow gave the alarm when I was drowning in the Regent's Canal in June 1886. It has always been a crow, not lark, robin, blackbird, raven, owl nor lapwing—no other bird but a crow!'

Or:

'Fethi had this tradition from the sage Abdul ibn Rashid, who had it from the sage Daoud ibn Zaki, who had it from his father who was a judge in Homs, who had it from his brother Ali the Copyist, who had it from Mahomed the guardian of the Mosque of Tarjid, who had it from his predecessor of the same name, who had it from [etc. etc.] who had it from Ali, the muezzin of Al Ragga, who had it from his father Akbar, the saddle-maker, who had it from the lips of the blessed Prophet Himself!'

But here are instances where the continued use of the same word becomes tedious. From a 'lay sermon':

'I admire the man who is man enough to go up to a man whom he sees bullying a child or a weaker man and tell him, as man to man, that he must lay off.'

This should read:

'I admire the man who is courageous enough to go up to someone whom he sees bullying a child or a man weaker than himself, and tell him plainly that he must lay off.'

The word 'of' is often a difficulty. From a report on broadcasting by the Committee of Convocation (1931):

'There has been . . . an honest dread on the part of many of the popularization of a form of godliness that lacked its power, of the substitution of an emotional appeal at the foreside for the organized fellowship. . . .'

This should have read:

> 'Many have honestly dreaded the popularization of a form of godliness that lacked its power, the substitution of an emotional appeal at the fireside for organized fellowhip. . . .'

The word 'in' is often a difficulty. From an agricultural report in a newspaper:

> 'In fact, in countless villages in England in this war and in a variety of ways, there has been a most astonishing adaptation of local products to war needs.'

This should have read:

> 'In countless English villages during this war, and in a variety of ways, there has been, indeed,' etc. etc.

Principle L

Words which rhyme or form a jingle should not be allowed to come too close together.

Though modern prose is intended to be read silently and two or three times faster than at the ordinary speaking rate, some people read with their mental ear not quite closed. Obtrusive accidental rhymes or jingles are therefore avoided by careful prose writers, as possibly distracting their readers' attention.

The terminations 'otion' and 'ation' are often a difficulty:

> 'The need of registration or re-registration at this station of all workers on probation is to be the subject of examination by the Administration.'

There is usually a way out—here, for example:

> 'The Administration will examine the need of registering or re-registering at this station all probationary workers.'

The termination 'ing' is often a difficulty. This is from a Gossip column (1940):

> 'I have heard something interesting which, anticipating the approaching ending of the Peiping Puppet Government, illustrates popular feeling in Northern China to-day.'

The way out here was:

> 'I have heard an interesting piece of news which illustrates popular feeling in Northern China to-day and anticipates the early collapse of the Puppet Government at Peiping.'

This is from *English Villages*, by Edmund Blunden:

> 'Our great game is cricket; our summer is incomplete without its encounters . . . and however the actual process of play may seem to the uninitiated visitor, the centre scene . . . with pigeons flying over and cuckoos calling across, and now and then the church clock measuring out the hour with deep and slow notes, cannot but be notable.'

To avoid the jingle with 'notes', 'notable' should have been 'memorable'.

Terminal 'y' is often a difficulty. From an article by Hilaire Belloc on air-superiority:

> 'We have established, and are increasing, our superiority in quality, while time makes steadily for ultimately establishing superiority in quantity as well.'

The way out was:

> 'We have established and are increasing our qualitative superiority, and are making steady progress towards the ultimate establishment of quantitative superiority as well.'

The persistent recurrence of the same vowel-sound is often very ugly. For example, this sentence from an article on the Baconian Theory:

'But my main contention is that, though great claims may be made for the name of Bacon, "Shakespeare's plays" remain unchangeably the same.'

Many of these 'a' sounds can be removed:

'But my chief contention is that, however strongly it may be urged that Bacon was the author of "Shakespeare's plays", this cannot result in the slightest textual alteration in them.'

Another example, from an article by Herbert Read:

'. . . Art as we know it now will have disappeared in the flames like so much plush, . . .'

Or like so much crushed, mushy, touchwood.

Principle M

Alliteration should be sparingly used.

The use of alliteration need not be altogether discarded. Indeed, when one writes with feeling in English there is a natural tendency for words to well up in a strongly alliterative way; and this should be checked only when the emphasis seems too heavy for the context. The foregoing sentence, for example, has got one 'w' too many in the middle of it: on reading it over we should naturally have changed 'well up' to 'start up', had we not seen that it illustrated our point.

In the following passage from a newspaper article, Mr. J. B. Priestley might well have cut out five of the eight 'w's' and two of the four rhymes in -*ore*.

'The world before the war produced the war, and we want no more such worlds. But we want . . .'

He could have written:

'There must be no more worlds like that which produced this war. Instead, there must be . . .'

The B.B.C. news-bulletin editors might well have trimmed off a few 'p's' from the following item (1940):

> 'A feature of to-day's news has been important public pronouncements on peace by the Pope and President Roosevelt.'

They could have written:

> 'Important declarations on peace are a feature of to-day's news: they have been made by the Pope and by President Roosevelt.'

Principle N

The same word should not be used in different senses in the same passage, unless attention is called to the difference.

If one searches in the kitchen-cupboard for a missing egg-cup and does not find it, though it is there, the chances are that it is doing duty as a mustard-pot—the eye refuses to recognize it as an egg-cup. Similarly, if the same word is used in different senses in a passage, the reader's eye will often fail to recognize the second word—it cannot grasp, as it were, that an egg-cup can also be a mustard-pot.

Here are examples. From a pamphlet by Dr. Hugh Dalton, M.P.:

> 'I have already said that Britain holds the key to this key-problem of Franco-German relations.'

The word 'key' is here used in two different senses. A key-problem is a metaphor derived from the key-stone of an arch; the key to a problem is a metaphor derived from unlocking a chest.

From a newspaper leader (1941):

> 'Roumania must remember that though she has now cho-

sen to take what she believes to be the safest course, namely, to *range* herself with Germany, the *range* of our heavy bombers based on Greek aerodromes constitutes a serious threat to her oil fields.'

From a newspaper report:

'The mob of frightened little children reached the fire-alarm, but were unable to reach it.'

The probable meaning is:

'The frightened little children ran in a mob to the fire-alarm, but none was tall enough to reach the knob.'

From the organ of the International Brigade Association:

'A few letters written in July have reached this country from German and Polish International Brigaders, interned at the concentration camp of Le Vernet. Two hundred prisoners still remain there. All efforts should be concentrated to save them.'

The odium in the word 'concentration camp' should have made the writer avoid using 'concentrated' in a good sense.

Principle O

The rhetorical device of pretending to hesitate in a choice between two words or phrases is inappropriate to modern prose.

Many orators have built their reputations on passages such as this:

'Mr. Hacksaw—oh, I beg his pardon, our friend served two whole days in the State militia, so I suppose I ought to call him *Captain* Hacksaw—well, this gallant Captain was born in Clay County getting on for thirty years ago, I reckon. His father was a dishonest, possessed Baptist minister—forgive the slip of the tongue, I should have said "an honest, dispossessed Baptist minister"—from a wretched living near Taunton, Conn. Well, this Rev. Jackstraw—I should say Chopstraw—oh, the devil take it, Hacksaw—was a sheep-stealer, or if that sounds too blackguardly, let us say he was a man who used to rob his fellow-ministers of their flocks and rush them down to the stream to be *dipped.* . . .'

Prose writers, however, are assumed to be able to correct their first inaccurate remarks before publication; so that their play with second thought is not amusing, but indicates mere indecision between two ideas.

From an article by Brigadier-General Morgan, K.C.:

'When the great explosion of 1914 occurred, the doctrine was there ready to the hands of the German armies to justify, or rather to excuse, every outrage they committed.'

From an article by Negley Farson:

'This might all be fruitless were it not that, in his self-overhaul, the Englishman has begun to question some of his traditions, or (let us call them correctly) his obsessions.'

From a woman's column in a weekly paper:

'Typewriting, from the very beginning, has been a woman's means of earning a livelihood—or, more correctly, a girl's perhaps because women, taking them all round, are nimbler with their fingers than men.'

From Sir Walter Citrine's *My Finnish Diary*:

'Below us were masses of trees fringing tracts of snow, which quite possibly were small lakes, or to put it more correctly, perhaps, creeks.'

(Or shall we say 'fjords'?)
In each of these cases, if second thoughts were best, the writer should have expunged the first.

Principle P

***Even when the natural order of its words is
modified for the sake of emphasis, a
sentence must not read unnaturally.***

The three following examples of inversion suggest too-literal
translations from a foreign language:

From a note by 'Atticus', the columnist:

> 'Colonel Bishop became a truly remarkable shot and the
> higher his score of victims amounted the more his china-blue
> eyes grew humorously pensive.'

(Here 'amounted' is probably a slip for 'mounted'.)

From an article by Ivor Brown:

> 'News comes of the death of a clown absolute . . . one of a
> dynasty adored . . . The clown absolute is quite a different
> person from the actor-droll.'

(Yes, quite a person different.)

From an unsigned book-review:

> 'That till he had installed himself at Ferney never, surely,
> in his whole life had he been so much of his fate the master,
> this was the burden, or under-song, of all Voltaire's later
> writings: . . .'

From an American news magazine:

> 'Unhappily, the Rome radio admitted: "There is a possi-
> bility of our having to yield some further points".'

The effect in this last instance is ambiguity. The writer did not
mean that he was made unhappy by the admission, but that
the Rome radio was unhappy.

Part II

EXAMINATIONS
AND
FAIR COPIES

Examinations
and Fair Copies

Explanation

While noting typical errors or shortcomings in English prose-works of the 1918-1941 period we came across numerous short passages, from each of which we could draw examples of several different sorts of error; and were surprised to see what eminent people some of the writers were. We then concentrated on the writings of eminent people, and the frequency of confusion or obscurity in their work supported our original contention: that English has for some time been written with great carelessness not only among the uneducated and semi-educated but also among the educated classes, who once prided themselves as much on their ability to write and speak well as on their lineage, wealth, or administrative capacities.

We do not claim that our system for classifying faults is the only practical one, or even the best one; or that, when we quote a passage, every one of the objections which we raise on behalf of the common reader is justified; or that the fair copies we offer are perfect; or that no faults in plain statement or shortcomings in the Graces of Prose are to be found in our own writing. But we hope at least that our inquiries will make people more conscious of the reader-writer relationship than they have hitherto been.

The quotations we use are chosen 'almost at random': which means that, having decided that so-and-so was eminent in such and such a profession, we took up the first popular book, pamphlet or article by him that came our way and read on at our usual speed until we found ourselves bogged in a difficult passage. This passage became the subject of our analysis. Often we were bogged in the opening paragraph; often we were not bogged at all and mentally apologized to the author—Godfrey Winn is an instance—for having suspected him of writing badly, merely because we did not much like his point of view, or because —Elizabeth Jenkins is an instance—popular reviewers whom we mistrusted had praised his or her work extravagantly.

We have had no intention of pillorying the writers whom we include in our list, or of suggesting that the passages chosen are characteristic of their work. We considered, at first, quoting examples of good prose by the same writers; but decided against this because one cannot profitably compare a straightforward account of one thing with a confused account of another, and because we did not wish to compile an anthology.

Our friend Captain Liddell Hart has suggested as a sub-title to this book 'A Short Cut to Unpopularity'. It is true that many small-minded people would almost rather be told that they have no sense of humour than that they have expressed themselves badly in prose: for every English writer considers himself, like the Emperor Sigismundus, to be 'superior to the grammarians'. But we shall not impute small-mindedness to any of those from whose writings we quote and shall assume that, like ourselves, they are always glad to have their errors pointed out, so long as this is done justly and without malice.

When we began making our comments, always from the reader's point of view, these were at first limited to surface faults or shortcomings; but we were soon reminded that good English is a matter not merely of grammar and syntax and vocabulary, but also of sense: the structure of the sentences must hold together logically. In analysing a passage we have often found ourselves in disagreement with the facts presented in it, but have not tampered with them in our fair copy, unless they seemed too contradictory to support their logical structure. If it is objected 'You really know what the writer means—why shouldn't he put it in his own way?—you can't pass a steamroller over individuality?', our reply is: 'In some cases we don't know at all what he means and doubt whether he is sure of it himself; in others we have guessed with varying degrees of certainty; in the remainder we have found out after only a slight delay.' Our contention is that each focusing of the reader's mind on an eccentricity or error or ambiguity interrupts the continuity of his reading and distracts him from a clear understanding of what the passage means. Every writer is entitled to make his own mistakes, if he is prepared to stand by the consequences and not expect the reader's gratitude for being given unnecessary work to do. But he must remember that even phrases which can be justified both grammatically and from the point of view of sense may give his reader a wrong first impression, or check his reading speed, tempting him to skip.

We do not attempt to stereotype English. The principles which we suggest, and which if adopted would, we believe, help people to read and understand books far more easily than now, allow full scope for individual style; just as the conventions of legible handwriting do. One cannot bind a lively intelligence to the dull regularity of copperplate script. In each fair copy we have tried to keep as close as possible to the style and spirit of the original.

If it is further objected that many of the points which we raise are so small as to seem hardly worth raising, our reply is that, though a single fly-spot does not make a dirty window-pane, twenty or thirty do. It is strange how insensitive English-speaking people are to faults in their own language, even those who pride themselves on the correctness of their French or Spanish. In our analyses we do not pass any fault or shortcoming however small; but to avoid tediousness we make a few of our more pettifogging points by implication in the fair copy rather than by direct comment in the analysis.

Here is a list of the twenty-five numbered categories which we use for tabulating errors in clear statement, and of the sixteen lettered categories we use for tabulating shortcomings in the graces, or decencies, of prose. With each category goes the principle which rules it.

1. WHO? *It should always be made clear who is addressing whom, and on the subject of whom.*

2. WHICH? *It should always be made clear which of two or more things already mentioned is being discussed.*

3. WHAT? *Every unfamiliar subject or concept should be clearly defined; and neither discussed as if the reader knew all about it already nor stylistically disguised.*

4. WHERE? *There should never be any doubt left as to* where *something happened or is expected to happen.*

5. WHEN? *There should never be any doubt left as to* when.

6. HOW MUCH? *There should never be any doubt left as to* how much *or* how long.

7. HOW MANY? *There should never be any doubt left as to* how many.

8. INAPPROPRIATE WORD OR PHRASE. *Every word or phrase should be appropriate to its context.*

9. AMBIGUOUS WORD OR PHRASE. *No word or phrase should be ambiguous.*

10. MISPLACED WORD OR PHRASE. *Every word or phrase should be in its right place in the sentence.*

11. UNINTENTIONAL CONTRAST. *No unintentional contrast between two ideas should be allowed to suggest itself.*

12. DUPLICATION. *Unless for rhetorical emphasis, or necessary recapitulation, no idea should be presented more than once in the same prose passage.*

13. SELF-EVIDENT STATEMENT. *No statement should be self-evident.*

14. MATERIAL OMISSION. *No important detail should be omitted from any phrase, sentence or paragraph.*

15. UNFULFILLED PROMISE. *No phrase should be allowed to raise expectations that are not fulfilled.*

16. UNDEVELOPED THEME. *No theme should be suddenly abandoned.*

17. FAULTY CONNEXION. *Sentences and paragraphs should be linked together logically and intelligibly.*

18. MISPUNCTUATION. *Punctuation should be consistent and should denote quality of connexion, rather than length of pause, between sentences or parts of sentences.*

19. CONFUSED SEQUENCE OF IDEAS. *The order of ideas in a sentence or paragraph should be such that the reader need not rearrange them in his mind.*

20. IRRELEVANCY. *No unnecessary idea, phrase or word should be included in a sentence.*

21. FALSE CONTRAST. *All antitheses should be true ones.*

22. OVER-EMPHASIS. *Over-emphasis of the illogical sort tolerated in conversation should be avoided in prose.*

23. LOGICAL WEAKNESS. *Ideas should not contradict one another, or otherwise violate logic.*

24. CHANGE OF STANDPOINT. *The writer should not, without clear warning, change his standpoint in the course of a sentence or paragraph.*

25. MIXED CATEGORY. *In each list of people or things all the words used should belong to the same category of ideas.*

A. MISMATING OF METAPHORS. *Metaphors should not be mated in such a way as to confuse or distract the reader.*

B. TOO MANY METAPHORS. *Metaphors should not be piled on top of one another.*

C. METAPHOR CONFUSED WITH REALITY. *Metaphors should not be in such close association with unmetaphorical language as to produce absurdity or confusion.*

D. POETICALITY. *Characteristically poetical expressions should not be used in prose.*

E. MISMATING OF STYLES. *Except where the writer is being deliberately facetious, all phrases in a sentence, or sentences in a paragraph, should belong to the same vocabulary or level of language.*

F. OBSCURE REFERENCE. *No reference should be unnecessarily obscure.*

G. CIRCUMLOCUTION. *All ideas should be expressed concisely but without discourteous abruptness.*

H. ELEGANT VARIATION. *The descriptive title of a person or thing should not be varied merely for the sake of elegance.*

I. OVERLONG SENTENCE. *Sentences should not be so long that the reader loses his way in them.*

J. MEMORY STRAIN. *No unnecessary strain should be put on the reader's memory.*

K. TOO MUCH OF THE SAME WORD. *The same word*

should not be so often used in the same sentence or paragraph that it becomes tedious.

L.   JINGLE.   *Words which rhyme or form a jingle should not be allowed to come too close together.*

M.   TOO MUCH ALLITERATION.   *Alliteration should be sparingly used.*

N.   SAME WORD IN DIFFERENT SENSES.   *The same word should not be used in different senses in the same passage, unless attention is called to the difference.*

O.   SECOND THOUGHTS.   *The rhetorical device of pretending to hesitate in a choice between two words or phrases is inappropriate to modern prose.*

P.   AWKWARD INVERSION.   *Even when the natural order of its words is modified for the sake of emphasis, a sentence must not read unnaturally.*

In the texts that we examine, a small letter following a numeral means that we have found more than one example of the same type of error; similarly, a small numeral following a capital letter means that we have found more than one example of the same type of shortcoming. The best way to follow our argument is first to read a text through without regard to numbers and letters; then to read it again, sentence by sentence, looking up each note in the EXAMINATION under the corresponding number or letter; then to read the FAIR COPY, comparing it with the TEXT, and finally the COMMENT.

Sir Norman Angell

from *Why Freedom Matters,* 1940

TEXT

. . . The new inquisitions[23a] and the new Popes assume infallibility. Stalin and Hitler pronounce [14] the true doctrine; decide on [18a] pain of death and torture,[P] that it shall not be questioned; decide what facts the millions[1a/H] shall be allowed to know, and what they shall not be allowed to know concerning those[2a] doctrines.[G]

And the new inquisitions[8a] are immensely more powerful, more efficient, more omnipresent[22a] than the old, because they possess instruments so immeasurably [22b] more efficient[8b] for reaching the mind of the million.[H] It will be[5] easier for the new Popes to crystallize error.[9]

From the day[22c] that a child is born in Germany or Russia, and to a lesser extent in Italy,[10a] it is brought under the influence of the State's doctrine; every teacher teaches it[2b] through the years of childhood and adolescence. In[4] every conscript, whether military or industrial, the process is continued;[18b] every book suggests the prevailing orthodoxy; every paper shouts it; every cinema gives it visual suggestion.[21/10b]

The effect of the process is, of course,[23b] to worsen the quality of the mass mind;[18c] to render it less and less capable of sound judgement.

The protagonist of dictatorship argues[1b] that the quality of the mass mind does not matter[18d] because the dictator rules[23c] and the mass only have to obey. . . .

EXAMINATION

1.   WHO?

(a) . . . decide what facts the millions shall be allowed to know . . .

Who are the millions? Their own nationals or the world at large?

(b) The protagonist of dictatorship argues . . .

A 'protagonist' is the leading character in a dramatic situation. Is Mussolini, Stalin or Hitler intended? Or does Sir Norman Angell mean merely 'enthusiastic advocates of the dictatorial form of government'?

2.   WHICH?

(a) . . . what they shall be allowed to know . . . concerning those doctrines.

Which doctrines? So far only one, true, doctrine has been mentioned.

(b) From the day that a child is born in Germany or Russia it is brought under the influence of the State's doctrine; every teacher teaches it through the years of childhood and adolescence.

At first one naturally reads the second 'it' as meaning the child; but this makes poor sense, so one decides that the doctrine is meant. 'The years of childhood and adolescence' are presumably the child's years, not the State's.

4.   WHERE?
   In every conscript the process is continued . . .

This 'in' conveys no clear location. It is probably short for 'in the case of'; but means literally that the process of education in State-doctrine is carried on by the conscript for himself.

5.   WHEN?
   It will be easier for the new Popes to crystallize error.

But it is said in the next paragraph that the process of bringing up children and adults in the way that (according to the Democrats) they should not go, is already complete in Germany and Russia.

8.   INAPPROPRIATE WORD OR PHRASE
   (a) And the new inquisitions are immensely more powerful, more efficient, more omnipresent than the old, because they possess instruments so immeasurably more efficient for reaching the mind of the million.

Is not 'inquisitions' too limited a word for the context? The task of the original Inquisitors was to smell out heresy, not to be missionaries of Christian doctrine—that was left to the priests and the friars. The Nazi and Communist parties as orders of priesthood should perhaps have been mentioned; the Inquistors—Ogpu or Gestapo—not being numerous compared with the mass of the party to which they belonged.

   (b) The new inquisitors . . . possess instruments so immeasurably more efficient for reaching the mind of the million.

The phrase 'efficient instruments' suggests people; 'efficacious', a word reserved for things as opposed to personal agents would be better—if microphones, the radio, modern newspaper plant and suchlike are meant. Also, 'efficient' has already been used in the sentence.

9. AMBIGUOUS PHRASE

It will be easier for the new Popes to crystallize error.

The argument is not at all clear. Play has been made with the ironical use of 'true doctrine' so that we do not know whether 'error' here is meant seriously or not. Real (as opposed to figurative) Popes may be said to crystallize error by their pronouncements against current heretical tendencies not previously regarded as erroneous. The edicts of these 'new Popes', however, unless Sir Norman is so violent an anti-Papist that he really means his readers to regard every pronouncement from the Vatican City as wilfully fraudulent, have, according to his argument, the effect, not of crystallizing error, but on the contrary of making it flow more freely.

10. MISPLACED PHRASE

(a) From the day that a child is born in Germany or Russia, and to a lesser extent in Italy, . . .

How can a child be born to a lesser extent in Italy than in Germany or Russia?

(b) Every book suggests the prevailing orthodoxy; every paper shouts it; every cinema gives it visual suggestion.

These are presumably the more efficient instruments hinted at in the second paragraph; and should have gone in there.

14. MATERIAL OMISSION

Stalin and Hitler pronounce the true doctrine . . .

This reads as though the Nazi and Communist doctrines were identical. They might have been emotionally allied in Sir Norman's mind in 1940, but in fact they were distinct and antagonistic to each other. He meant that Stalin and Hitler pronounced each his own true doctrine.

18. MISPUNCTUATION

(a) Stalin and Hitler . . . decide on pain of death and torture, that it shall not be questioned; . . .

With punctuation, it is often difficult to know whether the author, the typist, or the printer is responsible for the omission of important commas. The one that has dropped out after 'decide' is an important one, because without it the sentence means that the dictators decide on inflicting pain by death and torture in order that the doctrine may not be questioned; rather than meaning that death and torture are inflicted only in cases where the doctrine is questioned.

(b) In every conscript . . . the process is continued; every book suggests the prevailing orthodoxy; every paper shouts it; every cinema gives it visual suggestion.

These three semi-colons and the stop suggest that the items which they terminate are parallels. But the first item is of a different order from the rest, which all have to do with the dissemination of orthodox beliefs, and belongs with the previous sentence; the conscript has orthodoxy preached to him as part of his education, but does not necessarily disseminate it. Nor is the first semi-colon a possible misprint for a colon. Not only conscripts but the whole public are subjected to propaganda by books, papers and cinemas.

(c) The effect of the process is, of course, to worsen the quality of the mass mind; to render it less and less capable of sound judgement.

The semi-colon makes the phrases 'to worsen the quality' and 'to render it less capable' parallel and independent of each other. What is needed is a colon, to show that the second phrase is an interpretative enlargement of the first.

(d) . . . The quality of the mass mind does not matter because the dictator rules . . .

One should be careful of commas dropping out before the word 'because'. Here the omission makes the sentence mean: 'it is not because of a dictator being in power that the quality of the mass-mind matters'—which is contrary to the argument.

21.   FALSE CONTRAST

Every book suggests the prevailing orthodoxy; every paper shouts it; every cinema gives it visual suggestion.

The implied contrast between the different degrees of emphasis used by newspapers as a whole, books as a whole, films as a whole, does not stand. Some Russian and German books shouted their propaganda; in some newspapers, especially scientific and technical ones, it was only suggested. And the implication that Russian and German films restricted their doctrine to visual suggestion, dispensing with the aid of sound, is unfortunate.

22. OVER-EMPHASIS

(a) **The new inquisitions are more omnipresent than the old . . .**

There are no degrees in omnipresence: any more than there are in absoluteness, or completeness. A thing is either everywhere, or it is not. Its absence even from a single locality would deny its omnipresence. But a thing can be said to be more nearly omnipresent, absolute or complete than another.

(b) **. . . they possess instruments so immeasurably more efficient for reaching the mind of the million.**

'Immeasurably' does not ring true. The Spanish Inquisition managed to inculcate orthodoxy pretty well with the crude instruments at its disposal; and the heretic of those times could not secretly switch on a radio-set and console himself with a free Lutheran broadcast in Spanish.

(c) **From the day that a child is born in Germany or Russia it is brought under the influence of the State's doctrine;**

One cannot believe that the German or Russian midwives and doctors exert their doctrinaire influence quite so early.

23. LOGICAL WEAKNESS

(a) **The new inquisitions and the new Popes assume infallibility.**

This suggests that the old Inquisition also assumed infallibility, whereas it was merely an instrument of the Pope's and could be censured by him for errors in carrying out its task. Nor did the Russian Ogpu assume infallibility: an Ogpu chief had recently been purged by Stalin for making grave mistakes. Similarly, in Germany Hitler had not delegated his 'infallibility' to the Gestapo.

**(b) The effect of the process is, of course, to worsen the
quality of the mass mind; to render it less and less capable of
sound judgement.**

'Of course' is gratuitous. It is arguable that the effect of
Communist or Nazi state-doctrine on the public mind was not
to worsen its quality, but only to give it a new set of axioms on
which to form its judgements. Either doctrine, whatever might
be said against it by democratic moralists, could surely be held
by a convert without impairing his faculty of judgement—by
the way, can a public mind be said to form spontaneous judgements even in the most favourable circumstances?—so long as
he had confidence in the axioms and adhered to them.

**(c) . . . the quality of the mass mind does not matter
because the dictator rules and the mass only have to obey.**

This argument is not fairly presented. Obedience is demanded from the people in all forms of government.

G.   CIRCUMLOCUTION
**Stalin and Hitler decide what facts the millions shall be
allowed to know, and what they shall not be allowed to know
concerning those doctrines.**

The rhetorical repetition of 'shall be allowed' would be
more effective if it led up to something that stirred the imagination more than the bald 'facts . . . concerning those doctrines'.

H.   ELEGANT VARIATION
**. . .what facts the millions shall be allowed to know, . . .
for reaching the mind of the million.**

Is there any justification for reducing the millions from
plural to singular?

P.   AWKWARD INVERSION
. . . on pain of death and torture; . . .

It is useless to torture a dead man; 'torture' should therefore come first. It is true that in the Middle Ages people were
sometimes sentenced to be 'hanged, drawn and quartered and
mulcted of 1000 marks', but the mulct was intended as a punishment of the criminal's heirs rather than the criminal himself.

FAIR COPY

'A modern dicatator, or lay-Pope, has his assumption of infallibility maintained by an ubiquitous priesthood of Party-men, which includes an Inquisition of secret police. Popes Stalin and Hitler have each a political faith to enunciate which nobody in his State may question, under pain of torture or death; they decide just how many of the authentic facts of history and science may safely be taught to their docile millions.

Both the Communist and Nazi priesthoods, because of the superior efficacity of their instruments for controlling the public mind, are immensely more powerful than was the Catholic priesthood in the times of the Inquisition. The new Popes, indeed, find it easy enough to disseminate and perpetuate error: they can ensure that every book and newspaper published in the countries which they control, every cinema-film shown, must at least suggest, if it does not forcibly present, the new faith.

Children in Germany and Russia are introduced to the orthodox doctrine of their State as soon as they begin to talk, and are continuously instructed in it by all their teachers throughout the years of childhood and adolescence, and by their officers when they become military or industrial conscripts; the effect, of course, is to make them incapable of forming judgements on other bases of thought than those thus provided. This is also true of party education in Italy, though there the system is not run so thoroughly.

Those who advocate dictatorship as a practical form of government argue that the capacity of the common people for forming sound judgements does not matter, because the dictator and his staff do all the thinking for them. . . .'

COMMENT

A biographical note to Sir Norman Angell's book explains that he spent his childhood in England, but was educated in France and French Switzerland, and then worked as a cowboy and prospector in America; that subsequently he took to journalism in the United States, France and England; that for the last thirty years his chief interests have been economics and peace agitation. Graces of all the schools of language from which he graduated may be discovered in this passage: French rhetorical tricks, a go-as-you-please Western-American sequence of ideas, journalistic brightness, the insensitivity of the twentieth-century economist to the graces of prose, the uncertain emotional emphasis of pacifism. The liberties that we have taken in suggesting an alternative version to the passage chosen are far greater than in most cases; but this is a complicated case.

Viscount Castlerosse
(later the Earl of Kenmare)

from *The Londoner's Log* (December 1940)

TEXT

The history of the times[12a] of the century before one[9] I find to be deeply interesting,[12b] for the reason that there[G] are so many incidents and situations which coincide[8] with[14a] the present day.[16] There are also[4] odd bits of interesting information.[12b]

Few people know that Napoleon was a British subject. But nevertheless, it is the truth anyway.[12c] He was thus placed technically[20a] and for a period.[14b]

It happened like this. A few months after Napoleon had distinguished himself at the taking of Toulon, Corsica[14c] proclaimed herself to be a monarchy under the sovereignty[23] of King George III, who once[5] addressed a most august assembly[3] as 'My dear Lords and Turkey Cocks.'[20b]

EXAMINATION

3.　WHAT?
　　. . . a most august assembly . . .

　　The House of Lords? A convocation of spiritual peers at Lambeth Palace/ The Lords of the Admiralty?

4. WHERE?

There are also odd bits of interesting information.

This perhaps refers to some book he has been reading, but he does not mention it.

5. WHEN?

... George III, who once addressed a most august assembly ...

Was this before or after Corsica put herself under the King's sovereignty?

8. INAPPROPRIATE WORD OR PHRASE

... many incidents and situations which coincide with the present day ...

Incidents and situations of 1790 cannot coincide with those of 1940; though historical parallels may be drawn.

9. AMBIGUOUS WORD OR PHRASE

The history of the times of the century before one I find to be deeply interesting, ...

'The century before one' may mean the century that lies ahead of one; or the century that one is examining; or (from the point of view of the reader of 1940) the nineteenth century. The only event here particularized took place in the 1790's. 'The century before one' therefore probably means 'one hundred years before my birth.'

12. DUPLICATION

(a) ... history of the times of the century ...

All histories of a century are necessarily histories of its times.

(b) ... the history of the times of the century before one I find to be deeply interesting, ...

There are also odd bits of ... information.

All history is composed of odd bits of interesting information, sometimes strung together on threads of argument, sometimes merely juxtaposed.

(c) But, nevertheless, it is the truth anyway.

It would have been enough to write either:

'But it is the truth,'
or: 'Nevertheless it is the truth,'
or: 'Anyway, it is the truth.'
Duplication has here been enlarged to triplication.

14. MATERIAL OMISSION

(a) . . . so many incidents and situations which coincide with the present day.

An incident or situation cannot coincide with a day, but only with another incident or situation.

(b) . . . Napoleon was a British subject. He was thus placed technically and for a period.

For a period should read: 'only for a short period'. A subject's technical subjection to the King lasts normally for the period of his life.

(c) A few months after Napoleon had distinguished himself at the taking of Toulon, Corsica proclaimed herself to be a monarchy . . .

It should have been explained to the millions of Sunday paper readers who knew no history that Napoleon was born in Corsica, and that it was as a citizen of France that he assisted in the recapture of Toulon from the British.

16. UNDEVELOPED THEME

The history of the century before one I find to be deeply interesting, for the reason . . . that so many incidents . . . coincide with the present day.

This generalization that so many incidents are always duplicated a hundred years later falls to the ground. When the next paragraph begins with the statement that Napoleon was British, one expects to read that Adolf Hitler was once British too; but one is disappointed.

20. IRRELEVANCY

(a) . . . Napoleon was a British subject. He was thus placed technically . . .

Every Briton's subject to the King has been 'technical' since at least 1688: the King has no power over his life or property.

(b) It happened like this. A few months after Napoleon

had distinguished himself . . . at Toulon, Corsica proclaimed herself to be . . . under the sovereignty of George III, who once addressed a most august assembly as 'My dear Lords and Turkey Cocks.'

The eccentricity of George III does not clarify the reasons for Napoleon's temporary subjection to him.

23. LOGICAL WEAKNESS

. . . Corsica proclaimed herself to be a monarchy under the sovereignty of King George III, . . .

A monarchy cannot be under a sovereignty. What is meant is 'proclaimed her independence and put herself under the sovereignty of King George III'.

G. CIRCUMLOCUTION

. . . for the reason that there are . . .

'Because there are' would surely have been simpler and more suitable to the context?

FAIR COPY

'Recently, I read a history of the 1790's and was deeply interested to find so many incidents and situations of the time—just a century before I was born—reminding me of 1940. I also came across some odd bits of unfamiliar information. Did you know that Napoleon was once a British subject? Few do. But he was, though only for a short period and without residing in this country.

It happened like this. A few months after Napoleon had distinguished himself at the recapture of Toulon from us, his native island of Corsica repudiated her allegiance to the French Republic. She proclaimed herself a kingdom under the rule of our George III. This was the George who later went mad and addressed the House of Lords [?] in august assembly as 'My dear Lords and Turkey-cocks'!

COMMENT

This writing is deliberately conversational, and Lord Castlerosse perhaps does not greatly care whether or not his readers understand just what he is trying to say. And perhaps they do not care, either; much can be forgiven a peer who consents to gossip with commoners in this genial way.

Bishop of Chichester

from *Christianity and World Order,* 1940

TEXT

Christianity[8a] sets a standard.[16a] Nothing that I have said[8b] about principles governing human relationships, or about the social implications[9a] of the Gospel, should be permitted for a moment to obscure the crucial[9b] importance of personal character.[8c] Life[14a] has been described as a perpetual offensive against the repetitive mechanism of the universe![18/A1] This is profoundly true of moral life,[14a] which is the overcoming and transforming[14b] of hostile or unfavourable conditions and temptations[10a] continually recurring.[10a/23] The Christian faith[H] demands integrity of conduct, uprightness, truth,[25] sincerity[12a] and a vigorous initiative. The Christian religion[H] reinforces man's resistance to the struggle. It does not deny it.[9c/19a] It[2/k] is neither[10b] quietism in social matters, nor is it 'socialism' or 'social reform' without[9d] the energy of faith, and the vitality of personal effort rightly[L] directed.[12b/16b] Christianity[H] is not a fugitive and cloistered[8d] religion. It does not slink out of the race. It endures dust and heat. It sallies out and seeks its adversaries.[A2] It is exercised and fully breathed.[9e/19b]

EXAMINATION

2.   WHICH?

The Christian religion reinforces man's resistance to the struggle. It does not deny it. It is neither quietism in social matters, nor is it 'socialism' . . .

Which of these concepts is 'neither quietism nor "social-ism" '? The Christian religion, man's resistance, or the struggle? In formal grammar it would be the one referred to by the preceding 'it'—which is probably, but not necessarily, 'the struggle'.

8. INAPPROPRIATE WORD OR PHRASE
(a) Christianity sets a standard.

Christianity is too large a word for the ensuing context, which concerns not the standard that Christians of all sorts set for Buddhists, Moslems, and the like, but the standard that the Gospel sets for sincere Christians.

(b) Nothing that I have said . . .

The word 'written' would have been better than 'said': it would have referred the reader plainly to the early chapters of the book, instead of making him wonder what the Bishop might have been saying in the pulpit.

(c) . . . the importance of personal character.

This figurative use of 'character' refers to the stamp put on coins as a token of their uniform goodness, though the word is sometimes facetiously applied to a thoroughly eccentric person, as *type* is in French. It should have been avoided here, where a distinction is made between man in his social setting and man as exercising free will. 'Character' refers more appropriately to social conformity than to free will exercised.

(d) . . . Christianity is not a . . . cloistered religion.

Then why has the word 'cloister' in Christian countries an almost purely religious sense?

9. AMBIGUOUS WORD OR PHRASE
(a) . . . the social implications of the Gospel, . . .

This might well mean 'the implications in the four Gospels as to social life in the Roman Empire in the first and second centuries, A.D.' To hope that it will mean 'the modifications of natural principles governing social behaviour that are implicitly ordered in the Gospels' is to put too great faith in the ordinary reader's understanding.

(b) Nothing that I have said about principles governing

**human relationships . . . should be permitted to obscure the
crucial importance of personal character.**

There are three senses of 'crucial', beside the scientific one
of 'in the form of a cross'. 'Crucial' may refer to Francis Bacon's
phrase *instantia crucis* and so mean 'pointing the logical course
where rival hypotheses are offered'. And if the rival hypotheses
are that men should think and act as individuals, and that they
should think and act as loyal members of Christian society,
then 'crucial' is properly used here in this sense. 'Crucial' may
also mean 'of the nature of a crux, or textual difficulty', and so,
loosely, 'testing one's intelligence'—also a possible sense in this
context. A third sense was given to the word by Elizabeth Bar-
rett Browning in *Aurora Leigh* in 1856. Apparently she thought
it had something to do with the word 'crucible'. 'Crucial importance of personal character' in this sense would mean 'the importance of personal character in purging away the dross of
social relationship'.

Since, however, the theme of 'crucial importance' is not
developed in the succeeding sentences, we never learn which of
these senses was intended.

**(c) The Christian religion reinforces man's resistance to
the struggle. It does not deny it.**

The second sentence may mean: 'The Christian religion
does not deny that the struggle exists.'
Or: 'The Christian religion does not deny that it reinforces
resistance.'
Or: 'The Christian religion does not deny (refuse) its help.'
Or: 'The Christian religion does not deny that man resists.'

**(d) . . . nor is it 'socialism' or 'social reform' without the
energy of faith, . . .**

This may mean: 'Christianity is not "socialism" or "social
reform", both of which lack the energy of faith.'
Or: 'Christianity is not "socialism" or "social reform" of a sort
that lacks the energy of faith.'
Or: 'Unless Christianity has the energy of faith it is not really
"socialism" or "social reform".'

(e) It is exercised and fully breathed.

Is 'breathed' formed from 'breathe' or from 'breath'? If from
'breathe' the phrase, which is an odd one, means having had

full opportunity to breathe after violent exercise; if from 'breath' it means that the lungs have a full capacity for drawing breath.

10. MISPLACED WORD

(a) . . . the overcoming and transforming of hostile or unfavourable conditions and temptations continually recurring.

The natural order of these words is 'the overcoming of continually recurring temptations and the transforming of continually recurring hostile or unfavourable conditions'. The word 'temptations' has been misplaced. It is difficult to see how one can 'transform an unfavourable temptation'. One can only reject, end, or yield to any temptation. And in what sense is a temptation 'unfavourable'? Does this mean that one cannot readily yield to it? The phrase 'continually recurring' is also misplaced. It has been put at the end of the sentence probably to avoid a clumsy repetition of '-ings'—'the overcoming and transforming of continually recurring temptations'—but reads there as though it were an afterthought, rather than an important step in the argument about the 'repetitive mechanism of the universe'.

(b) It is neither quietism . . . nor is it 'socialism' . . .

This should have read: 'Neither is it quietism, nor is it "socialism".' Or: 'It is neither quietism, nor socialism'. Or: 'It is not quietism, neither is it "socialism".' The two phrases, as they stand, are not parallel.

12. DUPLICATION

(a) The Christian faith demands integrity of conduct, uprightness, truth, sincerity . . .

'Uprightness' and 'sincerity' are included in 'integrity of conduct'.

(b) . . . nor is it 'socialism' or 'social reform' without the energy of faith and the vitality of personal effort rightly directed.

'The vitality of personal effort rightly directed' surely includes the 'energy of faith'? 'Rightly', to a Bishop, means 'by the guidance of God sought in Faith'

14. MATERIAL OMISSION

(a) **Life has been described as a perpetual offensive against the repetitive mechanism of the universe! This is profoundly true of moral life.**

Since the unnamed natural philosopher expressed himself very loosely, the Bishop might well have restated the phrase in his own words. He could then have qualified 'life' as physical life, and afterwards shown moral life as analogous to it. This would have been far better than quoting the phrase just as he heard it, without commenting on its heretical implications, and drawing a pious conclusion from it which the originator might well have disavowed.

(b) **. . . moral life, which is the overcoming and transforming of hostile or unfavourable conditions . . .**

Transforming them into what?

16. UNDEVELOPED THEME

(a) **Christianity sets a standard.**

What kind of standard? The next sentence should explain, but does not. One has to guess from 'the crucial importance of personal character' that a moral standard for personal behaviour is meant.

(b) **. . . nor is it 'socialism' or 'social reform' without the energy of faith and the vitality of personal effort rightly directed.**

'Rightly directed' should be expanded. Does it mean 'under ecclesiastical tutelage'?

18. MISPUNCTUATION

Life has been described as a perpetual offensive against the repetitive mechanism of the universe!

An exclamation-mark after a quoted opinion usually denotes surprise that such an opinion has been expressed. Very occasionally it denotes intense admiration for the opinion: e.g. 'Christ said that I should love my neighbour as myself! What a noble ideal!' The opinion quoted by the Bishop does not seem to merit either surprise or intense admiration.

19. CONFUSED SEQUENCE OF IDEAS

(a) **The Christian religion reinforces man's resistance to the struggle. It does not deny it.**

'Does not deny it' reads weakly after 'reinforces', which it should perhaps have preceded.

(b) Christianity . . . does not slink out of the race. It endures dust and heat. It sallies out and seeks its adversaries. It is exercised and fully breathed.

The last sentence belongs to the racing metaphor and should have introduced it. And it would have been better to attach this brisk metaphorical passage to the strongly alliterative preceding one—about man's resistance to the struggle—from which it is separated by a long-winded sentence in another style.

23. LOGICAL WEAKNESS
Life . . . a perpetual offensive against the repetitive mechanism of the universe! This is profoundly true of moral life, which is the overcoming and transforming of hostile or unfavourable conditions and temptations continually recurring.

'The repetitive mechanism of the universe' is identified by all sects of Christians with the 'immutable laws of God'. Personal morality, by the Bishop's argument, consists in a perpetual offensive against these laws. He surely cannot mean this?

25. MIXED CATEGORY
The Christian faith demands integrity of conduct, uprightness, truth, sincerity and a vigorous initiative.

'Truth does not fit in with the other qualities here listed: it is one of the prime words, like 'love', 'death', 'God'. What is doubtless meant is 'truthfulness'. Nor does 'a vigorous initiative' belong to the list. 'A vigorous initiative' is an action, like 'a vigorous offensive'; whereas sincerity and uprightness are qualities. The 'a' should be omitted to make initiative into a quality too.

A. MISMATING OF METAPHORS
1.   . . . a perpetual offensive against the repetitive mechanism of the universe!

One undertakes an 'offensive' only against a living enemy; one attempts to break a mechanism or to throw it out of gear.

2. Christianity is not a fugitive . . . religion. It does not slink out of the race. It endures dust and heat. It sallies out and seeks its adversaries.

Though Homer and Virgil celebrate one or two very irregular incidents in Classical foot-races, the modern athlete at least would not 'sally out' of his race, struggle and overthrow his adversaries, and then return to the track; if he did so he would be disqualified for going out of bounds and dismissed from his club for disorderly conduct. Moreover, 'religion' is a feminine abstract, like 'the Church'. Translation of this passage into Latin would bring out the singular impropriety of the metaphor. The Christian is an athlete, perhaps, but to picture Mother Church lumbering half-naked round the dusty Stadium, and carrying on a perpetual running-fight with her adversaries on the side-lines—this will never do.

H.   ELEGANT VARIATION

Christianity sets a standard . . . The Christian faith demands integrity of conduct . . . and a vigorous initiative. The Christian religion reinforces man's resistance to the struggle. . . . Christianity is not a fugitive religion . . .

'The Christian faith', 'the Christian religion', 'Christianity', are used indiscriminately in this passage. If more than a single loose concept had been intended, this would have been shown by making Christian *religion* demand integrity of conduct, and Christian *faith* reinforce man's resistance to the struggle against mechanized evil.

K.   TOO MUCH OF THE SAME WORD

The Christian religion reinforces man's resistance to the struggle. It does not deny it. It is neither . . .

These three *its*, the second two of which are not clear in their reference, would be avoided if the sense of 'It does not deny it' were given its natural place in the previous sentence.

L.   JINGLE

. . . the energy of faith, and the vitality of personal effort rightly directed.

One would not perhaps notice the succession of 'y's' if 'vitality' and 'rightly' were not so similar in sound. The sentence has a far more gracious sound with 'well' substituted for 'rightly'.

'The Gospels set a moral standard for the Christian. Nothing that I have here written about the natural principles governing social behaviour, or about the necessary modifications of these implied in the Gospels, should have made my readers forget that man is an individual as well as a social being. Physical life has been described by a natural philosopher in some such terms as "a perpetual reassertion of individual uniqueness against the mechanical repetitiveness of the universe". This is a profound saying, if not read as a disparagement of the wonderful mechanical structure of Creation, and can be applied analogically to moral life also: Christian morality consists in overcoming, time after time, the same recurrent temptations, and transforming into blessings the same recurrent trials.

The Church does not counsel quietism but demands vigour of action, as well as integrity of conduct, from the Christian; and, without belittling the severity of his struggle against sin, fortifies him to survive it. He must be no fugitive from the world, self-immured in a cloister, but (to adopt St. Paul's imagery) an athlete, well-exercised, with unlabouring breath: one who does not avoid the race or slink from it before he has finished the course, but who endures the dust and heat. He must be no passive defender of the soul's citadel, but sally boldly thence to seek out his adversary. Yet neither does the Church counsel "socialism" or any other secular means of "social reform"—unless the Christian be supported therein by faith in God's guidance of himself personally, rather than by vain partisan enthusiasm.'

COMMENT

It will be seen that whereas some of the alternative versions that we offer—for example, in the cases of G. D. H. Cole and J. N.

W. Sullivan—are far shorter than their originals, this one is far
longer. The Bishop, in fact, has too much, not too little, to say.
In trying here to urge his fellow-Christians to a vigorous moral
effort he writes with more succinctness than clarity; and grafts
modern concepts ('the offensive', 'a vigorous initiative', 'repetitive mechanism of the universe', 'socialism', 'social reform') on
the stock of Church rhetoric, with rather too hurried a hand.

POSTSCRIPT

Since writing these pages of comment, and too late to recast
them, we have accidentally come across a passage in Milton's
Areopagitica:

> 'He that can apprehend and consider vice with all her
> baits and seeming pleasures, and yet abstain and yet distin-
> guish, and yet prefer that which is truly better, he is the true
> wayfaring Christian. I cannot praise a fugitive and cloister'd
> virtue unexercised and unbreath'd, that never sallies out and
> sees her adversary, but slinks out of the race, where that
> immortal garland is to be run for, not withstanding dust and
> heat.'

Milton was pleading that the reading of immoral books helped
a Christian to distinguish evil from good.

The Bishop should have looked up the passage, made sure
that it was appropriate to his theme, and then either quoted it
whole, with acknowledgements to Milton as its author, or translated its substance into modern language. If he had done this he
would have avoided several mistakes. He would not have
changed the subject of Milton's metaphors from 'a cloister'd
virtue' to 'Christianity', which is too large a concept for them;
nor would he have run together and confused the two metaphors which Milton kept separate; nor misquoted 'sees' as
'seeks'; nor changed 'unbreath'd' to the ambiguous 'fully
breathed'. Milton's original is, admittedly, not very good prose:
his metaphors 'wayfaring Christian', 'fugitive virtue', 'sallies

out', 'slinks out of the race' are too similar, without being allied, to be safely juxtaposed. We would mark this passage of Milton's with a 'B' to signify 'too many metaphors'. Milton was normally a careful writer; but Parliament had recently been petitioned (August 24th, 1644) by the Stationers' Company to take action against him for publishing two editions of his Divorce pamphlet without Parliamentary licence. Milton, alarmed, worked himself into an angry, bitter mood and because the Divorce pamphlet meant so much to him, dared to hit back with the *Areopagitica,* a plea for the liberty of the Press—a liberty which, by the way, as Assistant Press Censor to the Council of State, he afterwards denied his political opponents. In most of the *Areopagitica* he kept his anger simmering quietly; but here, where he was excited by the dangerousness of his theme, it boiled over in a stream of ill-assorted metaphors.

T. S. Eliot

from *Elizabethan Essays,* 1934

TEXT

Massinger has been more fortunately[3a] and more fairly judged[1] than several of his greater[8a] contemporaries. Three critics have done their best by him, the notes of Coleridge exemplify Coleridge's[22a] fine and[17a] fragmentary[10] perceptions;[23a] the essay of Leslie Stephen is a piece of formidable destructive analysis[23b]; and the essay of Swinburne is Swinburne's[22b] criticism at its best.[12a] None of these, probably,[17b] has put Massinger finally and irrefutably into a place.[3b]

English criticism is[8b] inclined to argue[8c] or to persuade[8d] rather than to state[8e]; and, instead of forcing the subject[8f] to expose himself,[8g] these critics have left in their work an undissolved residuum of their own[22c] good taste,[3c] which, however impeccable,[23c] is something that requires our faith.[3d] The principles which animate[8h] this taste remain unexplained.[12b] Canon Cruickshank's book[17c] is a work of scholarship; and the advantage of good[20a] scholarship is that it presents us with evidence which is an inivitation to the critical faculty of the reader: it bestows a method[9] rather than a judgement.

It is difficult—it is perhaps the supreme difficulty of criticism—to make the[2] facts generalize[8i] themselves; but Mr. Cruickshank at least presents us[24] with facts which are capable of generalization.[8j/13] This is a service of value; and it is therefore[23d] wholly a compliment[20b] to the author to say that his appendices are as valuable as the essay itself.[3e]

EXAMINATION

1. WHO?

Massinger has been more fortunately and more fairly judged.

By whom? Playgoers of his own time? Historians of Elizabethan drama? A few discerning critics?

2. WHICH?

It is difficult—it is perhaps the supreme difficulty of criticism—to make the facts generalize themselves; . . .

Which are 'the facts'? A great many have been introduced into this passage but no particular set is here indicated. Does he perhaps mean just 'facts'?

3. WHAT?

(a) Massinger has been more fortunately and more fairly judged . . .

'Fortunately' is not parallel with 'fairly'. A writer cannot be judged 'fortunately', though he may have the good fortune to be judged by understanding critics.

(b) None of these, probably, has put Massinger finally and irrefutably into a place.

Does this perhaps mean 'his place'—an undisputed niche, however humble in the Hall of Fame?

(c) . . . these critics have left in their work an undissolved residuum of their own good taste . . .

This is perhaps intended to mean that, when each stage of the critical argument has been examined by the reader, some expression of praise or dispraise unrelated to it will be found to remain, which he will accept as true because he knows the writer to have good taste. But this is not what is said. 'An undissolved residuum left in their work' can only be found after an examination by the reader—who, however, is not mentioned. And to what sort of critical process 'undissolved' refers is not clear. A writer does not *dissolve* his own good taste in criticism: he proves it, or *resolves* it (in the sense of making it clear to others).

(d) . . . an undissolved residuum of their own good taste, which . . . is something that requires our faith.

The comma after 'taste' plainly shows that it is the residuum, not the taste, which 'requires our faith'. This means merely that 'we' are asked to believe that a residuum exists. Is this what is intended?

(e) . . . it is therefore wholly a compliment to the author to say that his appendices are as valuable as the essay itself.

This is 'an undissolved residuum' of Mr. Eliot's 'own good taste'. We are given no indication of what sort of facts, or how many, are contained in the essay or in the appendices.

8. INAPPROPRIATE WORD OR PHRASE

(a) . . . than several of his greater contemporaries.

The words 'great' and 'greater' must always be defined when applied to people; otherwise, this 'leaves a residuum of good taste undissolved'. It would have been enough here to say that these contemporaries were more deserving of critical appreciation than Massinger.

(b) English criticism is inclined to argue . . .

No: it is the critics who argue; criticism is the argument.

(c) English criticism is inclined to argue . . . rather than to state . . .

As this seems to be intended as a derogatory remark, perhaps what is meant is 'to wrangle'. Criticism is necessarily argument: that is to say, it is the orderly demonstration of the critic's opinion.

(d) English criticism is inclined to . . . persuade . . .

Even if 'persuade' is a slip for 'try to persuade', this is

surely not the required meaning? All critical writers try to 'persuade'. Mr. Eliot apparently wishes to point out that the difference between effective and ineffective critical writing lies in whether or not the critics' opinions are substantiated by quotation. Perhaps what is meant is 'coax and charm'.

(e) English criticism is inclined to argue or to persuade rather than to state . . .

An argument, whether persuasive or not, and whether in good taste or bad, is a statement, unless put in the form of a rhetorical question. Perhaps what is meant is 'rather than to substantiate opinions'.

(f) . . . and, instead of forcing the subject to expose himself.

The 'subject' is not necessarily a person: there can be criticism of, say, a whole body of religious or philosophical opinion, or of national character. If Massinger is here expressly referred to, then 'the subject' is a misleading alias for him.

(g) . . . and, instead of forcing the subject to expose himself, . . .

Criticism is not necessarily destructive: 'expose himself' should have been 'reveal himself', because exposure implies the revelation of weakness or badness.

(h) the principles which animate this taste remain unexplained.

Surely they do not 'animate' it? Natural talent, vigour, or appetite may be said to animate taste; but principles 'control' rather than 'animate'.

(i) . . . it is perhaps the supreme difficulty of criticism— to make the facts generalize themselves.

Anyone who lets the facts do all the work of sorting themselves into generalizations is not a critic, but a literary spectator. A critic makes his own generalizations out of the facts.

(j) . . . facts which are capable of generalization.

Rather: 'suitable for generalization'. This phrase, too, makes the facts responsible for sorting themselves into generalizations.

9. AMBIGUOUS WORD OR PHRASE

. . . scholarship . . . bestows a method rather than a judgement.

Does this mean a method of delivering judgement? A scholar classifies facts methodically, but the method of delivering a judgement by interpretation of these facts is for the critic to provide.

10. MISPLACED WORD OR PHRASE

. . . the notes of Coleridge exemplify Coleridge's fine and fragmentary perceptions.

Surely 'fragmentary' belongs with 'notes', not with 'perceptions'? Coleridge's mental eye did not have a cracked retina: more than any other poet of his time he saw things whole, not in fragments (as, say, Milton and Keats may be said to have seen them).

12. DUPLICATION

(a) Three critics have done their best by him . . . the essay of Swinburne is Swinburne's criticism at its best.

It would have been enough to say: 'Three critics, including Swinburne in an essay, have done their best by him.'

(b) . . . an undissolved residuum of their own good taste, which . . . requires our faith.

The principles which animate this taste remain unexplained.

If the first sentence had been more clearly expressed, the second would have been unnecessary.

13. SELF-EVIDENT STATEMENT

. . . Mr. Cruickshank at least presents us with facts which are capable of generalization.

A generalization of sorts can be made from every collection of facts, though not necessarily an informative or stimulating one.

17. FAULTY CONNEXION

(a) . . . Coleridge's fine and fragmentary perceptions.

This is like speaking of a 'fine and leaky kettle'. To be fine is good; to be fragmentary is not good. 'But' is the obvious connexion between 'fine' and 'fragmentary'.

(b) Three critics have done their best by him; . . . None of these, probably, has put Massinger finally and irrefutably into a place.

A 'But' or 'However' is needed to introduce this obscure second sentence.

(c) English criticism is inclined to argue and persuade rather than to state . . . these critics have left in their work an undissolved residuum of their own good taste. The principles which animate this taste remain unexplained. Canon Cruickshank's book is a work of scholarship . . . it bestows a method rather than a judgement.

The connexion between the first two sentences and the last is obscure, though a close connexion is implied by their inclusion in the same short paragraph. The argument appears to be: 'Some critics deliver a judgement without substantiation; Canon Cruickshank, on the other hand, provides material for forming and substantiating a judgement but does not deliver one'. This should have been made clear.

20.   IRRELEVANCY

(a) Canon Cruickshank's book is a work of scholarship; and the advantage of good scholarship is . . .

The word 'good' is irrelevant unless it carries a suggestion that Canon Cruickshank's book, or essay, does not deserve to be called good.

(b) . . . it is therefore wholly a compliment to the author to say that his appendices . . .

It is difficult to see what place the ceremonious giving or withholding of compliments has in what purports to be a critical essay. A critic 'bestows a judgement'; a courtier 'bestows a compliment'. Dr. Johnson rightly distinguished 'compliment' from 'praise' as being 'usually understood to mean less than it declares'.

22.   OVER-EMPHASIS

(a) . . . the notes of Coleridge exemplify Coleridge's . . . perceptions . . .

No need to repeat Coleridge's name. Why not 'Coleridge's notes exemplify his . . . perceptions' . . .?

**(b) . . . the essay of Swinburne is Swinburne's criticism
at its best.**

No need to repeat Swinburne's name. 'Swinburne's critical essay shows him at his best'?

**(c) . . . these critics have left in their work an undissolved
residuum of their own good taste, . . .**

Of whose else could it have been? The word 'own' should
have been omitted. It suggests that other people's taste may
have been more successfully dissolved.

23. LOGICAL WEAKNESS

**(a) Three critics have done their best by him: the notes
of Coleridge exemplify Coleridge's fine and fragmentary perceptions. . . .**

This suggests that Coleridge's critical perceptions (or perhaps the records he has left of his critical perceptions) were,
even at their best, fragmentary. This is not so: probably Mr.
Eliot is thinking only of the fineness of Coleridge's perceptions
when he was at his best, not of the fragmentariness.

**(b) Massinger has been more fortunately and more fairly
judged . . . Three critics have done their best by him . . . the
essay of Leslie Stephen is a piece of formidable destructive
analysis. . . .**

It is not clear how Leslie Stephen can be said to have
'done his best by.' Massinger in a destructive analysis of his
work; or how Massinger can be said to have been 'fortunately
judged' by him—unless the analysis was so formidable to its
readers that it made them sympathize with Massinger as un-
justly treated. If they considered the analysis fair they would
have been discouraged from reading his plays.

**(c) . . . their own good taste, which, however impec-
cable . . .**

The word 'however' denotes degree: e.g. 'however hot',
'however cold', 'however bright'. But 'impeccable' does not admit of degrees: one is either impeccable or peccable.

(d) . . . Mr. Cruickshank at least presents us with facts

which are capable of generalization. This is a service of value; and it is therefore wholly a compliment to the author to say that his appendices are as valuable as the essay itself.

It does not necessarily follow that because it is a service of value to provide facts capable of generalization, it is a compliment to say that Canon Cruickshank's appendices are as valuable as the essay itself.

24. CHANGE OF STANDPOINT

. . . the advantage of good scholarship is that it presents us . . . with . . . an invitation to the critical faculty of the reader . . . Mr. Cruickshank presents us with facts . . . capable of generalization.

First it is 'us', then 'the reader', then 'us' again. Are 'we' not readers?

FAIR COPY

'Celebrated critics, including Coleridge, Stephen and Swinburne, have written more interestingly and passed fairer judgements on Massinger's dramatic work than on that of several of his contemporaries who were more deserving of their attention. However, Coleridge's notes, though characteristically illuminating, are fragmentary; Stephen's impressive analytic essay emphasizes only Massinger's demerits; and not even Swinburne, whose essay deals equally with merits and demerits [?], has passed convincing judgement on his status as a dramatist. Like most English critics, each of these three tries to persuade readers to share his taste without either sufficiently explaining his critical principles or—a supremely difficult task—substantiating his general conclusions with relevant generalizations: his taste may be impeccable, but readers are obliged to take it largely on faith. Canon Cruickshank's valuable book, which consists of an essay and appendices, is free from faults of this sort. Indeed, it is a work of pure scholarship rather than of criticism: by a just and methodical arrangement of the necessary material he invites his readers to pass judgement on Massinger, but abstains from doing so himself.'

COMMENT

Comment on this passage is embarrasing, because T. S. Eliot is now widely regarded as the leading poet and critic of his generation. It will be noticed that no shortcomings in the Graces of Prose appear, but that, by the standards of ordinary intelligible English, his failures to choose the appropriate word and to connect his argument lucidly are more frequent here than in any passage we have examined—even from the works of his fellow-critics. This is due less, perhaps, to a wilfully individualistic vocabulary than to critical nervousness. In his poems Mr. Eliot uses words with 'impeccable taste'; but in prose seems to shrink from the responsibility of 'bestowing judgement' and often slides into a conversational looseness which belies his 'fine perceptions'.

Major-General J. F. C. Fuller

from *Pegasus*, 1925

TEXT

The fire of Prometheus is[14] as a rush-light[18a/21a] compared to[8a] the volcano of steam[F] which, like all great world forces, is a mixture of Pandora and her box[23/18b/A]; for it has given us beauty and wealth, and[17] also ugliness and starvation. It revived the world, bled white by the Napoleonic wars,[22] and, in place of conquering[21b] the world as the great Corsican[H] attempted, it recreated it.[B,K]

. . . Nations grew and doubled, trebled and quadrupled[G] their populations, and the wealth of Crœsus is[8b] to-day but the bank balance of Henry Ford. Yet out of all this prosperity,[5] created by steam-power, arose the Great War of 1914-1918, which, in its four years[12] of frenzy, was to show a surfeited[9] civilization the destructive power of steam.

EXAMINATION

5. WHEN?

   . . . the wealth of Crœsus is to-day but the bank balance

of Henry Ford. Yet out of all this prosperity . . . arose the
Great War of 1914-1918 . . .

General Fuller speaks of the size of Henry Ford's bank
balance 'to-day'—1925—and then goes on to mention the
Great War as having arisen destructively out of this prosperity.
It would have been better to have mentioned John Rockefeller,
who belonged to the Steam Age more obviously than Henry
Ford.

8.   INAPPROPRIATE WORD OR PHRASE

(a) The fire of Prometheus is as a rush-light compared to
the volcano of steam . . .

The forms 'compared to' and 'compared with' have different meanings. One may compare a girl to a flower, a summer's
day, an angel, a harpy or a vampire—but not *with* those things:
'to' is used to express any likeness that is emotionally felt, but
'with' is reserved for comparisons in which judgement is delivered only after critical examination. 'A rush-light compared to
the volcano', in fact, will be understood by the reader as meaning: 'though the rush-light gives out only a feeble light and
heat, it is as powerful in its way as the volcano'; but this meaning contradicts the theme.

(b) . . . the wealth of Crœsus is to-day but the bank
balance of Henry Ford.

The wealth of King Crœsus of Lydia is no longer in existence: it was taken from him during his life-time by King Cyrus
of Persia. 'Is' should therefore be 'would be'.

9.   AMBIGUOUS WORD OR PHRASE

. . . out of all this prosperity, created by steam-power,
arose the Great War of 1914-1918, which, in its four years of
frenzy, was to show a surfeited civilization the destructive
power of steam.

With what was civilization 'surfeited'? With the frenzy of
war, or with prosperity?

12.   DUPLICATION

. . . the Great War of 1914-1918, which, in its four years
of frenzy . . .

The reader is capable of doing this sum himself: subtracting 1914 from 1918 and getting the answer 'four'.

14. MATERIAL OMISSION
The fire of Prometheus is as a rush-light . . .

Can the reader be expected to know about the fire of Prometheus? Should he not be reminded that this was the fire, stolen from Heaven, that lit the first domestic hearth and thus prepared for steam-power by giving water the heat necessary for making it boil?

17. FAULTY CONNEXION
. . . a mixture of Pandora and her box; for it has given us beauty and wealth and also ugliness and starvation.

Should this not be '*but* also ugliness and starvation'—if only to avoid connecting 'beauty and wealth' with the contrastive pair 'ugliness and starvation' by means of another 'and'?

18. MISPUNCTUATION
(a) The fire of Prometheus is as a rush-light compared to the volcano of steam . . .

Without a comma at 'rush-light' it is the rush-light, not the fire of Prometheus, which is being compared to the volcano.

(b) The fire of Prometheus is as a rush-light compared to the volcano of steam, which . . . is a mixture of Pandora and her box; for it has given us beauty and wealth, and also ugliness and starvation.

This suggests that the comparison of the fire of Prometheus to a volcano of steam is justified by the explanation that 'it' (whichever of the two 'it' may be) has given us a mixture of blessings and curses. The mistake lies in not having put a long dash at 'steam' and a comma at 'box'.

21. FALSE CONTRAST
(a) The fire of Prometheus is as a rush-light compared to the volcano of steam . . .

This suggests that the fire of Prometheus would have seemed of one-rush-light-power when compared with a volcano in eruption, but only when so compared—that it was in reality very much brighter. But, according to the legend, Prometheus stole the merest spark from Heaven, concealed in the pith of a dry fennel stalk—a lighted rush-light would have been detected by Celestial, the porter.

(b) . . . in place of conquering the world as the great Corsican attempted, it recreated it.

The contrast here is between Napoleon attempting the conquest of the world but failing, and the steam-engine successfully re-creating the world. A truer contrast would be between a cannon and a steam-engine, or between Napoleon with his marshals and James Watt with his industrialist successors, each attempting to conquer the world in a different way.

22.   OVER-EMPHASIS

It revived the world, bled white by the Napoleonic wars . . .

Only France and Spain were bled white. Many other parts of the world were unaffected.

23.   LOGICAL WEAKNESS

The fire of Prometheus is . . . a mixture of Pandora and her box; for it has given us beauty and wealth, and also ugliness and starvation.

The legend of Pandora is that she was the first woman created, and was given a number of presents by her godfathers and godmothers, the Olympian gods. Jove's gift was a box which was to be kept shut until further orders. Pandora's companion, Epimetheus, foolishly opened it and out flew all the Spites—the disasters that afflict mankind. However, Pandora found that Hope had also been shut in the box, and this became her consolation for what she suffered from the Spites. Epimetheus was Prometheus's brother and acted against his advice.

General Fuller in his 'mixture of Pandora and her box' perhaps means 'a mixture of delightful gifts given by the other gods to Pandora, and the gift, given by Jove, which proved noxious in the main—though it had its compensatory blessing'. But, if he means this, he has not expressed himself clearly; and he has confused Pandora herself with the gifts given her. It would perhaps have been tedious to tell the whole legend at length in order to make this complicated point; but had the contrast of the Spites with Hope been clearly drawn in the steam-power connexion, only the Box would have needed a mention—the other gifts could have been omitted.

A. MISMATING OF METAPHORS
... the volcano ... a mixture of Pandora and her box ...

Could this figure be intelligibly illustrated, even in a grotesque cartoon? This is a convenient question for testing the legitimacy of metaphors, because a metaphor that does not convey a clear picture has a distracting effect on the reader's attention. The answer here is 'no!'

B. TOO MANY METAPHORS
The fire of Prometheus is as a rush-light compared to the volcano of steam which ... is a mixture of Pandora and her box. It revived the world, bled white by the Napoleonic wars, and in place of conquering the world ... recreated it.

Generally speaking, a single metaphor is enough for any short paragraph.

F. OBSCURE REFERENCE
The fire of Prometheus is as a rush-light compared to the volcano of steam, which ... has given us beauty and wealth, ... ugliness and starvation.

What is this volcano of steam? The simile is confusing, because volcanoes do blow out steam, in purposeless clouds, but do not emit much *light* while doing so—the light comes with the lava. Perhaps the invention of the steam-engine is meant. If so, the reference to Henry Ford, who made his money by exploiting the steam-engine's rival, the internal combustion engine, is most misleading.

G. CIRCUMLOCUTION
Nations grew and doubled, trebled and quadrupled their populations ...

'Doubled' and 'trebled' are included in 'quadrupled'.

H. ELEGANT VARIATION
It revived the world, bled white during the Napoleonic

wars, and, in place of conquering the world as the great Corsican had attempted . . .

It is probably because he had just used 'Napoleonic' that
General Fuller finds it necessary to use 'the great Corsican'
instead of 'the Emperor Napoleon'.

K. TOO MUCH OF THE SAME WORD

It revived the world . . . and in place of conquering the
world . . . it recreated it.

'It' is repeated three times and 'world' twice. This could
have been avoided by: 'it revived and re-created, rather than
conquered, the world'.

FAIR COPY

'The spark of fire that the demi-god Prometheus stole from
Heaven for Man's domestic hearth has never been put to such
astounding uses as since James Watt's invention of the steam-
engine. The tremendous power of Steam, first introduced into a
world impoverished by the futile conquests of Napoleon,
brought hope of beauty, wealth and re-creation, rather than
fear of future wars. The enormous enrichment of the leading
nations of Europe and America during the century which followed was shown by the increase of their populations, which in
some cases were quadrupled. Industrialists became multi-mil-
lionaires: Mr. John Rockefeller habitually kept in his bank-
account a sum that cannot have been less than the entire capital of the legendary King Crœsus of Lydia. Yet Watt, like most
famour inventors, had opened Pandora's Box: not only Hope
was contained in it, but a crowd of Spites, including Ugliness
and Starvation. For prosperity brought surfeit, and surfeit
brought the frenzy of the Great War of 1914-1918—when
Steam was used to destroy wantonly the very riches it had
created.'

COMMENT

This writing is the product of a highly imaginative and impa-
tient mind. Unless the reader thinks at a furious rate, he will

find that the word-pictures succeed one another too rapidly for his comfort: the impression of the first will not have faded before the third and fourth are imposed upon it. Since these pictures are not interrelated, the result will be a confusion, like that of a camera-film which has been several times exposed to different objects, but each time under-exposed. First comes Prometheus stealing fire—then a rush-light is compared to a volcano—then out flies a cloud of steam and pushes along as a world force—then Pandora is mixed up with her box.

The faults are those of over-confidence in the reader's intelligence and knowledge: it is dangerous to use such brevity.

Earl Halifax

from an Address after the German reoccupation
of the Rhineland, November 19th, 1936

TEXT

We[1a] have been witnessing[14a] the gradual substitution in Europe of a new order[15]—which in some degree[20a] many have long deemed[E] inevitable[14b]—for the order[N] constituted by the Versailles Treaty. For years the attempt was[5] made to find some simultaneous solution for the twin[8] problems of German equality[3a] and general security[9] and when a simultaneous solution was not found,[22] it was not unnatural that they,[1b] still to some extent under the influence of the earlier order[N] of ideas,[2] should naturally[12] feel[5] that same doubt[3b] whether German equality unilaterally[E] achieved[3a] would not[23] in fact[20b] be found[1c] compatible with security.[19/L]

EXAMINATION

1.   WHO?

     (a) We have been witnessing the gradual substitution in Europe of a new order . . . for the order constituted by the Versailles Treaty.

By making the undefined 'we' vague enough to include all Europe, Lord Halifax, speaking as a member of the Government, is hinting that Britain will raise no objection to the Nazi assertion of Germany's right to rearm. (The word 'witness' suggests passive contemplation of a scene.)

(b) . . . it was not unnatural that they, still to some extent under the influence of the earlier order of ideas . . .

'They' have not been mentioned before. Perhaps 'they' are included in 'we' who 'have been witnessing the gradual substitution in Europe of a new order'. 'They' are certainly not the 'many' who 'have long deemed inevitable' this new order. Lord Halifax disapproves of these 'they': perhaps this is why he has failed to identify them.

(c) . . . whether German equality . . . would not in fact be found compatible with security.

By whom? It might even be by the Germans, who had hesitated fearfully before the reoccupation of the Rhineland.

2. WHICH?

. . . they, still to some extent under the influence of the earlier order of ideas . . .

Which order of ideas? Strictly speaking, this cannot refer to the 'order constituted by the Versailles Treaty', which was not an order of ideas, but a political ordering of conquered nations.

3. WHAT?

(a) . . . German equality and general security . . .
. . . whether German equality unilaterally achieved . . .

The phrase 'German equality', here probably standing for 'the right of Germany to rearm as she pleases, just as other European states do', means literally 'equality of all Germans with one another', an equality which could not be 'unilaterally achieved'.

(b) . . . should naturally feel that same doubt . . .

The doubt has not been mentioned; perhaps he means 'an old doubt'.

5. WHEN?

We have been witnessing the gradual substitution in Eu-

rope of a new order . . . for the order constituted by the Versailles Treaty. For years the attempt was made to find some solution for the twin problems of German equality and general security and when a simultaneous solution was not found, it was not unnatural that they . . . should feel that same doubt . . .

There is a change of tense early in this sentence. The phrase 'we have been witnessing' assumes the old order as already practically succeeded by the new. 'For years the attempt was made', if it refers to the years previous to this change, ought to be 'had been made', and 'it was not unnatural that they should feel' ought to be 'it was not unnatural that they should have felt'; but if the attempt was still being made at the time Lord Halifax was speaking, then it ought to be 'the attempt has been made' followed by 'it is not unnatural that they should feel'.

8. INAPPROPRIATE WORD OR PHRASE
    . . . some simultaneous solution for the twin problems of German equality and general security . . .

Twin problems are connected problems closely resembling each other: for example, the problems of how to buy chocolate and how to buy sausages, in the same village, after closing hours, in wartime, during a food-shortage.

The problems hinted at by Lord Halifax were not two problems, but a single one: how to satisfy German military aspirations without danger to Great Britain and France.

9. AMBIGUOUS WORD OR PHRASE
    . . . the twin problems of German equality and general security . . .

Does this mean 'general German security' or just 'general security'?

12. DUPLICATION
    . . . it was not unnatural that they . . . should naturally feel that same doubt . . .

No, naturally not.

14. MATERIAL OMISSION
    (a) We have been witnessing the gradual substitution in Europe of a new order . . .

This should have been supplemented with an explanation of why no attempt was made to check the process, or at least with a clear confession either of indifference or of impotence.

(b) ... which ... many have long deemed inevitable ...

If Lord Halifax had wished to be plain he would have identified himself with these 'many' (or spoken against their view); and would have pointed out that the 'New Order' was a Nazi concept, connecting it with the 'unilaterally' that follows; and would have admitted that the 'new order' which 'many deemed inevitable' was not by any mans the sort that the Nazis were proclaiming.

15. UNFULFILLED PROMISE

We have been witnessing the gradual substitution in Europe of a new order—which in some degree many have long deemed inevitable—

The reader expects '*by* a still newer order' but finds that the new order is being substituted *for* another.

19. CONFUSED SEQUENCE OF IDEAS

The natural sequence of ideas in this argument is:

(1) Britain and France have watched the rise of Nazidom for some years.

(2) Their problem has been whether or not to concede to Germany the same right to arm which other states enjoy.

(3) Some of their politicians, possessed by the vengeful spirit of Versailles,

(4) have believed that this concession would be incompatible with the security of Europe.

(5) Others have believed that the Treaty is obsolescent

(6) and that a new settlement, in making which Germany will have an equal voice with other states, must supersede it.

(7) Owing to these disagreements, the two governments have not been able to find any common solution to the problem,

(8) though they hoped, until the other day, that Germany would at least not assert her sovereign rights by unilateral action.

The order hesitantly followed in the original is:

1, 6, 5, 2, 4, 7, 3, 8.

20. IRRELEVANCY

(a) . . . a new order which in some degree many have long deemed inevitable . . .

To what word does 'in some degree' refer?

Not to 'inevitable'—there are no degrees of inevitability.

Not to 'many'—there are no degrees of maniness.

Not to 'deemed'—there are no degrees of deeming.

Not to 'a new order'—there are no degrees of a new order.

The phrase has been slipped in as a general reservation.

(b) . . . should naturally feel that same doubt whether German equality unilaterally achieved would not in fact be found . . .

'In fact' suggests that there has been a contrast made with 'in theory'; this is not so, and 'would not be found' is quite sufficient.

22. OVER-EMPHASIS

. . . to find some simultaneous solution . . . and when a simultaneous solution was not found . . .

By this heavy repetition Lord Halifax is making it seem due to a mere technical failure, in synchronizing the solutions to two connected problems, that France and Britain could not decide what to do about Germany. Actually, there was only one problem, and neither in France nor Britain was there any unanimity about its solution between 1919 and 1939. The failure of the two nations to have a 'Be Kind to Germany' party in power at the same time is perhaps what Lord Halifax means; but does he think that this would have been a solution?

23. LOGICAL WEAKNESS

. . . it was not unnatural that they, still . . . under the influence of the earlier order of ideas, should naturally feel that same doubt whether German equality unilaterally achieved would not in fact be found compatible with security.

Lord Halifax has introduced this conclusion in so negative a style that he has contradicted his theme by putting in one 'not' too many, after 'would'.

E. MISMATING OF STYLES

... which in some degree many have long deemed inevitable ...

... whether German equality unilaterally achieved ...

The 'deemed' is archaic except in school translations from the Classics; but 'equality unilaterally achieved' is Genevan modernism.

L. JINGLE

> ... should naturally
> feel that same doubt whether German equality
> unilaterally
> achieved would not, in fact, be found compatible with
> security.

'Equality' and 'unilaterally' come awkwardly together and call attention to the other two words ending in 'y'.

N. SAME WORD IN DIFFERENT SENSES

... and new order ...

This is a translation of the German *'Ordnung'*, meaning 'ordering' or 'organization'.

The order constituted by the Versailles Treaty ...

This is 'order' in the similar sense of (imposed) political harmony.

The earlier order of ideas ...

This is 'order' in the very different sense of 'class' or 'sort'.

FAIR COPY

'For some years now we British and French have watched, but not ventured to check, a gradual troubling of the European peace by the National Socialists for the furtherance of their "New Order". Our common problem has been whether or not we should restore Germany to equal status with her neighbours, by allowing her to maintain whatever armed force she pleases in any part of her territory. Some politicians, both here and in France, have believed that to do so would be incompatible with the general security of Europe; and have still been possessed by the spirit of revenge which animated the victorious Allies at the time of the Versailles Conference. Others, including myself, have for some years believed that the Versailles Treaty is obsolescent and that a new European settlement, in making which Germany will have an equal voice with all other states concerned, must one day supersede it. Owing to these differences of opinion, the two Governments have found no solution to the problem, though, until only the other day, both hoped that Germany would at least not reassert her sovereign rights by taking action without the formal consent of the League of Nations.'

COMMENT

Lord Halifax in making this speech, as a Minister without portfolio, was restrained by many considerations from saying frankly what he meant. First, whatever he said would be regarded as the mature opinion of the British Cabinet, from whose unanimous decisions and collective responsibility no member could dissociate himself except by resignation. Yet he was also a sincere Christian and did not wish to misrepresent the situation, which was that in both the British and the French governments great difference of opinion existed as to whether or not Germany should be permitted to become a first-class power again—it was not a case of France unanimously approving the Versailles Treaty and of Great Britain unanimously disapproving. The common irresolution encouraged the Nazis to defy both powers.

The large French army of 1936 might have successfully opposed the reoccupation of the Rhineland, which was an overt breach of the Treaty of Versailles, and so have suppressed the Nazi power before it had fully entrenched itself. But the French High Command did not feel strongly enough about the matter to force the issue; and the British Government, believing that the Nazis merely wanted to regain for Germany the sovereign rights forfeited at Versailles, decided to take no action—though annoyed that the Nazis had acted 'unilaterally'. Lord Halifax could not mention the Nazis by name, because their anti-Semitic activities had already made them extremely unpopular to the masses of the French and British people. Indeed, he had to omit every controversial word, since the Government was al-

ready committed to a policy of appeasement. It is remarkable
that with all these handicaps he managed to convey as much as
he did to readers patient enough to unravel his tangled sentences. The Fair Copy that we have given represents what he
would no doubt have said, had he been in a less delicate position.

Sir James Jeans

from *The Stars in Their Courses,* 1931

TEXT

[Scientists can weigh stars by calculating the amount of gravitational pull that components of the same stellar system exert on
one another.]

The results are interesting. Our[20] sun proves[8a] to be of about
average weight, or perhaps somewhat over.[0] Taken as a
whole,[23] the stars shew only a small range in weight[12/ H1]; if we
compare[14a] the sun to a man of average weight, most[10] of the
weights of the stars lie[14b] between those of a boy[8b] and a heavy
man. Yet a few exceptional stars have quite exceptional
weights.[12/16] A colony of four stars,[H2] 27 Canis Majoris, is believed to have a total weight[8c] nearly 1,000 times that of the
sun,[H3] although this is not certain. An ordinary binary system,[H2] Plaskett's star, is believed, this time with fair certainty,[8d] to have a total weight of more than 140 suns.[H3] But such
great weights are very exceptional.[12] It is very rare[3] to find a
star with[14c] ten times the weight of the sun,[H4] and no star yet
found[14d] has as little as a tenth of the sun's weight.[H4] Thus on
the whole the stars shew only a very moderate range in
weight.[H1/12]

EXAMINATION

3.   WHAT?
        It is very rare to find a star with ten times the weight of
the sun, . . .

'Very rare' is hardly admissible as a scientific expression except when applied to occurrences of particular birds, flowers, diseases and other organic phenomena, of which a cenus is impracticable. Here the reader deserves to be told whether one in fifty, or one in five hundred, or one in five thousand, of the star-weights recorded at reputable observatories is ten times as much as that of the sun.

8.   INAPPROPRIATE WORD OR PHRASE

(a) **Our sun proves to be of about average weight, or perhaps somewhat over.**

If Sir James really has scientific proof of the stars' comparative weight, then there is no need for a 'perhaps'; but if he doubts the accuracy of the calculation, then the results *suggest* rather than *prove* to him that the sun is a little heavier than the average star.

(b) **. . . if we compare the sun to a man of average weight, most of the weights of the stars lie between those of a boy and a heavy man.**

A 'boy' is a term implying sexual immaturity, not weight. Some boys weigh more than an average man; some are infants and weigh only a few pounds. Here 'boy' must be qualified by some phrase suggesting a narrower range of weight than from five pounds to one hundred and fifty.

(c) **. . . 27 Canis Majoris, is believed to have a total weight . . .**

An astronomer should avoid the word 'believe' wherever the question is one of reckoning rather than faith.

(d) **. . . Plaskett's star, is believed, this time with fair certainty . . .**

An astronomer should also avoid such illogical colloquialisms. A thing is either certain, or it is uncertain. It would be better here to say that the second reckoning is less widely disputed than the first.

10.   MISPLACED WORD

. . . most of the weights of the stars . . .

It should be 'the weights of most of the stars'.

12. DUPLICATION

Taken as a whole the stars shew only a small range in weight; . . .

Yet a few exceptional stars have quite exceptional weights. . . .

But such great weights are very exceptional. . . .

Thus on the whole the stars shew only a very moderate range in weight.

Sir James should have remembered that the Bellman in 'The Hunting of the Snark' was considered eccentric because he said things merely three times over, if he wanted them to be true.

14. MATERIAL OMISSION

(a) . . . if we compare the sun to a man of average weight . . .

The intended comparison is not of the sun to a man, but of the weight of the sun to that of a man of average size.

(b) . . . most of the weights of stars lie between . . .

A logical link has been omitted: 'it will be found that, proportionately, . . .'

(c) It is very rare to find a star with ten times the weight of the sun, and no star yet found has as little as a tenth of the sun's weight.

If it was necessary for the sake of clarity to put 'as little' into the second half of the sentence, then 'as much' should have been put into the first half, before 'ten times the weight of the sun', to show that 'ten times or more' is meant, not merely 'ten times'.

(d) . . . and no star yet found has as little as a tenth of the sun's weight.

Many stars have been found but not yet examined: 'and weighed' should therefore have been inserted after 'found'.

16. UNDEVELOPED THEME

Yet a few exceptional stars have quite exceptional weights.

Unless the stars are exceptional in other ways also, which

should be briefly summarized, there is no point in classifying them 'exceptional'.

20. IRRELEVANCY

Our sun proves to be of about average weight. . . .

'Our' is used perhaps to remind the reader that besides the Solar system there are others that consist of sun and planets; and that 'our' sun is not, as has for centuries been assumed, the Lord of the Visible Universe. But this 'our' is a dangerous irrelevancy in a passage containing the phrase 'a weight of more than 140 suns'—for these 140 then seem to be suns selected from 140 systems, rather than 'our sun' multiplied by 140.

23. LOGICAL WEAKNESS

Taken as a whole, the stars shew only a small range in weight . . .

He probably means 'most stars show only . . .' But 'taken as whole', they show a very wide range: for 'the whole' includes the exceptionally heavy ones, which are two or three thousand times heavier than the exceptionally light ones.

H. ELEGANT VARIATION

(1) . . . only a small range in weight . . .
. . . a very moderate range in weight . . .
(2) . . . a colony of four stars . . .
. . . an ordinary binary system . . .
(The second phrase means a colony of two stars.)
(3) . . . a total weight nearly 1,000 times that of the sun . . .
. . . a total weight of more that 140 suns . . .
(4) . . . ten times the weight of the sun . . .
. . . as little as a tenth of the sun's weight . . .

This variation, pardonable in a copy of ornate Latin verses, seems out of place in a scientific exposition.

O. SECOND THOUGHTS

Our sun proves to be of about average weight, or perhaps somewhat over.

It confuses the reader to be told something, and then to

have this qualified with a contradiction. What is meant is: 'of perhaps a little more than average weight'.

FAIR COPY

[Scientists can weigh stars by calculating the amount of gravitational pull that components of the same stellar system exert on one another.]

'The results are interesting. They suggest that the sun is a star of little more than average weight. On the whole, stars have only a small range in weight. If the weight of a medium-sized man were to stand for that of the sun, then the weights of most other stars would, in proportion, be found to lie between those of a large man and a ten-year-old boy. Of all the stars that have been weighed, only one in every [so many] has proved to be as much as ten times heavier than the sun; none has yet proved to be as little as ten times lighter. Among the few exceptionally heavy stars are the four components of the system *27 Canis Majoris:* they have been reckoned as being, together, nearly 1,000 times heavier than the sun. The accuracy of this figure is disputed by astronomers; but at least they generally agree that the two components of a system named "Plaskett's Star" are, together, over 140 times heavier than the sun.'

COMMENT

Sir James Jeans has set himself the task of translating the theories of physicists from mathematical formulae into ordinary English. A late-Victorian education seems to have taught him to shun a bald style; and his experience at Cambridge and Princeton to have taught him that the best way to make students in the lecture-room remember things is to repeat himself constantly. But such repetition is unnecessary in writing, if the points are clearly made in the first place: a reader can turn back the pages and refresh his memory whenever he wishes. And when repetition is disguised by constant variation of language, with the object of making the passage seem less tedious, the reader becomes confused. He is not quite sure whether the second and third repetitive phrases are the exact equivalent of the first or whether there is meant to be a subtle difference between them.

It is remarkable that nearly all scientists, at the point where they turn from mathematical or chemical language to English, seem to feel relieved of any further obligation to precise terminology. The sentence 'It is very rare to find a star with ten times the weight of the sun, and no star yet found has as little as a tenth of the sun's weight' would, if the words were translated into a mathematical formula, be found lacking in three necessary elements, and to have an inexplicable variation of symbols in the elements given. A more scientific presentation of the sentence is: 'Of all the stars that have been weighed, only one in every [so many] has proved to be as much as ten times heavier than the sun; and none has yet proved to be as little as ten times lighter.' If the second part of the sentence is thus phrased in the same style as the first, they both become easier to understand and remember.

Professor J. M. Keynes
(later Lord Keynes)
from *How to Pay for the War*, Spring 1940

TEXT

[How we are to decide on the best use of our productive resources in war time, considering the rival demands of the fighting services, exporters and civilians. We should be producing as much as possible and importing as much as we can afford, using as much as we need for war purposes, exporting as much as we can spare, and leaving a sufficiency for civil consumption.]

It is extraordinarily difficult to secure the right outcome for this resultant[12a] of many separate policies.[8a]

We[1a] can start out either[14a] by fixing the standard of life[3a/8b] of the civilian[H1] and discover what is left over for the service departments and for export; or by adding up the demands of the latter[1b] and[17] discover what is left over for the civilians.[H1/14b] The actual result will be a compromise between the two methods.[23a] At present it is hard to say who, if anyone, settles such matters. In the final outcome[11/22a] there seems to be a larger element of chance than of design.[12b] It is a case of pull devil, pull baker[J]—with the devil so far on top[1c/4]. . . .

On the assumption[15] that our[1a] total output is[5a] as large as we know how to organize,[6a] a definite residual[H2/12c] will be left over which is[5b] available for civilian consumption. The amount of the residue[H2] will certainly be influenced[8c] by the reasonable requirements of the civilian[8d] population.[H1] . . .

[The civilian—the baker—will have to be humoured to some extent.[14c]]

. . . But unless we[1a] are to fall far short of our maximum war effort, we cannot allow[1a] the amount of mere money in the pockets of the public[H1] to have a significant influence, unjustified by other considerations,[6b] on the amount which is released to civilians.[H1]

This leads up to our[1a] fundamental proposition.[19] There will be a certain definite[22b] amount[H2] left over for civilian consumption.[12d] This amount may be larger or smaller than what perfect wisdom and foresight[22c] would provide . . . [But this amount will depend far less than in peace time on what people can afford to spend. Before the war they were accustomed to produce less than they were capable of producing.] In such circumstances if we[1a] have more to spend, more will be produced and there will be more[14d] to buy. Not necessarily in the same proportion.[3b] . . . [The demand for some sorts of goods may exceed the supply and producing power may thus be reduced.]

. . . Nevertheless, when men were working harder and earning more, they have[5c] been able to increase their consumption in not much less than the same proportion.

In peace time, that is to say, the size of the cake[J] depends on the amount of work done. But in war time the size of the cake is fixed. If we[1a] work harder, we[1a] can fight better. But we must not consume more.[1a/H1]

This is the elementary fact which in a democracy the man in the street[H1] must learn to understand[12e] if the nation is to act wisely—that the size of the civilian's[H1] cake is fixed.[23b]

What follows from this?

It means,[24] broadly speaking, that the public[H1] as a whole cannot increase its consumption by increasing its money earnings.

EXAMINATION

1. WHO?
   (a)   i. We can start out either by fixing the standard of life of the civilian . . .
       ii. On the assumption that our total output . . .
       iii. But unless we are to fall far short of our maximum war effort . . .
       iv. . . . we cannot allow the amount of mere money in the pockets of the public to have a significant influence . . . on the amount . . . released to civilians.
       v. This leads up to our fundamental proposition.
       vi. . . . if we have more to spend, more will be produced . . .
       vii. If we work harder, . . .
       viii. . . . we can fight better.
       ix. But we must not consume more.

Readers would welcome a definition of 'the little word we' by Professor Keynes, even a paradoxical one, as in the song:

> 'We', *the little word* 'we':—
> *She said,*
> *She didn't do it;*
> *I said,*
> *I didn't do it.*
> *Who did it?*
> We *did it*—
> We, *my honey and me.*

In i, the 'we' is apparently a group of economic statisticians anxious to assist the puzzled Government.

In ii, it is apparently the united workers of Great Britain.

In iii, it is apparently the workers, fighters and exporters.

In iv, it is an ideally prudent War Cabinet.

In v, it is Professor Keynes.

In vi, it is probably the civil population of Great Britain, including the idle mouths.

In vii, it is the united workers again.

In viii, it is the fighters.

In ix, it is probably the civil population again.

(b) . . . we can discover what is left over for the service departments and for export; or by adding up the demands of the latter . . .

'The latter' apparently does not mean the export trade, but the service departments and the export trade.

(c) It is a case of pull devil, pull baker—with the devil so far on top.

It is not made clear until several lines further down that the baker is the civilian. Then is the devil the service departments and the export trade? Or is he only the service departments?

3. WHAT?

(a) We can start out by fixing the standard of life of the civilian . . .

At a minimum or a maximum rate of consumption?

(b) In such circumstances if we have more to spend, more will be produced, and there will be more to buy. Not necessarily in the same proportion . . .

This is puzzling. Does he mean perhaps that the ratio between production of goods and purchasing power is not necessarily constant in boom periods?

4. WHERE?

It is a case of pull devil, pull baker—with the devil so far on top. . . .

Since, as subsequently appears, the devil and the baker are tugging for possession of a cake, neither will be pictured by the reader as on top of the other. Are they perhaps scrambling, for the cake, as in the Westminster School pancake scramble? If so, does 'on top' mean 'on top of the cake' or 'on top of the baker who is clutching it'?

5. WHEN?

(a) **On the assumption that our total output is as large as we know how to organize . . .**

The most ignorant economist would not have assumed this in the Spring of 1940. What is surely meant is 'will eventually be as large . . .'

(b) **A definite residue will be left over which is available . . .**

Is it available now? Or will it be available later?

(c) **Nevertheless, when men were working harder, they have been able to increase their consumption . . .**

'Have' suggests that this ability continues, despite the war.

6. HOW MUCH?

(a) **. . . is as large as we know how to organize . . .**

'As we know how to organize' is no measure of size. He means perhaps that the maximum power to produce goods will presumably be exerted.

(b) **. . . we cannot allow the amount of mere money in the pockets of the public to have a significant influence, unjustified by other considerations, on the amount which is released to civilians.**

'Mere money' is a very loose way of talking about money; 'significant influence' is a vague extension of 'influence'; 'unjustified by other considerations' is a vague qualification of the preceding bold statement. The question here implied, 'What proportion of goods to money available for their purchase should be released to the public?' is not faced.

8. INAPPROPRIATE WORD OR PHRASE

(a) **It is extraordinarily difficult to secure the right outcome for this resultant of many separate policies. . . .**

Hardly 'many separate policies'. Already in the Spring of 1940 there was national agreement on a single policy, that of winning the war, though it was found difficult to assess the needs of civilians, fighting services and exporters in the light of this policy.

(b) **We can start out . . . by fixing the standard of life . . .**

'Standard of life' is a social, rather than an economic, concept. The normal phrase is 'standard of living'.

(c) The amount of this residue will certainly be influenced by the reasonable requirements of the civilian population.

An 'amount' can hardly be 'influenced', as an animate or semi-animate thing can be; an 'amount' is 'affected'.

(d) . . . the reasonable requirements of the civilian population.

Either 'the civil population' or 'civilians'.

11. UNINTENTIONAL CONTRAST

At present it is hard to say who, if anyone, settles such matters. In the final outcome there seems to be a larger element of chance than of design.

The phrase 'at present' is unnecessary and induces 'In the final outcome' (which does not refer to time but to arithmetic) to become its partner in a contrast between 'now' and 'eventually'.

12. DUPLICATION

(a) It is extraordinarily difficult to secure the right outcome for this resultant of many policies.

An outcome *is* a resultant.

(b) At present it is hard to say who, if anyone, settles such matters. In the final outcome there seems to be a larger element of chance than of design.

The second sentence is implied in the first.

(c) . . . a definite residual will be left over . . .

A residual *is* what is left over.

(d) . . . a definite residual will be left over . . . for civilian consumption.

There will be a certain definite amount left over for civilian consumption.

The second sentence does not add anything material to the argument; it was already clear that the goods were to be consumed.

(e) This elementary fact which . . . the man in the street must learn to understand . . .

Either 'understand' or 'learn' would have sufficed.

14. MATERIAL OMISSION

(a) **We can start out either by fixing the standard of life of the civilian . . .**

The total national production of goods would first have to be assessed.

(b) **We can start out either by fixing the standard of life of the civilian and discover what is left over for the service departments and for export; or by adding up the demands of the latter and discover what is left over for the civilians.**

This is too exclusive an alternative. Another method would be to give priority to the service departments, then satisfy the civilians and finally export what goods remained.

(c) **[The civilian—the baker—will have to be humoured to some extent.]**

Why? This should be explained at length.

(d) **. . . if we have more to spend, more will be produced and there will be more to buy.**

The first 'more' means money, the other two mean goods; this should be made clear.

15. UNFULFILLED PROMISE

On the assumption that our total output is as large as we know how to organize, a definite residual will be left over.

After 'on the assumption', one expects something like 'we can count on'.

17. FAULTY CONNEXION

We can start out either by fixing the standard of life of the civilian and discover what is left over for the service departments and for export; or by adding up the demands of the latter and discover what is left over for the civilians.

In each case 'and discover' should be 'so as to discover'; the 'or' is separated from its 'either' by an idea not relevant to the alternative methods of starting out.

19. CONFUSED SEQUENCE OF IDEAS

This leads up to our fundamental proposition.

The fundamental proposition, 'a definite residual will be left over which will be available for civilian consumption', has already been stated. It is now restated: 'There will be a certain definite amount left over for civilian consumption.'

22. OVER-EMPHASIS

(a) In the final outcome there seems to be a larger element of chance than of design.

This happens, apparently, not merely in the final outcome but at every stage.

(b) There will be a certain definite amount left over . . .

'Certain definite' suggests, falsely, that he knows what this amount will be.

(c) This amount may be larger or smaller than what perfect wisdom and foresight would provide.

'Perfect wisdom and foresight' are too high-sounding conceptions to introduce into so chancy a subject as this.

23. LOGICAL WEAKNESS

(a) The actual result will be a compromise between the two methods.

Not if 'we' follow one or other of the methods he has sketched out.

(b) . . . when men were working harder and earning more, they have been able to increase their consumption in not much less than the same proportion. In peace time, that is to say, the size of the cake depends on the amount of work done. But in war time the size of the cake is fixed. If we work harder, we can fight better. But we must not consume more. This is the elementary fact . . . that the size of the civilian's cake is fixed.

In peace time this cake apparently represents something different from what it does in war time. In peace time it is the total amount of consumable goods which the public can afford to buy; in war time it is apparently the amount of consumable goods which the Government would be wise to let the public buy, because 'we must not consume more'. To call both these concepts 'cake' confuses the argument. Moreover, whichever of these concepts is meant, a war does not 'fix' the size of the

civilian's cake. The amount of cake may vary not only season-
ally but according to military gains and losses.

24.   CHANGE OF STANDPOINT
      What follows from this? It means, broadly speaking ...
      Either: 'What does this mean? It means, broadly speak-
ing ...'
      Or: 'What follows from this? Broadly speaking, that ...'

H.   ELEGANT VARIATION
     (1) ... the standard of life of the civilian.
     ... what is left over for the civilians.
     ... the reasonable requirements of the civilian popula-
tion.
     ... mere money in the pockets of the public. ...
     ... the amount which is released to civilians.
     ... men ... were able to increase their consumption ...
     But we must not consume more.
     ... the man in the street must learn to understand ...
     ... the public as a whole cannot increase its consump-
tion.
     All these are apparently the same character: the civilian-
worker-consumer.
     (2) ... a definite residual will be left over ...
     The amount of this residue ...
     There will be a certain definite amount left over ...
     These are all the same thing.

J.   MEMORY STRAIN
     It is a case of pull devil, pull baker. ...
     In peace time, that is to say, the size of the cake depends
on the amount of work done.
     The reader has to wait all this time before he discovers
that the devil and the baker are pulling at a cake.

FAIR COPY

[How we are to decide on the best use of our productive resources in war time, considering the rival demands of the fighting services, exporters and civilians. We should be producing as

much as possible and importing as much as we can afford, using as much as we need for war purposes, exporting as much as we can spare, and leaving a sufficiency for civilian consumption.]

'It is extraordinarily difficult to coördinate all these different parts of our war policy. One sensible approach to the problem, after first assessing the country's maximum productive power (which will, presumably, be exerted), would be to fix a strict ration for civilian consumption of goods and then to see what was left for distribution between the fighting services and the exporters. Another sensible approach would be to determine the needs of the fighting services and the exporters and then see what goods were left for civil consumption. But nobody in authority has yet tried either way: it has been a case of "pull devil, pull baker" at the cake of available goods. Demands coming from all sides have been met by manufacturers, or by the Ministries which regulate the production and marketing of goods, without any common formula for reckoning proportionate needs. On the whole, the fighting and exporting devil has had a stronger pull than the civilian baker, who has had to go short of cake. However, when British production is fully organized, there will be quite a large surplus of cake after the devil's immediate needs have been satisfied; the baker will then probably be allowed more than his bare rations. He must be humoured to some extent because it is he who does the baking. Then the harder he works, the better will the devil be fed and so the better will the devil fight and export on the baker's behalf; but since there will not be an unlimited amount of cake, the baker must be prevented from eating as much as he would like.

How great a quantity, in fact, of consumable goods the civil population will be allowed to buy during this war—it may be more or less than is prudent—will depend far less than in peace time on what they can afford to spend. Before the war, they were accustomed to produce less than they were capable of producing, which meant that occasional increases in production resulted in higher wages and more goods to spend them on. The ratio between production and purchasing power is not necessarily constant in such boom periods—the demand for some sorts of goods may exceed the supply, and purchasing power may thus be reduced—but in practice there is not much variation. In war time, then, under a democratic system, the civil population should be forced to understand this: that the amount of goods, imported or manufactured, that they are allowed to buy, must be limited in the national interest—that they cannot, as a body, expect increased consumption of goods in proportion to their increased earnings.'

COMMENT

The bright modern way of writing about what is generally regarded as a dry subject seems inseparable from conversational carelessness. A dry subject is one in which one cannot afford to be inaccurate, because it concerns facts and figures. Here, in explaining the principles of prudent war-time expenditure, it would have been well to choose and keep consistently to the recurrent elements in the argument: for it is better to be dull than obscure. No amount of brightness ever made a naturally dry subject less dry, and a neatly developed argument on however dry a subject may convey a certain pleasure even to readers who are not particularly interested in it. Here the happy-go-lucky economic argument is interrupted by omissions, obscurities and even illogicalities. The last six paragraphs could have been compressed into half the space they occupy, without material loss; whereas the whimsical 'it is a case of pull devil, pull baker—with the devil so far on top' needs explanatory expansion to three or four times its space.

An expert on a dry subject who writes down to inexpert readers is tempted to indulge, and even imitate, their mental confusions. When, for example, scientific hypotheses are put into simple popular language they are removed as far from their originals as Catholic peasant superstitions are from orthodox Patristic theology. It is ridiculous to fob off on the inexpert reader any non-mathematical account of the structure of an atom, brightening it with a diagram of little electric balls whizzing round a solid nucleus, much as the planets whizz round the sun. This (to use a Puritan metaphor) leads to 'mere idolatory'. If the inexpert reader has never even made the step from Euclid to algebraic geometry he cannot begin to understand how an atom works; and it is flattering his vanity to pretend that he can. He will take the little balls literally.

The popular 'interpretation' of poetry and art for the inexpert person is equally open to objection. Either he has the poetic faculty, or he has not; either he has the artistic eye, or he has not. There are no substitutes for direct understanding or vision.

Sir Cyril Norwood
(then Headmaster of Harrow School)

from *The English Tradition of Education,* 1929

TEXT

The practical man[8a] who theorizes[14a] is seldom accounted wise by his own generation, or, for that matter, by any other,[8b] and the Headmaster who theorizes may be[8c] a conspicuous example of the saying.[3] Thring is remembered as the creator of Uppingham,[14b] not as the author[H1] of *Education and School,* which no one would buy,[14c/22a] nor yet as the writer[H1] of the *Theory and Practice of Teaching,* for which he did indeed received fifty pounds.[14d] Headmasters cannot[8d] even write novels[14e] about school life,[23a] for it is generally agreed that to this poor branch of literature their contributions have been the worst.[8e] They are men of action who should forswear the pen.[22b] If then I venture to tread where many predecessors have fallen, I do so because, like all authors,[22c] I have something which I want at this present time[23b] to say,[H2] and, since it belongs neither to the realms[11] of imagination[8f] nor to the province[11] of pure theory,[23c] I hope that even an active Headmaster[14f] may not be wholly ineffective[G] in stating[H2] it.

EXAMINATION

3. WHAT?
     The practical man who theorizes is seldom accounted wise by his own generation, or, for that matter, by any other,

and the Headmaster who theorizes may be a conspicuous example of the truth of the saying.

What saying? 'Don't-care was made to care', 'Republicans are always the worst masters', 'Of every ten men eleven have the itch' are typical sayings. There may be a saying 'Men of action should forswear the pen' (though it is not a familiar one), but there certainly is no saying cast in the form: 'The practical man who theorizes is seldom accounted wise by his own generation, or, for that matter, by any other.' Is Sir Cyril trying to give proverbial force to a generalization of his own?

8. INAPPROPRIATE WORD OR PHRASE

(a) **The practical man who theorizes is seldom accounted wise by his own generation, or . . . by any other, . . .**

The statement is so patently untrue that one naturally questions whether the word 'practical' is the one meant. A later sentence '. . . men of action should forswear the pen' suggests that what is meant is: 'men engaged in responsible executive jobs are seldom . . .'

(b) **. . . by his own generation, or, for that matter, by any other . . .**

'Or by any other' would have been the right phrase to tag on to a generalization about a theorist not being honoured by his own *country*. Here 'by any later generation' is what is meant.

(c) **The practical man who theorizes is seldom accounted wise . . . the Headmaster who theorizes may be a conspicuous example of the truth of the saying.**

'May be' adds an unnecessary qualification to a remark that has already been sufficiently qualified with 'seldom'. What is meant is: . . . 'the Headmaster who theorizes is a conspicuous example of this'.

(d) **Headmasters cannot even write novels about school life . . .**

He means 'should not'. They both can and do write them.

(e) **. . . to this poor branch of literature their contributions have been the worst.**

The 'worst' suggests that they have been morally the worst, as well as exceedingly dull and ill-constructed. Their badness should be more accurately defined.

(f) . . . Since it belongs neither to the realms of imagination nor to the province of pure theory, . . .

'Imagination' perhaps refers to the novels about school life, and therefore should have been 'fiction'. He surely does not consider that his own work lacks imagination?

11. UNINTENTIONAL CONTRAST

. . . neither to the realms of imagination nor to the province of pure theory, . . .

It is unlikely that the contrast between 'realms' and 'province' is intended. Of what realm is pure theory a province?

14. MATERIAL OMISSION

(a) The practical man who theorizes is seldom accounted wise . . .

This perhaps means that, like the proverbial water-beetle who skates easily on the surface of the water 'But if he ever stopped to think just how he did it, he would sink', the executive who stops to think about the general theory of his own profession is unwise: that where tradition does not help him he should trust to instinct and deal with problems empirically. Here 'theorizes' is not enough, since nobody can be practical who does not form theories. For example, even a practical plumber must have a theory as to where a drain is clogged before he sets to work on it. Also, 'or by any other generation' suggests that 'theorizes' is restricted to literary expression; it should be made clear whether this is intended.

(b) Thring is remembered as the creator of Uppingham . . .

It should have been explained that Uppingham had been, and was, considered a very fine public school; otherwise ignorant readers might take it for the name of a character in a play or novel by a more literary Thring than the Headmaster.

(c) . . . *Education and School,* which no one would buy . . .

'No one' would buy Shakespeare's *Sonnets* in 1609 or for two centuries later; but this did not mean that Shakespeare, as a practical actor-manager, should have forsworn the pen. It should be indicated here that Thring's theoretical works were on a par with the school-novels, written by Headmasters, which are mentioned in the next sentence.

(d) . . . *Theory and Practice of Teaching,* for which he did indeed receive fifty pounds.

On the strength of Thring's scholastic reputation some publisher may have bought the book outright for fifty pounds— and may then have sold a great many copies, or very few. The argument suggests that the book did not do much better than the first, but this is not specifically stated.

(e) Headmasters cannot even write novels about school life . . .

This is an irrelevant remark, unless such novels are cloaks for the unwise theorization which is the subject of this passage.

(f) I hope that even an active Headmaster . . .

'Such as I am', should have been inserted.

22. OVER-EMPHASIS

(a) . . . *Education and School,* which no one would buy . . .

Perhaps it only sold two hundred copies, perhaps only fifty; that nobody at all bought it is unbelievable.

(b) They are men of action who should forswear the pen.

What is meant is perhaps 'the pen with which they record their general theories'. It would be very awkward for a Headmaster to go without a pen altogether.

(c) I do so because, like all authors, I have something which I want at this present time to say.

Many authors feel no such incentive—as Sir Cyril ought to know from class-room observation of boys composing Latin verses or English essays.

23. LOGICAL WEAKNESS

(a) Headmasters cannot even write novels about school life, for it is generally agreed that to this poor branch of literature their contributions have been the worst.

That Headmasters have written bad school novels may be a reason for not expecting a good school novel from a Headmaster, but not for pronouncing such a thing to be impossible.

(b) . . . like all authors, I have something which I want at this present time to say.

'All authors' do not want to say something 'at this present time'. Many are taking a rest, or waiting for an idea.

(c) They are men of action who should forswear the pen.

If then I venture to tread where many predecessors have fallen I do so because . . . something which I want to say belongs neither to the realms of imagination nor to the province of pure theory . . .

Unless he literally means that men of action, as such, should not write books of any sort—which would rule out many of the best English writers from Chaucer to the present day—and that therefore he, too, should not write books, then 'if I venture to tread where many predecessors have fallen' must refer to Headmasters who have 'fallen' when writing directly or indirectly about educational theory. Yet unless he also is writing about educational theory, they are not his predecessors; and if he is not, then this excuse for authorship breaks down.

G. CIRCUMLOCUTION

If then I venture to tread where many predecessors have fallen, I do so because, like all authors, I have something which I want at this present time to say . . . and . . . I hope that even an active Headmaster . . . may not be wholly ineffective in stating it.

This means only, 'Undeterred by the literary failures of many other active Headmasters, I am writing because I have something to say.'

H. ELEGANT VARIATION

(1) . . . as the author of *Education and School* . . .

. . . as the writer of the *Theory and Practice of Teaching* . . .

There seems to be no reason for this variation.

(2) . . . something which I want . . . to say . . .

. . . even an active Headmaster may not be wholly ineffective in stating it.

Nor any reason for this.

FAIR COPY

'Books written about the general theory of a profession by one of its executive members, however able as such he may be, are seldom admired either by his own or by a later generation.

Books written by Headmasters about the theory of education are a case in point. Thring is famous for having made Uppingham one of the best public schools in England, not for having written either *Education and School,* which sold wretchedly, or *The Theory and Practice of Teaching,* which did little better—though indeed a publisher paid him fifty pounds for the rights and probably just recovered his outlay [?]. Nor, frankly, did these books deserve a kinder reception. Perhaps Headmasters who are not content merely to follow tradition should restrict themselves to the empiric practice of education: they should avoid theorizing upon it generally, even under the cloak of novels about school-life. (Certainly the dullest and most artificial contributions to that poor branch of literature have, it will be agreed, been written by Headmasters.)

However, though myself an active Headmaster, I remain undeterred by the literary failures of so many of my predecessors, and have here ventured to write about education. I have two excuses: that the impulse to authorship has been irresistible, and that this is a work neither of general theory, nor of theory disguised as fiction, but of school history—and with a direct bearing on present-day problems in education.'

COMMENT

This is the first paragraph of a first book by an eminent Headmaster. He is not sure how to break into his subject, and tries to hide his embarrassment by alternations of pride and humility— ranging himself beside the famous Thring of Uppingham as a man of action—and at the same time hinting that Thring could not write for toffee. (Perhaps he is not so great a Headmaster as Thring, but at least he hopes to be more successful as an author.)

This embarrassment leads him to write in block-phrases, borrowed from the grand oratorical tradition, like those that Headmasters memorize for delivery on school Speech Days:—

. . . seldom accounted wise by his own generation.

. . . men of action who should forswear the pen.

If then I venture to tread where many predecessors have fallen . . .

It is generally agreed that to this poor branch of literature their contributions have been the worst.

. . . and, since it belongs neither to the realms of imagination nor to the province of pure theory, I hope that, etc.

The block-phrase system ensures the continuity, but not the logical articulation, of an argument. As a speech this passage would doubtless have carried conviction, the heaviness of the style being relieved by playful intonations; the omission of important links in the argument, and the conversational looseness, would not have been noticed.

Headmaster, like bishops, suffer from an occupational disability: it is very seldom that people venture to criticize their literary style. The headmaster style is usually a uneasy mixture of semi-ecclesiastical oratory, Government Department English, and colloquialisms intended to disarm the natural hostility of schoolboys.

J. B. Priestley

from an Article in the Sunday Press, 1941

TEXT

The Government will have to come out into the open and choose a road.

There are two roads. One is the nationalist-imperialist-big-business-and-privilege road.[22a] **Hitler is to be defeated not because**[14a] **his very existence challenges**[8a] **any attempt to bring into being the good life,**[3/12a] **but because his lust for power conflicts with other people's lust for power. He wants what 'we' have got. He must be put out of the way so that 'we' can get on with the old job,**[12b] **and, indeed, perhaps with more power to our elbow. . . .**

The other road, the mere thought of which must give Goebbels a headache, is international instead of nationalist[21]**; is truly and sharply**[22b] **democratic, and proclaims its faith**[8b] **in every value that Hitler's existence challenges.**[12a/ 22c] **It is the road of peoples**[N] **really on their way to a genuine freedom**[22d]**. . . .**

Every move we[1a] made along that road would create hope and faith in the people[N] here and elsewhere. . . .

'A grand life if we don't weaken'.[14b] It is not a grand life. It is a filthy life, with most of the things that raise us above the level of fearful cowering savages rapidly disappearing. But on that true road, where the decent ordinary folk[11] who are suffering most for our past[1b] idiocies can look for a recompense, we[1c] shall not weaken. Men can endure toil and sweat and tears[1d] and the pointing finger of death[8c] if they know that one day their children can come running out[4] into a cleaner world.

EXAMINATION

1. WHO?

(a) **Every move we made along that road would create hope and faith in the people here and elsewhere.**

Who is the 'we'? It cannot logically be 'the people here'. The only previous 'we' mentioned is the wicked capitalist 'we', hoping to get on with 'our old job': perhaps this 'we' is now reformed by its change of road.

(b) **. . . our past idiocies . . .**

Who committed 'our past idiocies'? Apparently not the decent ordinary folk, but the fearful, cowering savages who, however, now shall not weaken. It is suggested, by 'men' in the next sentence, that they include no women. Perhaps the women *will* weaken.

(c) **. . . on that true road where the decent ordinary people . . . can look for a recompense, we shall not weaken.**

Who is the 'we' here? It is apparently not the decent, ordinary folk, but the 'we' who are in a fair way to becoming fearful cowering savages.

(d) **. . . men can endure . . . tears. . . .**

Whose tears? The women's and the children's? One cannot 'endure' one's own tears; they are, indeed, a relief to suffering.

3. WHAT?

. . . his very existence challenges any attempt to bring into being the good life. . . .

The virtue of this good life is not indicated. Yet 'the' implies that it is a good life of a particular sort. Is it perhaps 'the good life' of Plato or some other philosopher?

4. WHERE?

. . . on that true road . . . men can endure toil and sweat . . . if they know that one day their children can come running out into a cleaner world.

Where will the children run? Along the road or into the road?

8. INAPPROPRIATE WORD OR PHRASE

(a) . . . Hitler . . . his very existence challenges any attempt . . .

An existence cannot 'challenge' an attempt: it can only hinder or prevent.

(b) The other road . . . proclaims its faith . . .

Roads do not proclaim faiths: this is done by the people on them.

(c) . . . men can endure . . . the pointing finger of death . . .

Death's pointing finger may be bravely disregarded; or the distress it causes may be endured; but the finger itself cannot be said to be 'endured'.

11. UNINTENTIONAL CONTRAST

It is a filthy life, with most of the things that raise us above the level of fearful cowering savages rapidly disappearing. But on that true road, where the decent ordinary folk . . .

Are the 'decent ordinary folk' on the road being intentionally contrasted with 'us', the cowering savages? Or are they the same people seen in different aspects?

12. DUPLICATION

(a) Hitler . . . his very existence challenges any attempt to bring into being 'the good life' .

The other road . . . proclaims its faith in every value that Hitler's existence challenges . . .

The phrase about Hitler's very existence challenging this or that need not have been repeated.

(b) Hitler is to be defeated . . . because . . . he wants what 'we' have got. He must be put out of the way so that 'we' can get on with the old job.

These two nearly equivalent statements should have been combined into one.

14. MATERIAL OMISSION
    (a) Hitler is to be defeated not because . . .

The reader may be slow to grasp that this is not Mr. Priestley's view, but that of the wicked politicians.

(b) 'A grand life if we don't weaken'. It is not a grand life. It is a filthy life, with most of the things that raise us above the level of fearful cowering savages rapidly disappearing.

Mr. Priestley hesitates to say outright either that Mr. Churchill is talking nonsense; or that the British people is weakening. But in the phrase 'fearful cowering savages' he hints at both these things.

21. FALSE CONTRAST
    The other road . . . is international instead of nationalist . . .

Why not 'internationalist'? Or 'national'?

22. OVER-EMPHASIS
    (a) The Government will have to come out into the open and choose a road. There are two roads . . .

Mr. Priestley asserts that the Government will be forced to declare which road it intends to follow. He knows perfectly well that the Government could never declare openly that Hitler's lust for power conflicted with that of British business-men and imperialists; that the most it could say would be that it intended to continue on traditional lines. He is concealing his view that the Government is already tacitly committed to the nationalist-imperialist-big-business-and-privilege road, which is certainly not one to which a government would change in wartime; but admits it later in the phrase 'the old job'.

(b) The other road, . . . is truly and sharply democratic . . .

It is difficult to see the force of 'sharply'. 'Truly democratic' is as democratic as anyone can be without overstrain, just as a musical note cannot be sung more than 'truly'. When a tremendous effort to attain true pitch is made by a singer who usually sings flat, the chances are that he will overshoot the mark and sing sharp.

(c) . . . **proclaims its faith in every value that Hitler's existence challenges.**

Hitler's existence also 'challenges' the pluto-democracy which is here being arraigned.

(d) . . . **peoples really on their way to a genuine freedom . . .**

Could peoples be really on their way to an illusory freedom?

N.   SAME WORD IN DIFFERENT SENSES

. . . **of peoples on their way to freedom . . .**

Every move . . . would create hope . . . in the people here and elsewhere.

Peoples in the first sentence means *nation*.

People in the second means persons.

FAIR COPY

'The Government will have to come out into the open and announce its intention either of maintaining its traditional policy or of making a sharp change of course. The traditional policy amounts to working for Hitler's defeat only because his lust for power conflicts with that of British nationalists, imperialists, big business men and members of the privileged classes in general—in other words, because he wants what "we" have already got and prevents "us" from grabbing still more. The new course would be to proclaim Britain's faith in internationalism, democracy and all the other noble ideals which cannot co-exist with Hitler—the course of a people on its way to true freedom at last, inspiring faith and hope in all others. And if it were taken, what a headache that would give Dr. Goebbels!

The Prime Minister has offered Britain a watchword: "It's a grand life if we don't weaken!" It is not a grand life yet, but a filthy one, and growing rapidly filthier as so many of the amenities disappear that can raise the civilized person above the crouching savage. But if the Government takes this nobler course, from which decent, ordinary folk may expect an eventual recompense for their sufferings, none of these will weaken. It is they who are paying the dearest price for all the idiocies of former governments; yet they will endure toil, sweat, sorrow and will not quail at the pointing finger of Death, so long as they know that, when all is over, their children will be able to run out for play into a cleaner world than this.'

COMMENT

J. B. Priestley is conscious of the extreme difficulty of forcing a fundamentally Conservative Government, during a party-truce and at a critical stage in a world-war, to change its domestic policy; and of the danger of seeming to interfere with 'the war effort'. He apparently has no plan worked out in detail for the betterment of social conditions, but only a burning sense of indignation that ordinary decent people should suffer for the idiocy of war-time governments, and that the war-time government consists largely of the same idiots as before. Caution and doubt therefore combine to keep his remarks extremely vague; but the genuine indignation will not be denied and boils up in over-emphatic phrases.

D. N. Pritt, K.C., M.P.

from *Light on Moscow*, 1939

TEXT

On balance, both before and after the advent[5a] of Hitler, Germany is entitled to more good marks for friendly conduct towards the U.S.S.R. than we[24a] are; and it is not even more than partly true[6] to say that she should also be given more bad

marks for unfriendly conduct. If one includes[15] the very early[11] days,[5b] when we were financing one semi-piratical[3] invasion after another[7] against the Soviet Republic,[2a] the score[2b] is heavily against us[14]; if one looks at the more recent[11] years,[5c/15/16] it is true that the leaders of Germany have fulminated[24b] against her[1] more vilely and more officially[22] than our leaders ever did, but is that not perhaps only[10] a difference of technique and manners?

EXAMINATION

1. WHO?

. . . against the Soviet Republic . . . It is true that the leaders of Germany have fulminated against her . . .

If 'Russia' had been used instead of 'the Soviet Republic' it would have been clear that 'her' does not mean Germany.

2. WHICH?

(a) . . . friendly conduct towards the U.S.S.R. . . .
. . . against the Soviet Republic . . .

This reminder that the Union of Soviet Socialist Republics was not formally inaugurated until 1924 is a little obscure.

(b) . . . Germany is entitled to more good marks for friendly conduct . . . and . . . not . . . more bad marks for unfriendly conduct . . . If one includes the very early days, . . . the score is heavily against us.

Which score? The good mark score, or the bad mark one? The notion of a single score, with good marks cancelling bad, has not been suggested.

3. WHAT?

. . . when we were financing one semi-piratical invasion after another . . .

What does semi-piratical mean? Great Britain had not yet diplomatically recognized the Soviet Republic as existing, and the invasions were made by forces of the exiled Tsarist Government in an attempt to restore it to power. A 'piratical' invasion means one by an army with no accredited diplomatic representatives. 'Semi-piratical' means nothing at all.

5. WHEN?

(a) On balance, both before and after the advent of Hitler, . . .

When did this advent take place? The Advent of Jesus Christ is dated from the year of His birth, but Hitler's advent, in this sense, preceded 1924, the foundation-year of the U.S.S.R. A likely date is 1923, when Hitler first achieved European fame in the Munich *putsch*. But perhaps 1933 is meant, which was when he became Chancellor.

(b) If one includes the very early days, . . .

The Russians first formed a Soviet Republic in 1917, when the representatives of the German Second Reich behaved with conspicuous unfriendliness, both at the Brest-Litovsk meeting and afterwards. The Tsarist invasions of Russia took place some time after the collapse, a year later, of the Second Reich.

(c) If one looks at the more recent years . . .

Which are these? Tsarist invasions of Soviet territory, financed by Britain, ceased in the very early 'Twenties. Did the leaders of the German Weimar Republic ever fulminate vilely against the U.S.S.R.? Or was it only the leaders of the Third Reich in 1933 and later?

6. HOW MUCH?

. . . and it is not even more than partly true . . .

How much truth does this indicate? The question which Mr. Pritt has asked himself is a simple one: 'Is it true that Germany should be given more bad marks for unfriendly conduct towards the U.S.S.R. than Britain?' The answer cannot be either 'Partly' or 'More than partly' or 'Not more than partly': it must be either 'Yes', or 'No', or 'I don't know'.

7. HOW MANY?

. . . one semi-piratical invasion after another . . .

This suggests at least half a dozen. How many were there?

10. MISPLACED WORD

. . . is that not perhaps only a difference of technique and manners?

Rather: '. . . a difference only of technique and manners'.

11. UNINTENTIONAL CONTRAST
     If one includes the very early days . . .
     . . . if one looks at the more recent years . . .

This suggests a misleading contrast between the first week
or two after the October Revolution of 1917 and later years.

14. MATERIAL OMISSION
     **If one includes the very early days, the score is heavily
against us; if one looks at the more recent years . . .**

In a discussion of comparative national scores over a period of twenty-two years, the eleven middle years should not be
left out of the account so brusquely as this.

15. UNFULFILLED PROMISE
     If one includes the very early days . . .
     . . . if one looks at the more recent years . . .

In both cases the reader expects 'one finds that . . .'

16. UNDEVELOPED THEME
     **If one includes the very early days . . . the score is heav-
ily against us; if one looks at the more recent years, it is true
that the leaders of Germany have fulminated against her more
vilely . . than our leaders, but is that not perhaps only a
difference of technique and manners?**

The total score from 1917 to 1939 is here computed to be
heavily against Britain; and even if one reckons only from—
(from when? Perhaps from 1933?)—well, what? Mr. Pritt with-
holds the required information about the comparative scores in
good marks and bad achieved by Britain and Germany in 'the
more recent years'.

22. OVER-EMPHASIS
     **. . . the leaders of Germany have fulminated against her
more vilely and more officially . . .**

When a leader of one state fulminates against another
state, he does so either in his official capacity, or unofficially. In
such cases there are no degrees to 'officially', though 'semi-
officially' is loosely used on news-reports to mean that though
unofficial they are issued by people in close contact with the
government concerned.

24. CHANGE OF STANDPOINT

(a) . . . Germany is entitled to more good marks . . . than we are; . . .

Either: 'Germany is entitled to more good marks than Britain . . .'

Or: 'the Germans are entitled to more good marks . . . than we are . . .'

(b) On balance, both before and after the advent of Hitler . . . if one looks at the more recent years, it is true that the leaders of Germany have fulminated . . .

The word 'after' implies that the period under review has since ended; but 'the more recent years' and 'have fulminated' makes it clear that it has not. This 'after' should be 'since'.

FAIR COPY

'Though the Government of the German Second Reich had imposed harsh peace-terms on the Soviets in 1917 and sponsored separatist movements in their territory, the Allied victory of 1918 changed German policy in the East. The Weimar Republic showed an increasing friendliness to the U.S.S.R., which was substantiated in several treaties and agreements. On the other hand, the British Coalition Government financed three [?] Tsarist invasions of Soviet territory between 1919 and 1921, and almost every succeeding Government, though abstaining from further warlike action, has treated the U.S.S.R. with suspicion and high-handedness. It is true that the leaders of the Third Reich have fulminated against the U.S.S.R; but if one compares the British political record as a whole with the German, awarding bad marks for unfriendliness and good ones for friendlienss, Britain makes by far the worse showing on both counts. She hardly makes the better one if the comparison is limited to the years since 1933: for, though public abuse of the U.S.S.R. has been official in Germany, and in Britain both unofficial and less vilely phrased, these are perhaps unimportant differences of technique and manners, and the Government of neither nation has earned any good marks during this period for acts of positive friendship [?].'

COMMENT

D. N. Pritt felt very strongly that the hostile policy of Britain to Soviet Russia had been indefensible, and did not hesitate to say so. But his book was published when Britain was already at war with Germany and not yet allied with the U.S.S.R. To say any good word for Hitlerite Germany at the expense of the British Government was dangerous.

This limitation has cramped his style. He has carried into prose the forensic habits of emphasizing the dramatic points of his case at the expense of the less dramatic; of purposeful vagueness in assessing degree; of sly innuendo.

I. A. Richards

from *Principles of Literary Criticism*, 1926

The arts[3a] are our storehouse of recorded values.[3b/12a] They[2] spring from and perpetuate hours in the lives of exceptional[14a] people,[12b] when their control and command[12c] of experience is[24a] at its highest, hours when the varying possibilities of existence are most clearly seen and the different activities which may arise[3c] are most exquisitely reconciled,[12d] hours when habitual narrowness of interests[23a] or confused bewilderment[12e] are replaced by an intricately wrought composure.[3d] Both in the genesis of a work of art, in the creative moment,[9] and in its aspect[8a] as a vehicle of communication, reasons can be found for giving to the arts[G1] a very important place in the theory of Value.[3e] They record the most important[K] judgements we possess as to[8b] the values of experience.[12a] They form a body of evidence which, for lack of a serviceable psychology by which to interpret it, and through the desiccating influence of abstract[12f] Ethics, has been left almost untouched by professed students of value.[3f] An odd omission,[23b] for without the assistance of the arts we[1a] could compare very few of our experiences and without such comparison we could hardly hope to agree as to which are[24b] to be preferred.[22] Very simple experiences—[14b] a cold bath in an enamelled tin,[14c] or running for a train—may to some extent[20a] be compared without elaborate vehicles[8c]; and friends exceptionally well acquainted with one another may manage some rough comparisons in ordinary conversation.[12g] But subtle or recondite experiences are for most men incommunicable and indescribable,[12h] though social conventions or terror of the loneliness of the human situation[3g] may make us[1b] pretend the contrary. In the arts we find the record in the only form in which these things[P] can be recorded[18] of the experiences which have seemed worth having to the most sensitive and discriminating persons.[12b/G2] Through the obscure[8d] perception[1c] of this fact[20b] the poet has been regarded as a seer and the artist as a priest, suffering from usurpations.[1d] The arts, if rightly approached, supply the best data available for deciding what[8e] experiences are more valuable than others. The qualifying clause is all-important, however.[H] Happily[8f] there is no lack of glaring examples to remind us of the difficulty of approaching them rightly.

EXAMINATION

1. WHO?

(a) Without the existence of the arts we could compare . . .

Who is 'we'? Unless this is explained, the argument is not complete.

(b) but subtle . . . experiences are for most men incommunicable . . . though . . . terror of the loneliness of the human situation may make us pretend the contrary.

Does 'us' refer to 'most men'? Does I. A. Richards, despite his long study of the arts, admit himself at the same disadvantage as the uneducated mass?

(c) Through the obscure perception of this fact . . .

By whom?

(d) . . . the poet has been regarded as a seer and the artist as a priest, suffering from usurpations.

Who have usurped their places?

2. WHICH?

The arts are our storehouse of recorded values. They spring from and perpetuate hours . . .

Is it the arts or the values that spring from the hours? Values do not spring from hours but from the works of art that perpetuate them; if the arts are meant, then these are not a storehouse but the fruits stored inside.

3. WHAT?

(a) The arts are our storehouse of recorded values.

'The arts'? Which are these? Traditionally the phrase means either Grammar, Logic, Rhetoric, Arithmetic, Geometry, Music, and Astronomy or else 'The Fine Arts'—Painting, Sculpture and Architecture. Elsewhere in the book, I. A. Richards writes of 'Literature and the Arts', but here the Arts apparently include Literature, because 'the poet' though distinguished from 'the artist' is mentioned as recording experience by means of 'the arts'.

(b) The arts are our storehouse of recorded values.

The modern habit of lumping poetry, music and the graphic arts together as 'the arts' has been one of the chief causes of critical confusion in writing about them separately. In literature one can define, but in painting only record, and in music only suggest, valuable experience. What are these 'recorded values'? Does he mean 'recorded experience'?

(c) . . . hours when the different activities which may arise are most exquisitely reconciled . . .

It is difficult to understand how activities which have not yet arisen and have not therefore clashed can be reconciled to one another. Perhaps 'may arise' should be 'have arisen'.

(d) . . . hours when habitual narrowness of interests or confused bewilderment are replaced by an intricately wrought composure.

Possibly what is meant is 'hours when habitual narrowness of interests is replaced by intricacy; habitual agitation by composure'. Our suggestion is perhaps too bold a reading of the original; but how 'composure' can be intricately wrought, or how it can replace 'narrowness of interests', which usually denotes composure, puzzles us.

(e) . . . giving to the arts a very important place in the theory of Value . . .

What is this particular theory of Value?

(f) . . . a very important place in the theory of Value . . .
. . . left almost untouched by students of value.

Are 'Value' and 'value' the same thing? If so, why is only the first one capitalized?

(g) . . . terror of the loneliness of the human situation.

What is this human situation? Man's position on the earth? Or some person's particular situation?

8.   INAPPROPRIATE WORD OR PHRASE

(a) Both in the genesis of a work of art . . . and in its aspect as a vehicle of communication, reasons can be found for giving to the arts a very important place.

The reasons are to be found, if at all, not in the work of art's 'aspect' as a vehicle, but in its quality as a vehicle: that is, not in what is seems, but in what it is.

(b) . . . the most important judgements . . . as to the values of experience . . .

The words 'as to' introduce a vagueness into what should be simple judgements upon the values of experience.

(c) . . . a cold bath in an enamelled tin, or running for a train—may . . . be compared without elaborate vehicles.

The word 'vehicles' should have been avoided because it recalls the train.

(d) Through the obscure perception of this fact . . .

The perception is 'dim'; the thing seen is 'obscure'.

(e) . . . for deciding what experiences are more valuable than others.

Since 'experiences' are mentioned, not 'experience', the 'what' should be 'which'.

(f) Happily, there is no lack of glaring examples to remind us of the difficulty of approaching them rightly.

'Unhappily', if one is more interested in critical successes than in failures.

9. AMBIGUOUS WORD OR PHRASE

Both in the genesis of a work of art, in the creative moment, and in its aspect as a vehicle of communication . . .

Is 'in the creative moment' an explanation of 'the genesis', or is it a separate occasion? 'Both' suggests that it is an explanation: if so, it is not a helpful one. No work of art is created in a moment.

12. DUPLICATION

(a) The arts are our storehouse of recorded values . . . They record the most important judgements we possess as to the value of experience.

If the first sentence had been more lucid the second could have been omitted.

(b) . . . they perpetuate hours in the lives of exceptional people . . . the record . . . of the experiences which have seemed worth having to the most sensitive and discriminating persons.

The first sentence seems to be contained in the second.

(c) . . . when their control and command of experience . . .

The distinction between control and command is not obvious enough to warrant the use of both words.

(d) . . . hours when the varying possibilities of existence are . . . most clearly seen, and the different activities which may arise are most exquisitely reconciled . . .

There does not seem to be any difference between the 'varying possibilities of existence' and the 'different activities which may arise', existence being proved by activity, whether mechanical or volitional.

(e) . . . confused bewilderment . . .

One cannot be bewildered unless one is confused.

(f) . . . the desiccating influence of abstract Ethics.

'Ethics' necessarily deal with abstractions; but 'ethology', 'ethnology' and 'anthropology' with concrete instances of human behaviour.

(g) . . . may to some extent be compared without elaborate vehicles.

. . . may manage some rough comparisons in ordinary conversation.

Surely these two phrases mean the same thing?

(h) But subtle . . . experiences are for most men incommunicable and indescribable.

Description is communication; 'incommunicable and' could therefore have been omitted.

14. MATERIAL OMISSION

(a) . . . they . . . perpetuate hours in the lives of exceptional people . . . hours when habitual narrowness of interests or confused bewilderment are replaced by . . . composure.

In what way are these people exceptional? Their range of interests is habitually narrow and their minds are habitually confused and bewildered.

(b) . . . a cold bath in an enamelled tin, or running for a train . . .

These experiences are not parallel unless something is inserted before 'a cold bath': either 'taking' or 'making up one's mind to take' . . .

(c) Very simple experiences—a cold bath in an enamelled tin . . .

Perhaps 'tin bath' was originally written, and 'bath' then struck out because the word has just been used in another sense. But 'a tin' means a small tin container for biscuits, cocoa, or the like. And the circumstances of the bath are not sufficiently indicated: the season at least should have been mentioned.

18. MISPUNCTUATION

In the arts we find the record in the only form in which these things can be recorded of experiences which have seemed worth having to the most sensitive and discriminating persons.

The commas omitted after 'record' and 'recorded' make it difficult for the reader to find his way about this sentence.

20. IRRELEVANCY

(a) Very simple experiences . . . may to some extent be compared without elaborate vehicles . . .

Since 'to some extent' suggests no measure of comparison it should have been omitted.

(b) Through the obscure perception of this fact, the poet has been regarded . . .

Here, as practically always in modern English, the word 'fact' can be omitted.

22. OVER-EMPHASIS

. . . without the arts we could compare very few of our experiences, and without such comparison we could hardly hope to agree as to which are to be preferred.

If 'the arts' mean the Fine Arts, or even the Fine Arts and Literature, this is an over-statement. Most people manage well enough to explain their preference for countless different sorts of experience without recourse either to Literature or the Arts. Moreover, there is more disagreement about the goodness or badness of works of art than there is about the goodness or badness of food, drink or the weather. 'Our' preference, since 'we' is left undefined, is not necessarily the popular preference. And popular preference is not synonymous with greater value. Most people prefer Murillo to El Greco; educated taste and the art-market at present favour El Greco.

23. LOGICAL WEAKNESS

(a) . . . hours in the lives of exceptional people . . . when habitual narrowness of interests . . .

If, as seems clear, these exceptional people are the same as the 'most sensitive and discriminating persons' mentioned later it seems odd that they should be restricted to a habitual 'narrowness' of interests which leaves them little opportunity for discrimination.

(b) . . . a body of evidence which, for lack of a serviceable psychology by which to interpret it, and through the desiccating influence of abstract Ethics, has been left almost untouched by professed students of value. An odd omission . . .

The omission is not odd: it has just been plausibly explained.

24. CHANGE OF STANDPOINT

(a) . . . when their control and command of experience is at its highest . . .

Either: '. . . when their control of experience is . . .' Or: 'when their control and command of experience are at their highest.'

(b) . . . without such comparison we could hardly hope to agree as to which are to be preferred . . .

Either: 'without such comparison we could hardly hope to agree as to which should be preferred . . .'

Or: 'without such comparison we can hardly hope to agree as to which are to be preferred . . .'

G. CIRCUMLOCUTION

(1) Both in the genesis of a work of art, in the creative moment, and in its aspect as a vehicle of communication, reasons can be found for giving to the arts . . .

This means no more than: 'Both the creation and the communicative power of a work of art suggest that the arts should be given . . .'

(2) In the arts we find the record in the only form in which these things can be recorded of the experiences which have seemed worth having to the most sensitive and discriminating persons.

This could have been written more clearly, in fourteen words instead of thirty-four: 'The arts provide the only possible record of the worthwhile experiences of discriminating persons'.

H. ELEGANT VARIATION

The arts, if rightly approached, supply the best data available for deciding what experiences are more valuable than others. The qualifying clause is all-important, however.

Better to have repeated the clause than to have forced the reader to look back and identify it.

K. TOO MUCH OF THE SAME WORD

. . . giving the arts a very important place in the theory of Value. They record the most important judgements we possess as to the values of experience.

The word 'important' can be justified in either of these two sentences, but to use it in both is careless: the two occasions are not parallel.

P.   AWKWARD INVERSION

(1) In the arts we find the record in the only form in which these things can be recorded of the experiences which have seemed worth having . . .

It is not immediately clear to what 'these things' refers; it proves to be 'the experiences', which have not yet been mentioned.

FAIR COPY

'Though good manners or a sense of loneliness may make ordinary people pretend that every experience, however elaborate or recondite, can readily be communicated in conversation, and even compared in value with analogous experiences, yet in fact only the simplest ones—for example, that of taking a cold bath in winter in an enamelled tin hip-bath, or running to catch the morning train to business—can be so communicated and compared even between close friends.

The working out of a theory by which to reckon, account for, and compare the intrinsic values of spiritual [?] experience, implies the study of poems and works of art—no other evidence being so helpful—in an investigation both of the circumstances in which they were produced and of the the communicative power which they exercise. Poems and works of art are accurate and lasting records of certain tranquil hours in the lives of exceptionally sensitive people, when their vision has been keener, their range of observation wider, their faculty for co-ordinating intricate facts and possibilities stronger, and their power of expression more felicitous than usual.

That philosophers and scientists have done little towards preparing the ground for such a theory is at first sight surprising, but can readily be explained: philosophers are restricted to the vocabulary of ethics, too dry for the purpose; scientists to the vocabulary of psychology, as yet not fully formulated. The popular view that the poet's divinatory function has been usurped by the scientist, and the artist's priestly function by the philosopher, shows a vague understanding that, when properly consulted, poems and works of art yield the right answer to many questions about the comparative value of experiences, which have baffled professors both of ethics and psychology. But alas, how improper have the methods of consultation usually been!'

COMMENT

If I. A. Richards really finds the communication of simple experiences so much more difficult than most people do, this is probably because he avoids defining the terms he uses: here, for example, he does not explain what 'the arts' are, what 'values' are, who it is who decides about 'values', or who is thought to have usurped the functions of the artist and the poet. Also, the argument is incomplete, repetitive and disordered, and the language an uneasy mixture of Victorian literary incantation:

—hours when the varying possibilities of existence are most clearly seen and the different activities which may arise are most exquisitely reconciled, hours when habitual narrowness of interests or confused bewilderment are replaced by an intricately wrought composure.

and bald modern laboratory exposition:

The arts, if rightly approached, supply the best data available for deciding what experiences are more valuable than others.

Our alternative version may not represent exactly what I. A. Richards had in mind; but it is the nearest that we can get to a coherent statement, with the materials supplied by him.

Bertrand Russell

from *On Education*, 1926

TEXT

[Education must be democratic.] **This matter of democracy and education is one as to which**[8a] **clarity is important. It would be disastrous to insist upon a dead level of uniformi-**

ty.[3a/12a] Some boys and girls are cleverer[14a] than others, and can derive more benefit from higher education. Some teachers[14b] have been better trained or have more native[20a] aptitude than others, but it is impossible that everybody[9] should be taught by the few best[7] teachers.[12b] Even if the highest education[3b] were desirable for all, which I doubt,[20b] it is[24] impossible that all should have it[12b] at present,[22a] and therefore a crude application of democratic principles[3c] might lead to the conclusion that none should have it. Such a view, if adopted,[8b/22b] would be fatal[8c] to scientific[20c] progress, and would make the general level of education a hundred years hence[22c] needlessly low.[12a/13] Progress should not be sacrificed to a mechanical quality[3d] at the present moment[15]; we must approach educational democracy[8d] carefully, so as to destroy[8e/10] in the process[3e] as little[8f] as possible of the valuable products that happen to have been associated with social injustice.[3f/14c]

EXAMINATION

3. WHAT?

(a) It would be disastrous to insist upon a dead level of uniformity.

Uniformity in what? In democracy, in educational method, in the educational attainment of teachers, or in the educational standard reached by their pupils?

(b) Even if the highest education were desirable for all . . .

Is this 'highest education' what would be given if the few 'best teachers' were reduced to fewer and better, and finally to the single paragon?

(c) . . . a crude application of democratic principles . . .

Define! Define!

(d) Progress should not be sacrificed to a mechanical quality at the present moment . . .

What is this 'mechanical quality'? Is it equivalent to 'a crude application of democratic principles'? Or to 'a dead level of uniformity'?

(e) We must approach educational democracy carefully, so as to destroy in the process . . .

The 'process' of an 'approach' to 'democracy' can cause no destruction; but only the action taken when one reaches it.

(f) . . . as little as possible of the valuable products that happen to have been associated with social injustice.

This is perhaps an embarrassed way of admitting that although the present social system is unjust in giving the governing class privileges denied to the working class, it has produced some very gifted educationalists (including Bertrand Russell himself) whom it would be absurd to throw on the scrap-heap. 'That happen to' suggests that the Cambridge Mathematical School, for example, an incidental product of capitalism, is politically blameless.

7.   HOW MANY?

. . . it is impossible that everybody should be taught by the few best teachers.

How many are 'the few best'? (How long is a piece of elastic?) 'The few good teachers' is a sober concept, so is 'a few of the best teachers'. But 'the few best' is a capricious one, there being always fewer, better, teachers, until a single paragon is left.

8.   INAPPROPRIATE WORD OR PHRASE

(a) This matter of democracy and education is one as to which clarity is important.

Clarity cannot be called important 'as to this matter of democracy and education'; but 'clarity about the relation of democracy to education' can be.

(b) . . . the conclusion that more should have it. Such a view, if adopted, . . .

Rather: 'Such a conclusion, if translated into action . . .'

(c) Such a view . . . would be fatal . . .

'Disastrous', perhaps; but no element of fate seems to enter into this hypothesis.

(d) . . . we must approach educational democracy care fully . . .

This should be 'democratic education'—a very different concept.

(e) . . . we must approach educational democracy carefully, so as to destroy in the process as little as possible of the valuable products . . .

The question of destroying University laboratories and professors does not arise; the question is whether they should, or should not, be allowed to fade away.

(f) . . . as little as possible of the valuable products . . .

Rather: 'as few as possible . . .'

9. AMBIGUOUS WORD OR PHRASE

Some teachers have been better trained . . . than others, but it is impossible that everybody should be taught by the few best teachers.

Does this refer to a course in pedagogy by the 'few best teachers', which the other teachers cannot all attend because they are too numerous? Or does it refer to the general 'higher education' of children? The use of 'everybody', instead of 'all children', suggests that a course in pedagogy is meant.

10. MISPLACED WORD

. . . we must approach educational democracy carefully, so as to destroy in the process as little as possible of the valuable products . . .

If the word 'destroy' had been put later in the sentence, the idea of destruction would not have time to register itself violently in a reader's mind, before being cancelled by 'as little as possible'. Thus: 'We must approach democratic education carefully, so that as few as possible of the valuable products . . . may be destroyed'.

12. DUPLICATION

(a) It would be disastrous to insist upon a dead level of uniformity . . .

Such a view, if adopted, would make the general level of education a hundred years hence needlessly low.

The first instance is not introduced by any explanatory argument, as the second is, and should have been omitted because it contains nothing that the second does not.

(b) . . . it is impossible that everybody should be taught by the few best teachers.

. . . highest education . . . it is impossible that all should have it . . .

The second statement is repetitive.

13. SELF-EVIDENT STATEMENT

. . . the highest education . . . the conclusion that none should have it . . . would make the general level of education a hundred years hence needlessly low.

Since 'the highest education' here apparently means no more than 'higher education', it is obvious that to deny this to all children would needlessly reduce the level of education.

14. MATERIAL OMISSION

(a) Some boys and girls are cleverer than others, and can derive more benefit from higher education.

'Cleverness' is not the only consideration: some clever children cannot, or do not wish to, concentrate on school subjects, and some are lacking in moral sense.

(b) Some teachers have been better trained or have more native aptitude than others . . .

It should be made clear that these are the teachers required for higher education, not those, however well qualified, who work in elementary schools.

(c) . . . we must approach educational democracy carefully, so as to destroy as little as possible of the valuable products that happen to have been associated with social injustice.

The simple solution, namely, to make higher education the privilege of intelligent children, rather than of children with moneyed or intellectual parents, should surely have been indicated?

15. UNFULFILLED PROMISE

Progress should not be sacrificed to mechanical quality at the present moment . . .

This suggests: 'but in a few years we shall be able to do so'.

20. IRRELEVANCY

(a) Some teachers have more native aptitude than others . . .

Aptitude is necessarily 'native': 'native' could have been omitted.

(b) Even if the highest education were desirable for all, which I doubt . . .

'Which I doubt' is unnecessary, the word 'even' has already indicated his doubt.

(c) Such a view, if adopted, would be fatal to scientific progress . . .

Why is 'scientific' progress mentioned? If education were, absurdly, limited to an elementary course, *all* intellectual progress would be disastrously affected.

22. OVER-EMPHASIS

(a) Even if the highest education were desirable for all, . . . it is impossible that all should have it at present.

The phrase 'at present' shows that what is suggested in the 'if' clause is something that might conceivably come about one day; this in turn shows that what is really meant is '*higher* education for all children, with degrees of height corresponding with the capacities both of teachers and children', not '*the highest* education'.

(b) Such a view, if adopted, would be fatal . . .

It should have been made clear that this argument is a *reductio ad absurdum* and that the view could not possibly be adopted.

(c) . . . would make the general level of education a hundred years hence needlessly low.

Immediately, not merely a hundred years hence. 'A hundred years hence' is a familiar conversational phrase used often to intensify a statement emotionally rather than to be taken literally.

24. CHANGE OF STANDPOINT

Even if the highest education were desirable . . . it is impossible . . .

Either: 'Even if the highest education were desirable . . . it would be impossible . . .'

Or: 'Even if the highest education is desirable, . . . it is impossible . . .'

'It is important to decide how far the crude democratic formula "equal opportunities for social advancement must be given to all" can, and should, be applied to education.

Since there are far fewer trained and gifted teachers available for higher education than could cope with all the boys and girls now completing their elementary schooling, a strict application of the formula would mean that no child at all would be allowed to pass the elementary stage; which would be absurd, as entailing a sacrifice of intellectual progress to political dogma and as further depressing the standard even of elementary education. But once it is admitted that some boys and girls can derive more benefit than others from higher education because they have greater intelligence or power of concentration, and that by no means all of these are children of the well-to-do families who form the greater part of the present "governing class", then the formula can be modified without loss of principle. Since, therefore, higher education for all children is at present impossible, even if it were desirable, and since it would be both foolish and disastrous to discard valuable products of the present social system merely on the ground that it is founded on injustices, the obvious course is to restrict equal educational opportunities for social advancement to those who are likely to make the best use of them: those children of well-to-do families who show little apitiude for higher education should be given only elementary schooling, and the resultant vacancies filled with promising children of the wage-earning, or "governed", class.'

Professor (now Earl) Russell's mind is reputedly exact and brilliant when it deals with problems of mathematics; when it deals with politics and education it tends to relax. Here he has omitted to define or even stabilize his terms. One moment the subject is 'democratic education'; then without warning it becomes 'educational democracy'. Similarly, 'higher education' becomes 'the highest education'; and what 'democracy', 'democratic principles' and 'social injustice' mean, the reader is left to guess. It should have been made clear that 'democracy' means government by a majority of the people, as opposed to 'aristocracy', which means government by the best people, or to 'oligarchy', which means government by a few people. Higher education is supposedly a way of teaching children to be 'the best' for governmental and similar functions. The paradox here is that Professor Russell upholds majority government against government by people who call themselves 'the best', but are not; but also upholds government by the best against majority government if the majority prove to be unscientific and dogmatic. He does not wish to own up to this paradox, perhaps for fear he should be mistaken for an aristocrat by principle as well as by birth. It therefore remains unresolved.

George Bernard Shaw

from a Letter to a Weekly Journal, June, 1941

TEXT

[Because the Führer had proved that he could get all he wanted without fighting, I said that there would be no war] ... **I was wrong. I am always making mistakes by imagining that other people are as clever as I am myself.**[23a] **The Führer was not the first statesman to take me in**[8a] **and is unlikely to be the last.** [There was a war, Hitler wiped the floor with us, and Mr. Churchill then told him that he was fighting with a rope round his neck. I blundered again about Russia: I could not believe the Führer would make Germany commit military suicide by attacking Russia in the middle of a very tough war.]

... **Can it be that he is as blind as all our own Tories and Clericals**[16] **who persist in believing what they have been telling themselves**[8b] **for twenty years: that Stalin is a vulgar brig-**

and and assassin whose rabble of tatterdemalions[5a] must scatter before the Nazi legions[5b] like autumn[20a] leaves before October winds? If so, he is lost; for[17] if he is as far behind the times and as obsolete politically as our Old School Ties,[22a] we[1] shall not be able to put the rope round his neck[23b] when Churchill, Roosevelt and Stalin have him finally by the collar. We shall have to send him to Broadmoor.[8c,22b] But he is not as mad as that. The only sane[20h] explanation possible[22c] is that when Russia refused to join the Axis he concluded that[14] Stalin was waiting to attack him in the rear when[8d] he was fully engaged on the west[21] with Britain and America, and that his only chance was to smash the Red army first.[24] The gambler's last throw: double or quits.[23c]

EXAMINATION

1. WHO?

. . . we shall not be able to put the rope around his neck when Churchill, Roosevelt and Stalin have him finally by the collar.

Who are we, as opposed to 'Churchill, Roosevelt and Stalin' who presumably represent the governments and fighting services of Great Britain and the Dominions, the U.S.A., and the U.S.S.R.?

5. WHEN?

(a) . . . our own Tories and Clericals who persist in believing what they have been telling themselves for twenty years: that Stalin is a vulgar brigand . . . whose rabble of tatterdemalions must scatter before the Nazi legions . . .

For several of these twenty years, Stalin was neither a combatant Red Army officer nor executive head of the U.S.S.R.

(b) . . . whose rabble of tatterdemalions must scatter before the Nazi legions.

In 1921 the Nazi legions were not in existence. Bernard Shaw is perhaps thinking of the Tsarist counter-revolutionary armies financed by Britain.

8.   INAPPROPRIATE WORD OR PHRASE

(a) **The Führer was not the first statesman to take me in and is unlikely to be the last.**

This suggests that the Führer deliberately hoodwinked Bernard Shaw; but it is unlikely that he considered him a person of sufficient political importance to hoodwink.

(b) **. . . who persist in believing what they have been telling themselves . . .**

Rather: 'in telling one another'. The word 'themselves' suggests that they all independently fell under the same obsession.

(c) **We shall have to send him to Broadmoor.**

Rather 'a criminal asylum'. If Churchill, Roosevelt and Stalin were to be all equally responsible for his arrest, would he necessarily be committed to an English asylum?

(d) **. . . he concluded that Stalin was waiting to attack him in the rear when he was fully engaged on the west with Britain and America . . .**

The 'when' should surely be 'if'. Stalin could not have been sure that the U.S.A. would enter the war, or that Britain and the U.S.A. together would ever be able to bring sufficient forces into action in the west to engage the Führer fully.

14.   MATERIAL OMISSION

. . . he concluded that Stalin was waiting to attack him in the rear when he was fully engaged on the west with Britain and America, and that his only chance was to smash the Red army first.

If Bernard Shaw believed that the Führer expected to be 'fully engaged on the west with Britain and America', he should have said so; there the word 'first' suggests that the Führer believed that the U.S.A. would enter the war, whether or not he attacked the U.S.S.R., and in June, 1941, this was doubtful.

16.   UNDEVELOPED THEME

Can it be that he is as blind as all our own Tories and Clericals . . .

A comparison between the British and German Tory-

Clerical blocs is suggested by 'our own'; but whether the German Tories and Clericals influenced Nazi political thought is not discussed.

17.   FAULTY CONNEXION

Can it be that he is as blind as all our own Tories and Clericals . . .? If so, he is lost; for . . . we shall not be able to put the rope round his neck . . . We shall have to send him to Broadmoor.

It is not clear why the Führer is described as 'lost' because his life will be eventually spared when he pleads 'guilty but insane'.

20.   IRRELEVANCY

(a) . . . must scatter like autumn leaves before October winds?

Since October is an autumn month, 'autumn' could have been omitted.

(b) But he is not as mad as that. The only sane explanation possible is that when Russia refused to join the Axis he concluded . . .

The word 'sane' has been introduced perhaps as a contrast to 'he is not as mad as that'. But whether the Führer is or is not mad is one thing, and whether political experts who debate the point are mad is another thing, and the two should not have been confused.

21.   FALSE CONTRAST

. . . to attack him in the rear when he was fully engaged on the west . . .

This suggests that all the German armies, including the Eastern frontier guards, would automatically face west if engaged on the Atlantic sea-board. The proper contrast is 'attack him from the east when he was fully engaged on the west'.

22.   OVER-EMPHASIS

(a) . . . if he is as . . . obsolete politically as our Old School Ties . . .

It was absurd to suggest in June 1941 that the 'Old School Ties' (if this means members of the British governing class with a public-school education and a clannish spirit) were politically obsolete. If by 'Old School Ties' is meant merely: 'our own Tories and Clericals who persist etc.' this should have been made clear.

(b) . . . if he is as far behind the times and as obsolete politically as our Old School Ties we shall not be able to put the rope round his neck . . . We shall have to send him to Broadmoor.

This suggests that 'our Old School Ties' deserve hanging but are, instead, usually sent to Broadmoor. Perhaps Mr. Shaw is referring to the popular outcry in the early 'Twenties when Ronald True, who wore an old-school-tie, was spared the rope and sent to Broadmoor; but True's crime was murder, not being politically obsolete.

(c) The only sane explanation possible is that . . .

There are many other sane, though not necessarily correct, explanations, such as that the Führer needed Russian oil, grain, factories, labour; that he counted on the Old School Ties and the American Isolationists to welcome the attack; that he wished to give his army something to do, since an immediate invasion of Britain was not practicable; that he hoped, by a further demonstration of military power, to discourage the U.S.A. from entering the war and from sending further help to Britain.

23. LOGICAL WEAKNESS

(a) I am always making mistakes by imagining that other people are as clever as I am myself.

He always imagines that other people are as clever as he is; this is a mistake; therefore, they are not so clever as he is; therefore, it is perhaps a sign of cleverness to be always mistaken; therefore, since they are not so clever as he is, they are perhaps less often mistaken than he; therefore, the German invasion of Russia is perhaps after all not a mistake; therefore, the Führer is perhaps clever after all; therefore, Bernard Shaw is not mistaken; therefore . . . etc.

(b) [Mr. Churchill then told him that he was fighting with a rope round his neck] . . . we shall not be able to put the rope round his neck.

Since it is 'the rope' and not 'a rope', the reference is

clearly to the figurative rope which Mr. Chruchill put there. How can it be put there again, if already in position?

(c) . . . **his only chance was to smash the Red army first. The gambler's last throw: double or quits.**

When the desperate gambler calls for 'double or quits', it means that he has had several serious losses but hopes to recoup them and return to the *status quo ante ludum* by staking all his remaining cash on a last throw. This metaphor does not correspond with the known facts. The Führer, so far, had been almost uniformly successful in his gambles. If 'winner take or lose all' is the phrase meant, it should have been made clear that a German victory over Russia would either discourage or make hopeless the feared Anglo-American invasion of Western Europe.

24. CHANGE OF STANDPOINT
. . . when Churchill, Roosevelt and Stalin have him . . . by the collar. . . . when Russia refused to join the Axis he concluded that Stalin was waiting to attack him in the rear when he was fully engaged on the west with Britain and America, and that his only chance was to smash the Red army first.

Since it is clear that Churchill, Roosevelt and Stalin could not literally take Hitler by the collar, these men must be understood as representing their nations. To switch from 'Stalin' to 'Russia', then back to 'Stalin' again, and from Stalin to the Red Army, and from 'Churchill and Roosevelt' to 'Britain and America' is confusing to the reader.

FAIR COPY

['Because the Führer had proved that he could get all he wanted without fighting, I said that there would be no war.] I was wrong, as I frequently am when I over-estimate people's intelligence: he was not the first statesman I had gone wrong about and is unlikely to be the last. [There was a war, Hitler wiped the floor with us, and Mr. Churchill told him that he was fighting with a rope round his neck. I blundered again about Russia: I could not believe the Führer would make Germany commit military suicide by attacking Russia in the middle of a very tough war.] Can it be that he is as far behind the times as those British Old School Ties and Clericals who for more than twenty years have blindly persisted in lying to one another about the military and political strength of Russia? Does he perhaps believe that Stalin is a vulgar brigand and assassin whose rabble of tatterdemalions must scatter before the Nazi legions like leaves before October winds? If so, he is lost. To invade Russia in reliance on such a misconception must inevitably lead to defeat; and when he is eventually dragged before an Anglo-Russo-American court of justice the verdict can only be "guilty but insane"; so that the other end of the rope will not, after all, be hitched to a beam. But I do not think him mad.

The only reasonable explanation of his attack on Russia, that I can suggest, is that he does not trust Stalin, fears an Anglo-American invasion of Western Europe, and has decided to forestall this by smashing the Russian army which, by a diversion in the East when he was fully engaged with the invaders, could alone give these a reasonable hope of success. Hitler's is a bold gamble: "winner take or lose all".'

COMMENT

Age, self-confidence, excitement at the Russian news, and, perhaps a slight annoyance at having made two wrong guesses, here combine to make Bernard Shaw write with unusual carelessness. Much of the passage is humorously intended, and was perhaps written with smothered guffaws and ogre-like grimaces; but a writer should be particularly careful when he is being humorous or ironical, because vocal inflections are not communicable in ordinary printed prose.

H. G. Wells

from *The Common Sense of War and Peace,* February 1940

TEXT

For the greater part of my life I have given most of my working time to[12] the problem of the human future,[5a/20a] studying the possibility of a world-wide re-organization of human society,[H1] that might avert[3a] the menance[14a] of defeat[3b] and extinction[20b] that hangs over our species.[E/H1] That has been my leading[20c] pre-occupation since I[5b] published 'The Time Machine' in 1893.[12] I have never thought, much less[6] have I asserted,[H2] that progress[3c] was[24a] inevitable, though numerous people chose[5c] to fancy that about me.[8a] I have always maintained[H2] that by a strenuous effort mankind[H1] *might* defeat the impartial destructiveness[14b] of nature,[23] but I have always insisted[20d/H2] that only by incessant hard thinking and a better co-ordination of man's[H1] immense but dispersed[8b] powers of self-sacrifice and heroism[E] was such[24b] a victory possible.[20d]

EXAMINATION

3. WHAT?

(a) . . . that might avert the menace of defeat and extinction that hangs over our species.

Does this mean that individual man might become physically immortal?

(b) . . . that might avert the menace of defeat and extinction . . .

A 'menace of defeat' by what? Flood? Fire? Disease? Exhaustion of food and fuel supplies? Moral degeneration?

(c) I have never thought, . . . that progress was inevitable . . .

Does this mean progress in his own studies? Or progress in the re-organization of human society? Or Progress, in the late-Victorian sense of the continuous betterment of mankind by civilization?

5. WHEN?

(a) . . . the problem of the human future . . .

H. G. Wells gives no clue as to whether he is speaking in terms of a few months, a few generations, or millions of years.

(b) That has been my leading pre-occupation since I published 'The Time Machine' in 1893.

Did the publication of *The Time Machine* have anything to do with his studies? He is probably referring to the writing, not to the publication. Was that all done in 1893? We should guess

1892 as the date of his first preoccupation if he means that the writing marked the end of some earlier preoccupation.

(c) **I have never thought ... that progress was inevitable, though numerous people chose to fancy that about me.**

On what particular occasion did they make this choice?

6. HOW MUCH?

I have never thought, much less have I asserted ...

How much is less than never? He means: 'I have never asserted, nor even thought'.

8. INAPPROPRIATE WORD OR PHRASE

(a) **I have never thought ... that progress was inevitable, though numerous people chose to fancy that about me.**

Why not: 'though numerous people chose to fancy that I did'.

(b) **. . . a better co-ordination of man's immense but dispersed . . .**

The sense of 'dispersed' is already contained in 'world wide'. He perhaps means 'dissipated'.

12. DUPLICATION

For the greater part of my life I have given most of my working time to the problem of the human future ... That has been my leading pre-occupation since I published 'The Time Machine' in 1893.

Unless H. G. Wells was a centenarian when he wrote this, and had started his literary career in early childhood, it would have been enough for him to write: 'I have given most of my working time to the problem of the human future since I published "The Time Machine" in 1893.'

14. MATERIAL OMISSION

(a) **. . . the possibility . . . of a . . . re-organization . . . that might avert the menace . . .**

Two subjects of study are concealed in this doubled contingency: what the nature of the menace is, and what social reforms will best avoid it. Both of these subjects should have been clearly stated.

(b) **. . . the impartial destructiveness of nature . . .**

This, as H. G. Wells knew, is offset by Nature's equally impartial constructiveness, e.g. the creation of fertile islands by coöperation between the coral insect, sea-birds, tides and currents.

20. IRRELEVANCY

(a) . . . I have given most of my working time to the problem of the human future, studying the possibility of a world-wide reorganization . . . that might avert the menace . . . that hangs over our species.

Since 'the problem of the human future' is set out at length in the remainder of the sentence, there seems no reason for this anticipatory mention of it.

(b) . . . the menace of defeat and extinction that hangs over our species.

The concept 'extinction' contains 'defeat', which could have been omitted.

(c) . . . my leading pre-occupation since I published 'The Time Machine'.

Any 'preoccupation' is a leading one: the 'pre' in the word denotes priority.

(d) I have always maintained that by a strenuous effort mankind *might* defeat the impartial destructiveness of nature, but I have always insisted that only by incessant hard thinking . . . was such a victory possible.

The phrases 'I have always insisted that' and 'was such a victory possible' could have been omitted without loss to the sense.

23. LOGICAL WEAKNESS

. . . our species.
. . . mankind might defeat the impartial destructiveness of nature . . .

H. G. Wells regards man as a species: and a species is a department of Nature. He wants man to survive as long as possible. Therefore he wishes Nature well. Yet he urges Natural Man not to co-operate with nature, but to defeat her; and promises him survival as a reward. Nature's impartial destructiveness, also characteristic of Natural Man, is the poor excuse offered for his waging war against her.

24. CHANGE OF STANDPOINT
    (a) I have never thought that progress was inevitable . . .
    Either: 'I never thought that progress was inevitable . . .'
    Or: 'I have never thought that progress is inevitable . . .'
    (b) . . . I have always insisted that only by . . . hard thinking . . . was such a victory possible.
    Either: 'I have always insisted that only by . . . hard thinking is such a victory possible.'
    Or: 'I always insisted that only by . . . hard thinking was such a victory possible.'

E. MISMATING OF STYLES
    . . . the menance of defeat . . . that hangs over our species.
    . . . man's immense . . . powers of . . . heroism . . .
    The word 'heroism' is used only in idealistic contexts; 'our species' in materialistic ones.

H. ELEGANT VARIATION
    (1) . . . human society . . .
    . . . our species . . .
    . . . mankind . . .
    . . . man's immense powers . . .
    The same word, probably 'mankind', would have served in all these four contexts.
    (2) I have never thought, much less have I asserted, . . .
    I have always maintained . . .
    I have always insisted . . .
    There seems no reason for the variation between 'asserted', 'maintained', 'insisted', which has a contrastive effect.

FAIR COPY

'Ever since 1892 [?], when I began to write "The Time Machine", the two chief subjects of my literary studies have been the process of moral and physical degeneration [?] that now threatens to make mankind extinct in a few hundred years [?], and the various theories of world-wide social reorganization that have been designed to arrest this process. Many people fancy me to have asserted, at some time or other, that nothing can prevent the beneficent progress of civilization from continuing indefinitely. They are wrong: on the contrary, I have often asserted that mankind's survival for thousands, rather than hundreds, or years [?] depends on whether it will make a strenuous effort to coördinate its immense but dissipated powers of thought, and on whether each individual will always be prepared to sacrifice himself intrepidly for the common good.'

COMMENT

This passage, which opens the book from which it is taken, seems to have been hurriedly dictated, and not afterwards revised. The resonance of the sentences suggests that H. G. Wells is proud of the immense effect that his novels and other works have had on contemporary imaginative thought. But the passage is not, perhaps, intended to be more than a clearing of the throat, a signal for attentive silence. He does not trouble to define the meanings of his words, confident that most of his readers will have read at least one or two of his important works and be able to make the definitions for themselves. Possibly the phrase 'though numerous people chose to fancy that about me' conceals a slight pique—pique almost always has a destructive effect on the orderly progress of prose.

Most readers will sum up vaguely: 'Oh, yes, H. G. Wells is reminding us that ever since 1893 he has been warning us of the danger that mankind will one day become extinct, by some means or other, if we don't do something about it.' And perhaps this is how they are intended to sum up.

Professor A. N. Whitehead

from *Science and the Modern World,* 1926

TEXT

If we attend[24a] to what actually has happened in the past,[14/15a] and disregard romantic visions[8a/9a] of democracies, aristocra-

cies, kings, generals, armies, and merchants,[25a] material power[9b] has generally been wielded with blindness, obstinacy, and selfishness, often with brutal malignancy. And yet mankind has progressed.[5a/16a] Even if you take[24a] a tiny oasis of peculiar excellence,[2a/15b] the type[12] modern man who would have most chance of happiness in ancient Greece at its best[3] period is probably (as now[4]) an average professional heavyweight boxer,[23a] and not an average Greek scholar from Oxford or Germany.[25b] Indeed,[17] the main[23b] use of the Oxford scholar[16b] would have been[5b] his capability[8b] of writing an ode in glorification of the boxer.[16c/23b] Nothing does more harm[22] in unnerving men for[24b] their duties[16d] in the present than the attention devoted to the points[2b] of excellence in the past as compared[8c] with[G] the average failure[9c] of the present day.[H]

EXAMINATION

2. WHICH?

(a) Even if you take a tiny oasis of peculiar excellence, the type of man who would have most chance of happiness in ancient Greece at its best period ... is ... an average professional heavyweight boxer, and not an average Greek scholar from Oxford or Germany.

It is not immediately obvious whether the tiny oasis of peculiar excellence is the Greek faculty of Oxford (or of Heidelberg) University, the modern heavyweight boxing ring, or 'ancient Greece at its best period'. Ancient Greece at its best period seems quite a large oasis: ancient Greece, with its colonies, stretched from Spain to the Caucasus, and from Marseilles to Alexandria.

(b) ... devoted to the points of excellence in the past ...

These points have not yet been specified, so 'points of excellence' is enough.

3. WHAT?

... ancient Greece at its best period ...

There are divergent views as to which this 'best period' was. It may well have been the Homeric age; or the Sixth Century B.C.; or even the age of Alexander and Aristotle. However, the view that Pericles's Athens was Greece at its best is held by most University professors who are Professor Whitehead's contemporaries.

4. WHERE?

. . . the modern man who would have most chance of happiness in ancient Greece at its best period is probably (as now) an average professional heavyweight boxer . . .

Does this really mean, as it seems, that only in modern Greece is an average professional heavyweight boxer the happiest man—happier even than a visiting scholar from Oxford or Germany? Or does 'as now' cover all Europe and America too?

5. WHEN?

(a) And yet mankind has progressed.

Since when?

(b) The type of modern man who would have most chance of happiness in ancient Greece at its best period . .

Indeed, the main use of the Oxford scholar would have been . . .

The change from 'would have' to 'would have been' throws the date back behind 'the best period of ancient Greece' to an archaic second-best one.

8. INAPPROPRIATE WORD OR PHRASE

(a) . . . and disregard romantic visions . . .

Surely 'versions' is meant? 'Visions' are of the future, as ghostly apparitions are of the past.

(b) . . . the main use of the Oxford scholar would have been his capability of writing an ode . . .

Capabilities are put to uses, but are not themselves uses.

(c) . . . the points of excellence in the past as compared with the average failure . . .

This is surely a case of contrast rather than comparison? One compares like with like; one contrasts dissimilars.

9. AMBIGUOUS WORD OR PHRASE

(a) . . . disregard romantic visions of democracies, aristocracies . . .

Does 'of' here mean that the democracies, aristocracies and so forth had the visions; or that the visions were had of them?

(b) . . . material power has generally been wielded . . .

Does 'material power' in this context mean 'power that matters'? Or is it an implied contrast with spiritual, or with intellectual, power?

(c) . . . compared with the average failure of the present day.

Does this mean that, on an average, people of the present day are failures? Or that the comparison is with an average case of failure—failures not necessarily being common?

12. DUPLICATION

. . . the type of . . . man . . . is . . . an average professional heavyweight boxer, . . .

'Type' here means 'an average representative of a class' and can be omitted; unless perhaps what is meant is that such people as dirt-track racers, rodeo-performers and caber-tossers would have been equally happy at Athens—which is historically doubtful.

14. MATERIAL OMISSION

. . . what actually has happened in the past . . .

To say 'has happened' implies 'the past', which need not be mentioned unless to distinguish it as a 'recent past' or a 'far past'. What past is this?

15. UNFULFILLED PROMISE

(a) If we attend to what actually has happened in the past . . . material power has generally been wielded with blindness . . .

The expected conclusion to 'if we attend' is 'we shall discover'; but this is not provided.

(b) Even if you take a tiny oasis of excellence, the type of modern man who would have most chance of happiness in ancient Greece at its best period is . . .

The expected conclusion to 'if you take' is 'you will find': but this is not provided.

16. UNDEVELOPED THEME
   (a) **And yet mankind has progressed.**

The form that this progress has taken is not indicated. The hypothesis of the scholar and boxer, intended perhaps to bear out the statement, only confuses it. Apparently, the heavyweight boxer is still the happiest man, though nowadays the scholar no longer glorifies his happiness for him.

   (b) **. . . the main use of the Oxford scholar would have been . . .**

What would the use of the German one have been?

   (c) **. . . his capability of writing an ode in glorification of the boxer.**

More than this is needed to make the point clearly. Average heavyweight boxers in Greece did not have odes addressed to them; only a champion who managed to win a laurel, ivy or parsley crown for his city-state was so rewarded.

   (d) **. . . his capability of writing an ode in glorification of the boxer. Nothing does more harm in unnerving men for their duties . . .**

The present position of the average scholar is left undefined; but 'mankind has progressed' suggests that, though the boxer nowadays is still the happier man, the scholar is the more highly honoured by the enlightened authorities.

17. FAULTY CONNEXION
   . . . the . . . man who would have most chance of happiness in ancient Greece . . . is probably (as now) an average professional heavyweight boxer, and not an average Greek scholar from Oxford or Germany. Indeed, the main use of the Oxford scholar would have been his capability of writing an ode in glorification of the boxer.

'Indeed' always emphasizes a point made in the preceding sentence. But here not a word has been said about happiness; nor can it be assumed that an Oxford scholar would *not* be as happy to write a graceful ode in glorification of a boxer as Pindar was.

22. OVER-EMPHASIS
   Nothing does more harm in unnerving men for their

duties in the present than the attention devoted to the points of excellence in the past . . .

A great many things obviously do more harm: such as domestic worries, fear of death, boredom, the tyranny of employers or the apathy of fellow-workers.

23. LOGICAL WEAKNESS

(a) . . . the type of modern man who would have most chance of happiness in ancient Greece at its best period is probably (as now) an average professional heavyweight boxer.

A professional boxer, unlike an amateur, would probably be disappointed at getting a perishable crown rather than a cartload of *minae* for his splendid victories; and an *average* professional heavyweight boxer would be less likely than a leading one to win any victories worth eulogizing by the Oxford (or German) scholar. And any modern boxer, whatever his status or skill, would be disgusted at the persistent fouling which characterized the Greek ring.

(b) . . . an average Greek scholar from Oxford or Germany. Indeed, the main use of the Oxford scholar would have been his capability of writing an ode in glorification of the boxer.

The *main* use of the Oxford scholar would no doubt have been his Homeric commentary and philosophic argument in the Schools. Odes were written by poets, not scholars.

24. CHANGE OF STANDPOINT

(a) If we attend . . .
Even if you take . . .

The change from 'we' to 'you' seems arbitrary. (Nor are 'we' and 'you' defined.)

(b) Nothing does more harm in unnerving men for their duties . . .

The sentence starts with the idea of 'unnerving men *in* their duties' and changes to that of 'incapacitating men *for* their duties'.

25. MIXED CATEGORY

(a) . . . romantic visions of democracies, aristocracies, kings, generals, armies, and merchants . . .

This catalogue begins with forms of government, and then suddenly switches to kinds of people. There seems no reason why it should stop here, or anywhere, once it has thus changed its theme: it might continue with a list of trusts, trade-unions, and courts of law.

(b) . . . **Greek scholar from Oxford or Germany** . . .

'Oxford' and 'Germany' are not parallel. It should be: 'Oxford or Bonn', 'Oxford or Heidelberg' or 'an English or German university'.

G. CIRCUMLOCUTION

. . . **attention devoted to the points of excellence in the past as compared with** . . .

Why not 'the greater attention devoted to past excellences'?

H. ELEGANT VARIATION

. . . **their duties in the present** . . .

. . . **the average failure of the present day** . . .

There seems no need for 'present day' to become 'present' in the same sentence.

FAIR COPY

'Those who study the authentic records, disregarding idealistic misrepresentations of the past, will discover that in democracies, aristocracies, monarchies, plutocracies and military dictatorships, alike, temporal power has usually been wielded with blindness, obstinacy and selfishness, often with brutal malignance. Yet, despite all this, mankind has slowly progressed during the last thousand years, at least in gradually adopting a more respectful attitude towards literary culture. If two moderns, a good Greek scholar, say, from Oxford or Heidelberg, and a good professional heavyweight boxer, were to be carried back in time to Pericles's Athens—often described as a small oasis of enlightenment in the desert of that semi-barbaric age— the boxer would be the one likely to receive the more handsome civic honours; though the scholar, if his literary capacities permitted, and if the boxer carried off the prize at some important festival, might perhaps win the approval of the authorities by an ode written in the boxer's honour. (Nowadays boxers, though still popular heroes, are never officially honoured with titles and orders, as scholars sometimes are.) It unnerves the modern worker to hear the successes of the past constantly cried up at the expense of the failures of his own day: as though the past had never had failures, nor modern times successes.'

COMMENT

Professor Whitehead is generally acknowledged to be the most thorough, acute and original of contemporary British philosophers. It is strange to find him unbending in this popular work: becoming as conversationally loose as any feather-headed undergraduate.

Sir Leonard Woolley

from *Ur of the Chaldees*, 1929

TEXT

Excavating the site, we found Ennatum's building standing on the stumps[8a] of the older walls which had been used by the new bricklayers[1] as a foundation, and so recovered at one time[8b] the ground-plan of both temples.

The building was a rectangle measuring 240 feet either way,[3a] and was surrounded by an enormously heavy[8c] wall[3b] through the heart of which[3c] a narrow paved corridor ran round three sides of it,[3d] leading from a gate-tower over the main[16] entrance to two fortified towers at the far corners[4]; a similar corridor cut straight across the building, dividing it into two unequal parts[3e] and affording quick access from one tower to the other.

EXAMINATION

1. WHO?

　　. . . we found Ennatum's building standing on the stumps of the older walls which had been used by the new bricklayers as a foundation . . .

Who were these new bricklayers? If Ennatum's, why not 'his'?

3. WHAT?

(a) The building was a rectangle measuring 240 feet either way . . .

Does he mean that the elevation was rectangular?—if so, what were the lateral dimensions? For though a square *is* a rectangle, it is usually called a square; 'rectangle' is reserved for a figure with two equal sides longer than the two other equal sides.

(b) . . . and was surrounded by an enormously heavy wall . . .

At what distance? Or was the heavy wall part of the structure?

(c) . . . through the heart of which a narrow paved corridor ran round three sides of it . . .

Usually 'through the heart of' means 'direct through the middle of an object, from a point outside and in front of it.' Here it apparently means 'transversely inside'. And at what height did the corridor run?

(d) . . . ran round three sides of it . . .

Which three sides?

(e) . . . a similar corridor cut straight across the building, dividing it into two unequal parts . . .

In which direction? Which part was the larger? How was this corridor similar to the other? Was it also enclosed in an enormously heavy wall? At what height did it run?

4. WHERE?

. . . two fortified towers at the far corners . . .

Does this mean the rear angles?

8. INAPPROPRIATE WORD OR PHRASE

(a) . . . the stumps of the older walls . . .

It is easy to imagine the stumps of pillars, columns, posts, or piles: but what are the 'stumps' of walls?

(b) . . . and so recovered at one time . . .

The phrase he wants is either 'At one and the same time' or 'at once'. 'At one time' means 'formerly'.

(c) . . . **an enormously heavy wall** . . .

Surely it is the massiveness of the wall that is being stressed, not the weight. If it had been built of stone it would have been far heavier.

15. UNDEVELOPED THEME

. . . **a gate-tower over the main entrance** . . .

Were there other entrances?

FAIR COPY

'When we excavated the site we solved two problems at the same time: for we found that Ennatum's bricklayers had used the broken lower courses of the original walls as foundations for the new temple, so that the ground plan, the outline of which was a square with a 240-foot side, had remained unaltered.

Fifty [?] feet above ground level along the interior of each of the massive main walls, except the rear one, ran a narrow paved passage, connecting a tower over the front gateway with two fortified towers at the rear angles. Easy communication between these two was provided at ground level [?] by a similar passage contained in an equally massive [?] inner wall standing parallel with the rear wall, fifty feet [?] from it.'

COMMENT

The failure to explain clearly the lay-out of a situation is due sometimes to uncertainty about one or more of the elements, sometimes to haste or emotion, sometimes to caring little whether or not the reader forms an accurate mental picture. Here the failure does not seem to be due to any of these causes. Probably Sir Leonard Woolley has himself so clear a memory of the temple that he forgets that his readers know only as much as he cares to tell them about it.

In the Fair Copy we have guessed at the heights and distances which the reader will want to be given; the correct ones are not to be found in the original.

Poet, novelist, critic, translator, essayist, scholar and historian, Robert Graves is one of the leading English men of letters. Born in 1895, he fought in World War I and won international acclaim in 1929 with the publication of his autobiography, *Goodbye to All That*, an appraisal of the effect of the war on his generation. After the war, he was granted a Classical scholarship at Oxford and subsequently went to Egypt as the first professor of English at the University of Cairo. In addition to *I, Claudius* and *Claudius the God*, he is the author of, among many other books, *The White Goddess, The Hebrew Myths,* and *Collected Poems.* He lives in Majorca.

Alan Hodge, for many years joint editor of *History Today*, is the author, with Robert Graves, of *The Long Weekend*, a study of England between the two world wars, and, with Peter Quennell, of *The Past We Share.* He lives in England.